IMPROVISATION
LEARNING THROUGH DRAMA

IMPROVISATION
LEARNING THROUGH DRAMA

David W. Booth   Charles J. Lundy

Consultants: Tony Goode Larry Swartz

THOMSON

NELSON

Australia   Canada   Mexico   Singapore   Spain   United Kingdom   United States

ISBN-13:978- 0-7747-1211-8
ISBN-10: 0-7747-1211-2

Canadian Cataloguing in Publication Data
Booth, David W. (David Wallace), 1938–
Improvisation : learning through drama

ISBN 0-7747-1211-2

1. Drama in education, 2. Role playing.
I. Lundy, Charles J., 1939– II. Title.

PN3171.B66 1985 · 371.3'32 C84-099321-8

Designer: Blair Kerrigan/Glyphics
Photographer: Philip Barton

This book was printed and bound in Canada.
3 4 5 6 08 07 06

Thomson Nelson
1120 Birchmount Road,
Toronto, Ontario, M1K 5G4
1-800-668-0671
www.nelson.com

For our students at
the Faculty of Education,
both in-service and pre-service,
past, present, and future.

Table of Contents

To the Reader

"Finding the Drama." This is a phrase that you will encounter again and again as you work and play your way through this book. It's a somewhat vague phrase, but that is because drama is very hard to define.

Drama doesn't simply mean theatre, although theatre is one of the events we participate in (as audience and performers) in the hope of finding drama.

It doesn't mean just sensitivity games, although tuning in to yourself and to others is an important aspect of drama.

It doesn't always mean fun and excitement, although excitement, tension, and satisfaction are important ingredients of drama.

And drama doesn't imply "serious theatre" as opposed to comedy or mystery or science fiction, although this is the way the word is often used in, for example, television guides.

Then what is drama? It is something that happens when all the participants in and witnesses to a make-believe situation find themselves believing in that situation, because somehow the situation has come to represent things that are important to everyone. The learning in drama is something like a voice saying: "This is what life is like; this is how people are; this is the way that human encounters work."

Drama is a group process: it works from the strength of the group and enriches the lives of everyone concerned. You find drama by working within the medium—by improvising, by exploring ideas through role-play, and then by replaying, discussing, arguing, and discovering new meanings in the situation.

You begin to work in drama with everyone in the whole class, free from anyone looking at you. This allows you to learn about yourself as you participate, building on your personal strengths, learning about how you think and feel, and, at the same time, developing your communication and theatre skills. Then there will be times when you may wish to revise, shape, and rehearse your work so that you can communicate your ideas to others in the class. And, as your experience and trust grow, you may want to share your drama explorations with other audiences.

Improvisation: Learning Through Drama is divided into five sections. Section A is about getting yourself prepared for the drama work. Section B prepares the whole group for the drama process. These two sections are filled with games and activities that can be played and worked with for their own sake. Section C is about the differences between playing yourself and playing a role. And in section D you cross over into the drama itself. The last part of the book, "Drama Projects," offers a few suggestions for exploring the performance aspects of theatre.

Each section is divided into chapters, and each chapter contains an introductory essay, a Workshop with its own Table of Contents, and a page for journal writing. The further you move into drama, the more necessary it becomes that you know how to find your way out of it. By keeping a drama journal, you can reflect on what happened within the drama, think about how you felt working inside the action, examine your feelings and ideas about working with your group, look at how the drama affected you, and add to your knowledge of how drama works. You may or may not wish to share your notes with others in the class.

Join in. Trust yourself. Trust your group. Explore and enjoy drama. Drama helps you build skills for life, so that you can feel confident and secure in dealing with others in the many situations in which you find yourself. Drama can be a powerful and significant experience.

David Booth
Charles Lundy   Toronto, April 1985

Moving into Drama

The preparatory work on a role can be divided into three great periods: studying it; establishing the life of the role; putting it into physical form.

Constantin Stanislavski
Creating a Role p. 3

Brook asked us not to look at the actor developing the movement. We were to watch the person directly opposite us in the circle. If the exercise was done in this way, each movement would flow more naturally into the next. But if one of us faltered, everyone faltered. It was an exercise in simplicity and awareness.

But when we began everyone got it wrong. The fact is that no one made a simple movement. When it came to it, the actors began to make the most involved and elaborate gestures, made to impress. The word 'simple' had been ignored, though no one intended to. Even for people as highly trained as these, their first instinct was to do what came most naturally—the complex. From the start, Brook had proved his point. It's more 'natural' to be complicated.

And it's easier.

John Heilpern
Conference of the Birds p. 158

Drama can be a way of learning about yourself and the world you live in. In drama, the way you learn is by joining in, by participating in activities with the rest of the group. In this section, you are going to move into the types of experiences and the kinds of learning that drama has to offer by taking part in various drama games and activities with the members of your class.

Some of the games and activities are designed to create a healthy atmosphere and to release tension. Others develop spontaneity and flexibility. There are some activities that help you find out about your senses, so that you can use your sensory experiences in your work. Some of the activities will help you to use your feelings honestly so that later on in the drama work you will be able to express your feelings to others. Many of the activities will involve movement—sometimes moving by yourself, sometimes moving with others. You gain physical confidence by learning to trust others and by expressing yourself through your body. These activities can enhance your abilities to focus and concentrate. And this in turn enables you to really join in: sharing, participating, and communicating with everyone while "thinking on your feet."

In this section, you will have opportunities to find out about your own abilities and strengths. Then, with the support of everyone involved, you will begin to build on these. As each of you discovers how to work with the others in a trusting, positive atmosphere, the group itself begins to boost the confidence of each of its members.

After working with this section, you will have a background of techniques that you can use in creating drama throughout your work during the year. If, later on, you are having difficulty in an area of work, you may wish to repeat some of the activities learned here. Indeed, you may find that some of these games actually work better when you are using them to solve a problem arising in the work.

Games and activities like these can be used in all aspects of drama learning. Sometimes they work as physical warm-ups before the actual drama begins, or they can be used near the end of a class to change the atmosphere, or to help everyone relax before the next class. At other times you can use a game within the drama lesson for a specific purpose, such as finding or understanding the conflict that is at the heart of the drama situation.

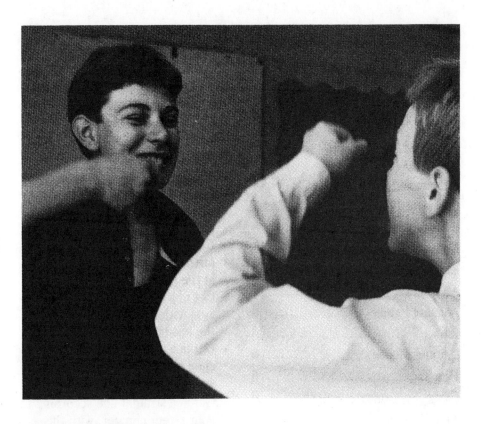

Joining In

What really makes a game is an attitude toward play that encourages everyone to benefit from the challenge of play and to share in the joys of play. We can carry the spirit of playfulness into our own work and our lives.

Andrew Fluegelman
More New Games p. 40

The games in this chapter are all ways for you to introduce yourselves and to get acquainted with one another. These games help to overcome shyness, inhibitions, and fears of making mistakes in front of others.

In this chapter each of you will be required to work with different partners, to work as a member of small groups, and to be a part of the whole group. Everyone gets to work with everyone else—a very important part of any work in drama. Eventually it will feel as if the group has a life of its own. This "group feeling" will help free you from nervousness and from the fear of working with people that you don't know well. At this stage it is important that you learn from the experience of joining in. When all of you feel free from criticism, you will all feel free to explore. Developing trust in your classmates is a very important part of moving into drama.

Workshop

Where Do I Belong?

1. Choose one person to call out the following instructions. This person picks a signal (a whistle, for example) which means "go." Try to follow the instructions as quickly as possible.

- Get in a straight line from shortest to tallest, with the shortest person at the head of the line.
- Get in a straight line according to birthdays, with January birthdays at the head of the line.
- Get in a straight line according to age, with the youngest person at the head of the line.
- Get in a straight line according to shoe size, with the smallest shoe size at the head of the line.
- Get in a straight line according to your street number, with the smallest number at the head of the line. If you share a number, stand side by side.
- Get in alphabetical order using first names only. If you share the same name, stand side by side.

2. Choose someone else to call out the instructions. The new "caller" can repeat any of the above in any order. Instructions may vary so that the order of the line is rearranged. For example, instead of shortest to tallest, the order may be tallest to shortest. You can also play these games by dividing your group in half, so that one team plays against another. When an instruction is called out, the first team to complete the task scores a point.

Shake!

Choose someone to lead you through this game. Your leader gives a signal such as a handclap or drumbeat and calls out "hands." You say "Hi, I'm (your name) ," and shake hands. On the next signal, the leader calls out "knees," and you introduce yourself to another, but this time shaking *knees*. The leader keeps changing the part of the anatomy to be shaken (elbows, ears, toes), and you try to introduce yourself to all the other people in the class.

Greetings

Invent a greeting that you might use if you came from another planet. Now, all of you walk about the room, and introduce yourselves using your new greetings.

Introducing...!

1. Stand in a circle. One of you begins by saying your name and making some gesture or movement such as clapping your hands above your head, wiggling, or bending over. As a group, repeat the name and the movement. Continue until you have all given your names.

Repeat the game. This time call out your name in some dramatic way (for example, as a whisper, a scream, a cheer), and use a new gesture.

2. Get into groups of five or six, and choose one person who will begin the game by saying his or her first name. The person on the right repeats the name and then gives his or her name. The third person repeats the first two names and adds his or her name. Go around the circle until you have all given your names. Then, go around the circle several more times with all of you repeating the entire list of names.

3. Combine two groups, and repeat the process.

4. Combine all your groups in a large circle, and repeat the process.

5. At this stage in the game, add an alliterative adjective in front of your name, such as "cheerful" Cheryl, "tiny" Tony, or "wonderful" Juan.

6. Walk around the room assuming an identity suggested by the adjective that you have chosen to describe yourself—"dynamic" David, "sad" Sue. When greeting a new person, call out the alliterative adjective followed by your name. After a while call out the adjective only and have the person you are meeting complete the phrase.

Crossword Names

Write your first name in capital letters on a piece of paper. Then begin looking for people who have first names beginning with any of the letters of your own first name. When you find such a name, write it in a crossword fashion below your own.

```
L A R R Y
O L O O V
I L N B O
S E   N N
N     N E
      E
```

When everyone is finished, sit in a circle. Choose one person to begin by introducing to the class all the people whose names are part of his or her crossword. Continue until you have all introduced your crossword people.

Bouncing Names

Stand in a circle. One person begins by bouncing a ball into the centre of the circle, while calling out the name of another person in the circle. The person whose name is called catches the ball, and then bounces it back with another name. Try to move as quickly as possible.

Name Quickdraw

You are all going to be Western gunfighters, looking for a duel. Walk slowly around the room, looking at the others. As soon as you make eye contact with someone, quickly draw a pretend gun and "shoot" the other person by loudly calling out his or her first name. The one who first calls the other's name correctly wins the duel, and the other must "drop dead." The person who stays up the longest is the fastest name-slinger in town.

Empty Seat

Sit on chairs arranged in a circle, leaving one chair empty. The person who is to the left of the empty chair begins. "The chair on my right is free, I want (name) sitting next to me." As soon as the person chosen moves to the new chair, there is, of course, a new empty chair in the circle. Whoever is to the left of that chair calls out the rhyme. Continue the game for several minutes, going at a quick pace.

All Change!

All but one member of your group sit on chairs arranged in a horseshoe. The remaining person is "it" and stands on a spot equidistant from the ends of the horseshoe. "It" calls out the names of two group members who must exchange places. "It," however, tries to sit on one of the chairs before the exchange can be completed. At any time "it" may call "all change!", and everyone seated must move.

Fox and Rabbit

1. Choose two people, one of whom will be "Fox" and the other "Rabbit." Now everyone get a partner. The partners join arms, hands to elbows, and become a series of "rabbit holes" spread around the room. Fox goes to one end of the room, and Rabbit goes to the other. On a signal, Fox chases Rabbit. Rabbit may take refuge in any hole. The person to whom Rabbit has his or her back becomes the new Rabbit. Whenever Fox manages to tag Rabbit, roles are switched.

2. Complicate the game by having two Foxes and two Rabbits. In this case, it is important that you use something to identify the Fox, for example, a strip of cloth for a tail.

Blob

Choose one person to be "it." "It" runs around and attempts to tag the rest of you. When one of you gets tagged by "it," you both continue, hand-in-hand, to chase and tag others who then join the growing "blob." As you are caught, join onto the ends of the blob and be the taggers. Continue until everyone is caught.

Cat and Mouse

Choose two people, one of whom will be "Cat" and the other "Mouse." Now, form two circles, one inside the other, with everyone facing inward. Everyone standing in the outside circle must have a partner standing in front of him or her in the inner circle. On a signal, Cat chases Mouse in and around the circles. Mouse is safe when standing directly in front of any other pair, but, because there can never be a group of three, the person who is standing in the outside circle immediately becomes Mouse. If Cat touches Mouse, roles are switched.

Hug Tag

Choose one person to be "it." "It" must try to tag someone else in the class. The only way for the rest of you to be "safe" is to hug someone. There can be only two people in a hug. You must keep moving (you cannot stay in a hug unless you're in danger of being tagged!). If you get tagged, you become "it," and the tagger becomes part of the class. (You must stay within set boundaries within the classroom.)

Clues

Take a piece of blank paper and write your first name in the centre of the page. In the top right-hand corner write down one of your accomplishments. In the top left-hand corner write down a food that you dislike. In the bottom right-hand corner write down something that you own that you're proud of. In the bottom left-hand corner write down an ambition that you have.

Take your paper, and walk about the room holding it in front of you. Try and meet as many people as you can, and become aware of the things that they have written down.

Sit in a circle and share the clues you've gathered in the following way: one person begins and states anything that he or she has learned about another person in the circle—for example, Jerry wants to be a dentist, Sylvia has written a book. The person who has been called upon tells something about somebody else in the circle. Each person can only be called upon once. Continue until everyone has had a turn. The last person can talk about anyone. This exercise can be repeated several times.

Third Person

1.   Choose a partner—someone you don't know very well. Tell your partner about yourself from the point of view of someone else who does know you, such as your father, sister, or best friend. For example, if your name is Harry and you've chosen your father's point of view, you might begin by saying, "Harry is so sleepy every morning. I have to call him ten times before he gets up." Go on to describe your physical characteristics, personality traits, hobbies, and so on, all from your father's point of view. If you are the person who is doing the listening, ask questions to get more background information. Here are some suggestions for questions you might ask "Harry's father":

– What is something that Harry's proud of?
– Does he have a nickname, and how does he feel about it?
– What is his favourite possession?
– What is the funniest thing that ever happened to Harry?
– What is the most embarrassing experience that he has had?
– How does he spend his time after dinner?
– What was the best vacation that Harry has had?
– What was the best book that he's read? Why?
– What was Harry's favourite toy as a child?
– What is something that he would like to change about himself?
– What is an ambition that Harry has?

When you've finished, switch roles.

2.   When you have both finished, go and sit in a circle, and wait for the whole class to join back in. Choose one person who begins and introduces his or her partner to the group by taking the role the partner did in describing himself or herself (for example, be the person's father describing his son).

Drama Journal

Did you feel most comfortable working with a partner, a small group, or the whole class?

Write down three things that you learned about yourself from "joining in."

How do you think that this type of activity will help your future work in drama?

What skills does a person have to have to take part in drama?

What skills do you think you will have to develop to work effectively with others?

Awareness Games

Cooperative games where there are no losers, along with friendly, low-key competition which reduces the importance of the outcome of the game, frees us to enjoy the experience of playing itself. We are given a new freedom to learn from our mistakes rather than to try to hide them.

Terry Orlick
*The Cooperative Sports
and Games Book* p.6

This is a chapter of games and activities that will help you become more aware of yourself, both as an individual, and as a member of a group. These activities also help to release tension and build a co-operative atmosphere for learning. Because everyone playing the games has to understand and stick to the rules, the group begins to work together in positive, helpful ways. Since competition is not stressed, these games will build co-operation, sensitivity, and communication.

In this type of atmosphere, you can focus and concentrate on exploring aspects of yourself such as your movement, your voice, your ideas, and your feelings. As well, you can begin to notice how your group functions as a whole. You begin to see your behaviour in terms of how you relate to the group, and of how the group relates to you. As you become more aware of the others, you find that you can put yourself in their situations and begin to consider their needs. Once you begin to see how others are working, you can start responding with more appropriate words and actions. In this way, you will be working towards building a sense of belonging to your drama group.

Nov 30

Workshop

Face to Face

1. Choose one person to be the "caller." Each of you finds a partner and you stand face to face. The caller calls out "face to face" or "back to back," and, with your partner, you respond to the instruction. When the caller calls out "change" everyone must find a new partner and stand either face to face or back to back. At some point the caller takes a partner, and someone else calls out the instructions.

2. Repeat the game, but this time the caller can call out different instructions, such as toe to toe, side to side, knee to knee, and so on.

In One Word

1. Choose a caller. This time the caller calls out adverbs, such as "noisily," or "happily," and the rest of you must move around the room accordingly.

2. Choose someone to leave the room. Now the rest of you choose an adverb, for example, "timidly." When the person returns he or she must find out what the adverb is by asking people to do things "that way." For example, he or she might say "Shake hands that way," and you would shake hands very timidly. Or, someone might say "I don't want to," in a very timid voice. After each command the person makes a guess at the word, and the game is over when the person either guesses correctly, or gives up.

Atom

Choose someone to be the caller. The rest of you move about the room according to the caller's instruction—"Jog!," "Hop!" or whatever. Whenever the caller calls out a number, "Atom 2!", "Atom 5!", you must form a group with that number of people in it. On "Atom 1!" everybody freezes in a "hugging" position. The caller may call any number and may repeat a number that has already been called. If people are left over, they may form a smaller group but they must not join a complete group.

Prui (Proo-ee)

All of you stand with your eyes closed. One person is secretly designated by your teacher to be the "PRUI" by a tap on the shoulder. PRUI remains still and silent, with eyes open. On a signal from your teacher you move towards each other with hands outstretched, keeping your eyes closed. When you touch another person, keep your eyes closed and ask, "Prui?". If the other person answers "Prui?", you both know that you have not found the real PRUI, and you must keep searching. When you ask "Prui?" of the real PRUI, you will not get an answer back. Then you open your eyes, link arms and become part of the PRUI, keeping still and silent. The game ends when you have all located and become part of the PRUI.

Look Twice

1. Choose a partner, and note as many aspects of that person's clothing, jewellery, and appearance as you can. Your partner will do the same by observing you. Now each of you turn away and alter one aspect of your appearance, for example, undoing one button, removing an earring. Turn back to face your partner, and identify the change that he or she made.

2. Repeat the exercise and this time make *two* changes.

3. Find a new partner and repeat the activity.

Killer

1. The class divides up into groups of seven or eight, and each group forms a circle. Have your teacher give everyone a slip of paper. One slip in each group has an X marked on it. The person who receives the X-marked slip is the "killer" who murders by winking at another person. If you get winked at, you must count silently to ten before announcing, "I'm dead." If someone else in the group thinks that he or she knows who the "killer" is, then that person makes an accusation. If correct, the game is over, and the slips are drawn again. If wrong, the accuser must withdraw from the game.

2. Repeat the game, joining two circles together. Make sure that there is only one piece of paper marked "X."

3. This time, perform the game in one large group. Everyone draws a slip, but this time there are four or five "killers." Now you all meander around the room. The game proceeds in the same way except that, if you get "killed," you count to ten, and then die in a very dramatic way.

Just a Squeeze

Stand in a circle holding hands. Choose one person who will begin by giving a short, sharp squeeze to the hand of the person on the left. Each of you passes the squeeze on so that it travels around your circle in a clockwise direction. Go around several times. At some point, the beginner can start passing the squeeze both ways at once.

This Is My Ear

Find a partner. The object of the game is to point to one part of your body while calling out another part of your body. For example, you might say "This is my eye," while pointing to your nose. Your partner might then point to his or her ear and say "This is my nose." Then you might point to your hand and say "This is my ear." You always call out the body part your partner has pointed to. See how long you can keep going without getting confused in the hand-eye-mouth co-ordination.

What's in a Word?

1. Choose a partner and call yourselves A and B. A calls out a noun—"chair" for example. B quickly says the first association that he or she has with "chair,"—"table," perhaps. A then adds another word—maybe "food"—and so on. Continue until your teacher gives a signal to stop.

2. Repeat the game. This time establish a rhythm that the word associations must fit into. Try clapping twice on your knees, twice in the air, for example.

3. Sit in groups of four, then in groups of eight, and repeat the game each time. As a final activity the whole class could establish a continuous word association game. Again a rhythm could be established to make the game flow spontaneously.

Fortunately/ Unfortunately

1. Choose a partner, and call yourselves A and B. A starts a story that begins with "fortunately." B continues the story with "unfortunately." Here is an example of how the game might go.

A: Fortunately I won a lottery.
B: Unfortunately I lost the ticket.
A: Fortunately my brother found it in his drawer.
B: Unfortunately the ticket blew away when he gave it to me.
A: Fortunately a bird caught the ticket in his beak.
B: Unfortunately the bird did not stop flying.

Continue telling the story until your teacher gives a signal to stop.

2. Sit in groups of five or six. Repeat the above exercise with each person using "fortunately" or "unfortunately" in turn, adding on a sentence to build a story. Go around the circle a few times until your teacher gives a signal to stop.

3. Repeat the activity with your whole group sitting in a circle.

Spinning a Yarn

1. Sit in groups of five or six. One person begin a story by saying one word. The person to the left adds one word and so on around the circle to create what will probably be a very imaginative story. Continue until your teacher gives a signal to stop.

2. Repeat the above exercise with each person giving two words.

3. Repeat the exercise with each person giving a sentence.

4. If you wish, you can repeat each of the three story building games with your whole group sitting in one large circle.

Fatal Story

Sit in a circle of ten to fifteen people. Choose one person to be the leader. The leader, who steps into the centre of the circle, is a pitiless, easily bored monarch, whose sole object in life is to be continuously entertained. The rest of you are courtiers. The monarch points to one of you, who begins telling a story. At some point the monarch indicates another courtier. The second courtier then takes up the story and continues until the monarch cues yet a third courtier. If a courtier falters or in some way breaks the story line, the monarch sentences him or her to death, and the courtier must mime a death scene. The rest of you, as courtiers, are quick to advise the monarch of your displeasure with any storyteller and may suggest to the monarch—through booing and hissing—that another courtier die. The monarch may accept or reject any advice that he or she receives. The last living storyteller must point out the moral of the story. If he or she cannot, or if the moral is unsatisfactory to the monarch or to the rest of you (who are now participating as ghosts), then the last courtier, too, must die.

Gibberish

1. Choose a partner, and call yourselves A and B. Each of you think up a situation or problem, and then, using only gibberish, try to communicate your problem to your partner. A's begin.

2. This time, you can use only numbers for your conversation.

3. Try using only letters of the alphabet for your conversation.

4. Sit in groups of four or five. You are all cave people, and one of you—choose one person—has just seen something strange while out hunting. Using gibberish and gestures, this hunter must report back to the other cave people to explain what he or she has seen. The rest of you can ask questions (in gibberish) in order to find out more information. This exercise should be repeated so that each of you has a chance to describe the strange animal or object that you have discovered.

Alibis

Sit in groups of five or six. Choose one person to be the detective. The detective thinks up a crime, stands in the middle of the group, states what the crime was, and where and when it was committed. Now the detective cross-questions one of the suspects. The trick of this game is that all the rest of you left in the group act as *one* suspect. You must each remember what the others have said when it is your turn to be questioned by the detective. The detective questions each of you several times, switching quickly back and forth, as if you were all one person. The detective's aim is to catch one of you when you disagree with yourself or contradict what someone else has said. Whoever gets caught becomes the detective and the situation starts again.

Interrogator

Get into groups of seven or eight and choose one person to be the interrogator. The interrogator questions one person, but it is the person on the right of the questioned person who must answer, and with a straight face. The questioned person must maintain eye contact with the interrogator and not laugh. Whoever cannot remain solemn throughout the proceedings becomes the next interrogator. Try going fast.

Join the Conversation

Get into groups of four or six, and choose two people who will secretly decide upon a topic of conversation. These two then discuss the topic in the presence of the rest of you. Their intent is to mislead you regarding the topic that they are discussing, but they may not use any false statements to do so. When you think that you know what the topic is, you can join the conversation. But, at any time after joining the conversation, you may be asked, by the original two, what the topic is. When this occurs, you must whisper what the topic is to one of the two conversation leaders. If correct, you can continue to participate in the conversation. If incorrect, you must become an observer again until you have a new guess. After three wrong guesses, you are out of the game. The game goes on until you have all either guessed correctly and joined the conversation, or have made three wrong guesses and are out of the game.

Gentle Persuasion

Choose a partner, and call yourselves A and B. Use one chair, which A sits on. B has to use any means whatsoever, except physical violence, to persuade A to give up the chair so that B can sit on it. After your teacher gives a signal to stop, switch roles. When you have both finished, you can discuss with the rest of the group the arguments that you used.

Arguing

Choose a partner. Decide what your favourite colour is and try to persuade your partner that your colour is better and is one that the other should favour. Your partner, at the same time, tries to convince you to switch. Any means of persuasion (except physical violence) can be used. Continue the argument until you are given a signal to stop. With the rest of your group, discuss the methods you used. Consider the following: Did anyone use bribery? flattery? Did anyone almost give in? Why? Why not? How can you get someone else to change his or her mind?

Holding Your Own

Choose a partner, and, to yourself, decide on a topic to talk about. Sit relatively close to your partner, and establish eye contact. Keeping eye contact the whole time, begin talking to each other at the same time about your topics. Both of you should continue talking and should not stop until a signal is given. The object of the exercise is to keep talking at all costs and to make your partner break his or her concentration. (No physical contact can be made.) Here are some suggested topics for consideration:

– tell the most embarrassing experience you've had;
– retell your favourite fairy tale;
– be a sales person trying to sell some kind of product;
– talk about the best vacation you have had;
– persuade the other person to see a movie that you enjoyed.

After the conversation, tell your partner the parts of the conversation—if any—that you paid attention to.

Picking a Fight

1. Choose a partner and call yourselves A and B. Without preparing, A begins a conversation by saying, "No you didn't," and B replies with, "Oh yes I did." Continue the conversation and quickly develop it into a natural argument. Don't continue at a "No you didn't," "Yes I did" level. (Here are some suggested situations: in a store, in a classroom, at a meeting, in the subway, at a dinner table, in a theatre.)

2. Repeat the exercise, this time with B starting off with "No you didn't" and so on.

3. Choose a new situation for developing the argument and improvise using one of the following instructions:

– argue with eyes closed;
– argue without words, in mime;
– clasp each other's wrists;
– sit on your hands;
– do not raise your voices at all.

Snake in the Grass

Choose someone to be the starter snake. The starter snake lies down on the ground on its stomach. Everybody else gathers fearlessly around to touch it. (One finger will suffice—you don't want to get too close to a snake.) When your teacher shouts "Snake-in-the-Grass!" everybody runs, staying within the bounds of the snake area, while the snake, moving on its belly, tries to tag as many as it can. Those touched become snakes too.

Non-snakes run bravely around in the snake-infested area, trying to avoid being caught. (For your own sake and the snake's sake, take off your shoes and watch out for snake-fingers.) The atmosphere gets even better if all the snakes are hissing. The last person caught is the starter snake in the next game.

Drama Journal

Which game did you feel involved you most completely?

Were these games competitive? Is competition part of classroom drama?

What elements in these games will help you in drama?

What did you become aware of in yourself and in others through playing these games?

Do people play these types of games in "real life"?

Growing Through Movement

Two worlds, the world of words and the world of movement, should be continually interwoven in life. Such interweaving can only increase and deepen the capacity to communicate—a capacity vital to life.

Joyce Boorman
Dance and Language Experience p. 64

We waited quite a while. Until at last, several women entered the room. They were old and beautiful. Their gray hair was plaited. They wore beads, dressed very simply. They were the reverse of intimidating. They were gentle and calm, smiling at us with shy eyes. I couldn't take my eyes off them. When they shook our hands they drew the hands close to them, kissed them and gently wiped their eyes with the kiss.

Two drummers sat at one end of the room.

They were younger than the women, very relaxed. They waved hello.

We hushed in anticipation of a start. But there seemed to be a delay. We talked among ourselves for a while, uncertain what was happening. We couldn't speak the same language as the women. They talked quietly in their own group.

Without warning, one of the drummers began.

The room was shot through with a thunderclap. The room shook. The women danced.

In that split second the atmosphere in the room was totally transformed. My eyes were opened and astonished. The old women danced and were young.

They danced alone within their group, flowing and amazing. Without effort or apparent will, their bodies vanished and burned. The old and beautiful women of the forest were spirits, dancing for joy. They were so proud and so gentle. The whole of life was held in their movements and gestures, rhythms of gods, changing and mesmerising. When the drums switched rhythm, the women changed and turned even before the signal had finished. Worlds turned on them. The spirits of the forest had shown themselves to us. Human bodies became a vehicle for the spirit. And the spirit spoke. Life of reason. Life of so much hope and love. Never had I seen even a dream like this. Yet I can neither describe nor explain it. That in a room I received a vision of sheer existence. And that God passed before our eyes.

John Heilpern
Conference of the Birds p. 311-312

The games and activities in this chapter are about movement. Sometimes you will be moving by yourself, sometimes with others. You will also experiment with gestures, facial expressions, and body language. All of these activities can help you learn how to express your feelings and ideas through your body and through interacting physically with the members of your group. Learning to communicate through movement brings physical confidence and the ability to get a message across in situations where words are not appropriate.

Many movement activities are co-operative efforts and involve learning to trust others. As you work through this chapter, you will have the opportunity to practise these vital group skills.

Musical Laps

1.   Form a circle, everyone facing in one direction, and put your hands on the waist of the person in front of you. On a signal from your teacher, sit down in the lap of the person behind you (carefully! take your time at first). Your goal is to get everybody sitting down without anyone falling on the floor.

2.   Repeat the exercise using music. When the music starts begin moving forward. When the music stops, sit down in the lap of the person behind you.

Stretching

Start out by stretching your whole body in every direction, using your arms, head, legs, fingers, and toes. (Can you stretch and be relaxed at the same time?) Move around the room, and if you come into contact with someone else who is stretching, try stretching with them. What kinds of stretching are possible when you work with a partner or two? Can you stretch without using your arms? What kinds of feelings (if any) do you get when you stretch while you change levels from high to low? Does stretching make you yawn at first? (If it does, it is because your active body is calling for more oxygen.) Can you stretch with one foot off the floor? What kinds of adjustments must you make to keep the quality of the stretch and still keep your balance?

Swinging

A swing is a loose, easy, relaxed movement that starts with energy, continues because of the momentum of the body, and ends with energy. A swing must have a free flowing ease about it which corresponds to the breathing cycle of inhalation (energy) and exhalation (relaxation of muscles). Try swinging various parts of your body separately: head, shoulders, arms, wrists, upper body, and legs. Can you swing using your whole body? Does your head move with your body? If your head does not move with the rest of your body, it is probably because there is a strain on your neck. Use extremes of range. Start small and low. Swing to full extension, then reverse the order. Pay attention to your own rhythm. Is it full and expansive or tight and cramped? Notice if your rhythm is different from that of others.

Bouncing

Bounces, which can be jumps or gentle bobbing, are easy up and down movements done by any part or all of your body. Bounces must be done without great effort and without a great range of movement. Pay special attention to how you use your feet. Land on your toes for an instant, then onto the ball of your foot, then your heel, and finish with a bending of the knee. (It is very important that you follow this technique, especially if you are working on concrete floors.) Try bouncing in place, then moving around the room. Your bounce shouldn't change when you move forward or backward. Keep the flow of energy free and easy. Try bobbing your head or shoulders. See whether you can bounce while crouching, when sitting on the floor, or when lying down. If your body does not "flop" while you bounce, then you know that you are

tense and should work to relax your muscles to produce easy, gentle movements. Bounce with different people in the class, adjusting your rhythm to their rhythm.

Striking

A striking movement uses any part of the body and is a short, sharp, clearly defined action that is the opposite of a stretching, languid movement. Striking motions require organization of the body and a fair amount of controlled tension. Striking is often a difficult kind of movement because it requires a definite commitment: you are either doing the movement or you are not. There is no half way. Try doing this movement in various positions. Remember to keep the movement short, sharp, and crisp. How does working with another person affect you? Does doing this kind of movement in a large group affect the way you feel?

Shaking

Shaking, or vibratory movements, are the hardest to do because they require the greatest muscle control. Shaking movements resemble shivering because they are tiny, quick, and constant. Try shaking in various positions, starting with isolated movements of your arm, leg, or face. If the movements are not extremely rapid, you know that you are not vibrating or shaking. When you learn to shake properly you will find it can be very useful in getting rid of fatigue that has accumulated in parts of your body that have

been worked very hard. For example, if you have been standing for a long time, your feet will probably feel tired. Lie down on your back, put your legs in the air and shake out your ankles as hard as you can. Stop, then repeat. Do not let your legs drop to the floor when you have finished shaking them out. Bend your knees and place the soles of your feet on the floor. If you have really shaken your ankles, you will feel much less tired when you stand up.

Collapsing

Collapsing or falling needs to be practised slowly, and from low levels, until you are relaxed and know what you are doing. When you fall, you must land on the padded parts of your body, your buttocks, the side of your upper arm. The back rounds to absorb the shock of falling and to protect the spine. Start your collapse from a sitting position. Try it again from a kneeling position. Start standing to see how and what you can do. When you are very sure of yourself, collapse after jumps and turns from high speeds. Avoid landing on your knee, wrist, elbow, shoulder, or tailbone. (Make sure your head is always the *last* thing to settle into place.) If you try collapsing forward, use your hands and the bottom side of your arm, keeping your fingers together and forward, to absorb the shock. Collapses can be partial (going from standing to crouching, using just the upper body) or total (from standing to lying). Work with a partner to see what kinds of partial and total collapses you can think up to do together.

Using Space

Move on your back or stomach *without* using your legs. Now move without using your arms. Now try moving without using your legs *or* arms. Sit down with your knees up, and move without using your hands. Walk on your knees. Move backwards around the room. Now spin like a top. Walk around holding on to your ankles. Now walk with your elbows on your knees. Tie yourself into a "knot" and move about the room. Roll around the room in a "closed" position. As you roll, "open" the position, then "close" it, open-close, and so on. Construct an obstacle course out of risers, boxes, chairs—whatever is available—and move through it. Choose a partner and move with your bodies joined at various places—your elbows, feet, head, shoulders, for example. Move around the room with variations in speed, level, and quality of movement (tense, relaxed, for example). Move through various environments (deserts, space, haunted houses, underwater), and join up with others who are moving in similar ways. When you have finished, tell the other people that you were moving with where you felt you were.

Using the Floor

1. Go across the floor, keeping as much contact with it as you can.

2. Now see how many other ways you can use the floor, besides the conventional methods of creeping and crawling. Try slithering, keeping your torso off the ground, using your feet and fingers for support. How can you use your hair or head to create unusual movement? Use sounds to help. Try working with a partner or a group.

Life Raft

1. The purpose of this game is to save as many people as possible. First, place a number of sheets of newspaper on the floor. These are the life rafts, and the floor is the water. Now choose someone to be the lookout. The lookout can yell "shark!" at anytime. When the game begins everyone mimes swimming and keeps moving continually. When the lookout yells "shark!", everyone must get on a life raft and help others on before the lookout counts aloud to five. If anyone has any part of his or her body touching the floor, that person has been eaten by the shark. After each shark attack, some of the life rafts are removed. Those who have been eaten can help judge if any others are touching the floor after the count of five.

2. Repeat the above game using a piece of music that your class has selected. Choose one person who will stop and start the music. When the music is on, move about the room. When the music stops, everyone must land on a newspaper. Again, your objective is to save as many people as possible. Your final task is try to get as many people as possible on a single sheet of newspaper!

Spiral

Everyone form a line holding hands. The person at one end of the line remains standing on the spot, while from the other end of the line the group is led into a tight spiral around the person standing still. When your group is wound up like a clock spring, the person in the centre ducks under everybody's arms, starting with those closest, and, *still* holding hands, leads the group back into the original line.

Tangles

Form a circle, holding hands. Move to get as tangled as you can without letting go of hands. When you are fully tangled, stop. (It is important that you understand that you should stop yourself rather than waiting for someone to stop you.) Work slowly so that no one yanks or forces you to move beyond your capacity. When everyone in the group is quiet, one person gives directions such as, "Make eye contact with as many different people as you can," or "Touch elbows of all the people near you," or "Extend your body as much as you can without pulling on someone else."

Untangling

1. Form groups of seven or eight. Send one member of each group out of the room. Now, each group form a line holding hands and, without breaking the handclasp, get tangled up in the most complicated manner. When each group is completely tangled, the people who are outside return to their groups, and attempt to untangle the bodies. Each group is co-operative in the untangling process and must avoid hurting anyone, but no one in the group should volunteer any information to make the process easier for the outsider. When each group is untangled, the people should be standing in the same line in which they started.

2. Repeat the exercise. This time the people who are brought in to untangle the groups may not give any verbal instructions. They must actually physically move the individual members of the group around until the group is back in the original line.

3. Join together two groups. This larger group tangles itself up in a complicated manner. This time you untangle yourselves on your own without anyone instructing you. To make it more difficult, do the exercise without talking.

4. Repeat the untangling exercise in any of its variations using everyone in your class. Be very careful at all times to work without hurting anyone. Be aware of the different physical limits of each person in your group.

Robots

1. Find a spot in the room where you won't interfere with anyone else's space. On a signal from your teacher, start walking in a straight line, as if you were a mechanical robot creature. When you touch another person or obstacle, make a ninety degree turn and continue in a straight line until you encounter another obstacle. Continue on until your teacher gives a signal to stop.

2. Repeat the above exercise, this time adding sounds to the movements. Each mechanical person creates an individual noise (for example, "clink," "breep"), and produces this noise whenever encountering an obstacle.

Building a Machine

1. Stand in a large circle, so that as much space as possible can be used. One person stands in the centre of the circle and performs an action in a mechanical, repetitive manner (for instance, swinging an arm from side to side). One by one, in no predetermined order, everyone enters the circle by creating a new action which corresponds or "interlocks" in some way with the movement already being performed. For instance, the second player may lie on the floor and raise one leg up and down in rhythm to the first person's arm movement. You may connect physically to one another or depend on someone for support. It is important that a variety of movements be used to create the machine.

Add a movement in an unexpected direction, in a different rhythm, or on a different level such as lying down, squatting, leaning, standing. Once everyone is in the centre you will have created the impression of a fantastic machine, composed of individual parts which move in a complex rhythm.

Try adding a vocal sound to accompany the movement that you invent.

2. On a signal from your teacher, try the following:

– the power is shut off and the machine comes to a halt;
– the machine begins to lose energy and works in slow motion;
– the machine begins to move quicker and quicker;
– the machine gets louder and louder;
– the machine explodes and comes apart.

Product Machine #1

(In the following four activities the instructions are the same as those for *Building a Machine*. However, in these activities, the machines have a purpose.)

Choose a narrator. All of you decide on a product that your machine is going to produce, and work to create a fully functioning unit. The narrator, as though narrating a TV commercial or conducting a tour of a factory, describes how the machine works.

Product Machine #2

Choose another narrator. This time the narrator decides on a product (which may be whimsical or real). As the narrator indicates for his or her imaginary audience each of the various mechanical parts and devices by which the machine functions, each of you will step forward to become the parts indicated. For example, the narrator might begin by saying to his or her imaginary audience, "This machine produces electric toothbrushes. Here is where the bristles are cut." A couple of people might come forward to perform the cutting of the bristles. "This is the vat where the paint is mixed to colour the handles." Two or three people might come forward and make a vat by kneeling and joining hands in a ring. Continue on like this until the entire machine is put together.

Service Machine

Your group decides on a real machine that performs some particular kind of function or service (a washing machine, vacuum cleaner, stereo, telephone, printing press). Now create the machine using movement and sound. This time, when the machine is all put together, instead of a narrator describing the machine, each of you, in turn, explains what your function is. You might also outline how important you are, how long you have been doing this job, what kind of shape you're in, how you get along with others, and whether or not you have any complaints.

Theme Machine

This time you are going to create a machine built on an idea or theme. The theme should be based on any ordinary social activity, for example, eating in a cafeteria, going to a football game, rush hour in the city, going shopping, a cast party, or dating. The aim in this activity is to assemble a machine that imitates people in the particular situation that you have chosen. There is no narrator in this activity to direct you.

Monster Creation

The following activity could be done in groups of four, then eight, then sixteen and eventually lead to the creation of a whole-group monster.

Creating a monster is much the same as developing a machine. One by one, in no special order, come forward and add movements and sounds which in some way fit in with the actions already started by other players. Your object in this exercise is to create a sinister creature that would cause some sort of unpleasantness for anyone who gets in its way. Do not plan beforehand how the monster will look or sound when fully created. Keep in mind that a monster is a living thing and not a machine. Like any real living creature, a monster should have some symmetry between its right and left sides. Suppose, for example, that a player begins the game by kneeling and moving his or her right arm forward and back at shoulder level, suggesting some sort of antenna. A second player might then kneel beside the first, facing the same direction, and perform the same action with his or her left arm. Each action and sound that is added should help suggest the monster's menacingly sinister qualities. A gesture might be claw-like, a movement of your foot might be a powerful thud. The monster should be able to move—walking, creeping, or slithering—about the room. To do this, you will have to be more closely synchronized with your group than you were in the machine games.

Mirror Images

1.   Choose a partner. One of you will be a "mirror." The other will stand in front of the mirror and move in slow motion, using only hands and arms at first. As the "mirror" becomes more confident in copying your movements, expand your movements to include your whole body. Change roles often so that each of you gets lots of practice being both the mirror and the reflected person.

2. Continue doing the mirror exercise, but freeze each time your teacher gives a signal.

3. The person in front of the mirror is getting dressed to go to a costume party. Decide what your costume is but do not tell your partner. After you have put the costume on, the mirror image has to describe the costume and guess what it is.

4. The person in front of the mirror decides on a famous person that he or she will be. This famous person could be real—dead or alive—or fictitious, but should be known by a distinctive costume. Do not tell your partner who you have decided to be. Stand in front of the mirror, and put on your outfit. The mirror image must then guess who you are.

5. Form groups of five people. Ask one person to turn around while you silently choose a second person as leader. The first person turns back around, and the rest of you, like several mirrors, copy your leader's actions. The first person tries to guess who the leader is. Discuss ways of disguising who the leader is—for example, by not looking directly at the leader—and ways of making the game more difficult.

6. Repeat the exercise by joining with another group. Keep repeating the game until you're playing it with the entire class.

Following a Leader

1. Form groups of six or seven, and choose someone to lead you. Stand in a straight line behind the leader. The leader begins with a movement, such as moving his or her arms, and the rest of you follow. It is important that you watch the person in front of you and *not* the leader. The leader can introduce additional movements when he or she feels that the group is ready. At some point, the leader goes to the end of the line and the second person takes over leading. Continue until you've all had a turn at leading. As you progress down the line, leaders can be more creative in their movements and try using many levels. Remember to aim for a flowing effect as the movement travels from one person to another. You may wish to use music to help this feeling of "flow."

2. Repeat the above exercise with the leader leading the group around the room.

3. Join two groups together, and repeat the original exercise. Continue expanding the group until your whole class is involved.

Any Port in a Storm

(The remaining exercises in this chapter can be done with your eyes shut, or using a blindfold. When it is your turn to be the "blind" person, try to trust all your remaining senses, as well as the people in your group.)

The class stands in a circle. One person is blindfolded and is pointed in a direction across the circle. The blindfolded person walks across the circle, trusting and confident that he or she will be stopped by the person towards whom he or she is walking. The person who stops the blindfolded person does so by gently holding him or her by the shoulders and stating his or her own name. The blindfold can be exchanged now or, if confidence is lacking, the first person should walk across the circle again.

Guide Dog

Choose a partner and call yourselves A and B. If you're A, close your eyes and let B lead you around the room. If you're B, then as well as guiding A carefully around other people and obstacles, you might try to find different surfaces for A to touch—rough, smooth, warm, cold, hard, soft. After about five minutes change over, and A leads B. If conditions allow and your group feels confident enough, you may want to lead your partner outside to explore the environment.

Listen Through the Dark

1.   Choose another partner. One partner is blind and the other will call out vocal instructions. This time, distance yourself from your partner. Those who are giving vocal guidance stay in one place, and call out instructions to try to get the blind partner to cross the room. Since your whole group will be working at the same time, it is important to be aware of the obstacles and obstructions that your blind partner may meet. Reverse roles.

2.   Repeat the exercise again, but this time, the person guiding only calls out his or her partner's name. Reverse roles. Repeat the exercise a third time, using a two or three syllable word (such as toothbrush, hamburger), so that the blind partner depends only on recognizing the voice of his or her partner. Reverse roles.

Amazing Rescue

Everybody in the room—except for eight people—create a maze using only your bodies. Make sure that the maze consists of different levels. The eight people pair off in four sets of partners. Decide which four people will be blind, and repeat the blind walk exercise, carefully moving the blind partners through the maze.

Reverse roles so that each partner has a chance to be blind. When the eight people have had the chance of being blind, exchange places with people who are creating the maze.

I'll Catch You!

Choose a partner, and call yourselves A and B. B stands about 45 cm behind A. A leans backwards keeping his or her knees straight. B catches and supports A by putting both hands on A's shoulders. This is repeated several times until A's confidence is built up. A then moves a little further away and repeats the "fall." The experience is usually heightened if A closes his or her eyes. Change roles.

Balancing Act

Choose a partner and stand facing each other. Your toes can be touching or not. Hold hands and lean backwards as far as you can. The idea is for each of you to balance the weight of the other, so that neither of you falls over. Close your eyes when you *both* feel balanced.

Russian Doll

Get into small circles of about five or six people, and choose one person to stand in the centre. He or she closes his or her eyes and leans back in the same way as in *I'll Catch You*. The person is caught, supported, and passed around your group, gently and slowly. Try to make this person "roll" around your circle smoothly. You can all take turns being in the centre.

Trust Lifts

Form groups of eight or nine people. One person lies on the floor on his or her back, with eyes closed. The rest of you station yourselves on either side of this person and place your hands underneath his or her body. Gently raise him or her in a rocking to-and-fro movement as high as possible. Then lower the person in the same way. Change around so that everyone can experience the trust lift.

Snake

Get into lines of six or eight people, and form a snake by holding onto the shoulders, waists, or hands of the person in front of you. Everyone closes his or her eyes except for the person leading the snake. He or she leads the rest of you around, negotiating real or imaginary obstacles, climbing stairs, going over, round, or through things, around tight bends, sometimes crouching, sometimes on tiptoe. Be aware of the person in front of you for receiving any signals.

Landing the Plane

Line up two rows of chairs to form a landing approach to an airport runway. Choose one person to be the pilot, another to function as the control tower. The airport is engulfed by fog, and obstacles such as books, clothing, and blackboard erasers are placed in the approach. Blindfold the pilot, and turn him or her around slowly several times. The pilot then begins the approach. The control tower talks the pilot through, around, and/or over obstacles. If the pilot touches an obstacle, the plane crashes. The game is over when the pilot crashes or lands successfully, and a new pilot and control tower take over.

Drama Journal

How did you feel doing these movement activities?

When did you feel most involved in an activity?

During which movement activity did you best communicate your ideas and feelings?

When one trains to be a professional actor, why is a great deal of time spent on movement activities?

Why is a sense of trust in others essential to dramatic expression through movement?

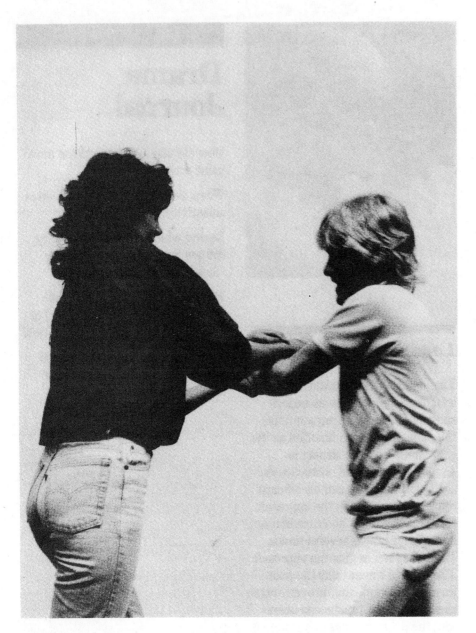

Drama Without Words

There is a mime inside you, and with mime, anything is possible. All you need are your body and your imagination. Mime is a language the whole world understands.

Kay Hamblin
Mime: A Playbook of Silent Fantasy p. 15

This chapter is about mime. Although mime is a classical art form that requires years of training, there are many elements of mime that you can learn and use in your drama work. Much of drama is about non-verbal expression, and mime, which teaches the art of carefully controlled movement, is certainly valuable training for you to have.

Mime can be as simple as a hand gesture indicating "stop!", or it can be a demonstration of some complicated action such as climbing a mountain. With experience in exploring mime, you can use its techniques in all of your drama work. You may choose to incorporate mime into the drama that your group is building, or you may choose to use mime as a way of beginning or ending the drama. You may decide to have some group members interpret in mime the story the other group members are narrating. However you decide to use mime, the goal of your work in this chapter—as well as adding to your store of drama techniques—should be to find out how you can use nonverbal language to build drama awareness.

The following excerpt from Peter Shaffer's play *Equus* has been included at this point to give you a sense of how carefully and skilfully mime must be used in drama. "Equus" is the Latin word for horse, and this is the description of how the horses are to be played. Consider as you read how the costumes described in the first paragraph could add to both the power and the difficulty of the mime work called for by the playwright.

THE HORSES

The actors wear track-suits of chestnut velvet. On their feet are light strutted hooves, about four inches high, set on metal horse-shoes. On their hands are gloves of the same colour. On their heads are tough masks made of alternating bands of silver wire and leather: their eyes are outlined by leather blinkers. The actors' own heads are seen beneath them: no attempt should be made to conceal them.

Any literalism which could suggest the cosy familiarity of a domestic animal—or worse, a pantomime horse—should be avoided. The actors should never crouch on all fours, or even bend forward. They must always—except on the one occasion where Nugget is ridden—stand upright, as if the body of the horse extended invisibly behind them. Animal effect must be created entirely mimetically, through the use of legs, knees, neck, face, and the turn of the head which can move the mask above it through all the gestures of equine wariness and pride. Great care must also be taken that the masks are put on before the audience with very precise timing—the actors watching each other, so that the masking has an exact and ceremonial effect.

Workshop

Statues

Get into groups of eight to ten people. One group at a time will perform this activity so that the rest of you can be the audience. In the first group, two "sculptors" form the rest of the group into a statue. The audience then suggests, what, who, and where the statues might be, if it were alive, and what might happen next. The group statue should then explore all or several of the suggestions. If the group runs out of ideas, the audience could offer qualifications such as: a giant is roaming the land; it is getting very cold; people are hungry. The statue can represent an event (planting a flag), a place (classroom), or an emotion (people being shoved into line at gun-point).

If someone has been in a difficult situation, let the person mold a statue re-creating part of this situation, and see how alternatives could be developed. Words should not be used if possible. Try having the statue group keep their eyes closed. Sounds can be made by the statue, or given by the sculptors. When one group has finished, another group should work. Although groups can work simultaneously, a great deal can be learned by watching others.

Silent Movie

Divide up into small groups. One person in each group starts an action. A second person silently determines the place, time, and activity of the first person, and joins in. Each person in the group adds an element until the scene is completed. For example: one person is eating; a second person sits down at the table; the third person is the waiter, the fourth the maitre d'. When everyone has contributed, make sure that you all remember your action and relation to the others, so that the piece can be repeated for the total group. Work nonverbally, but discuss after sharing.

Frozen Together

Divide into small groups. One person makes a shape and freezes. (Choose positions that can be maintained without discomfort.) A second person finds a way, with movement and sound, to use the first person's shape, and the two people freeze in the resulting position. A third person uses their shape, and all three freeze. Repeat the process until everybody is part of the freeze.

Statues Come to Life!

One person makes his or her body into a shape. When finished, a second person finds some empty space defined by the position of the first person and moves into it, without touching the first person. When finished (this is established nonverbally), the first person finds a new space around the second person. On a signal from the leader, both people freeze. Using action, and, if necessary, words, think of an activity that you could be doing. If you both have different ideas at the same time, try to use both. Repeat this activity with several different people.

Share work with the group, so different possibilities can be demonstrated. With practice, you could

work in threes and fours. Experiment with the effect of tension levels by doing one activity with little, then greater degrees of tension. If you tend to talk a lot, try working nonverbally. Afterwards, discuss problems, new ideas, and general responses.

Pictures

1. Divide into two groups. Each group stands in a circle facing inward. One person in each group begins by going silently into the centre of the circle and adopting the frozen pose of a person doing a job, such as building a house or repairing a road. The rest of you decide, silently, on how you can fit into the picture, and, when ready, go into the centre and adopt a pose that contributes to the picture. When everyone is involved, hold the picture for a few moments. Unfreeze, and discuss what each of you thought the picture was and who the other people in the picture were.

2. Instead of freezing the pose, the first person invents an action which is repeated over and over. The rest of you create actions which contribute to the whole group action.

3. This time, pick a piece of music which has a definite theme or concept (for example, military march music). Play it and create a frozen picture that is appropriate to the music.

Slow Motion Movie

Get into groups of six or eight. Choose an activity that can be mimed in slow motion—a baseball game or a snowball fight, for example. Discuss with your group what will take place during the action, and then begin your work.

A slow motion activity should look like a movie played at half speed. Remember to make your movements and gestures large, flowing, almost overemphasized. Your object is to sense and adapt to the group tempo.

Aggressive activities, such as fights, also work well in slow motion. In such activities, you can use a variety of hostile and evasive actions—lunging, dodging, swaying, falling—all in slow motion and without actually making physical contact. Imaginary obstacles such as a

Slow Silent Movie?

wall, moat, or swamp can help make interesting mock battles. A slow motion activity can also be improvised around a musical theme. For example, you might improvise a bank robbery or an old-fashioned melodrama with exaggerated movements and gestures conforming to the rhythm patterns of the music.

In Double Time

In groups of six or eight perform activities similar to those of the slow motion game above—pie fights or cops and robbers chases, for example. However, all your movements and gestures are performed faster than normal. And again, you can use background music to make the game fun.

Tableau

Divide into groups of eight to twelve people. Choose one person in each group to be the leader. Divide your classroom area up so that each group has its own space. Now each group moves around energetically in several directions like a crowd on a busy downtown street. At any time your leader calls out a word, and you must freeze, forming a tableau which in some way reflects or illustrates the word. For instance, if your leader calls "Homework!", quickly assume a position which displays your reaction to the idea of homework. Your position may or may not relate to another person's position. For example, one person might appear to be reading silently; another might appear to be reading aloud to another person, who in turn might

appear to be puzzled or to be taking notes. The tableau is held for about five seconds. Your leader then releases you, and you again move about until another key word is called. Repeat this process several times, responding to a new key word each time.

While you are displaying your individual reactions to the key word, you must also be aware of the group as a whole. The object is to form a tableau, an overall picture, composed of individual reactions. If someone were to come unsuspectingly into the room, he or she should be easily able to guess approximately what the key word had been. Try to use a wide variety of stage positions, levels (kneeling, lying down, stretching upward), and gestures. Don't be finicky about composing the picture, but attempt to supply enough individual variety for an interesting tableau to occur.

Beyond Words

This is a series of short exercises which explores your means of communicating. Choose a partner and call yourselves A and B. Your teacher will be the leader.

1. Sit facing each other. A explains the workings of an imagined machine to B, and B questions A when necessary. At some point the leader calls "Change!" A and B continue the discussion in gibberish as though nothing had happened. A and B revert to English on the next "Change!" and so on.

2. Sit back to back with your partner. Have a discussion about any topic at all, but do not turn around to look at each other.

3. Sit face to face, with your eyes closed, and continue your conversation.

4. Sit face to face. This time neither of you can speak or hear. B has a problem or a need and tries to convey it to A by mime, and A attempts to help.

5. Sit facing each other. A, a young person in a busy post office, has a partial hearing-impairment. A wants to send a parcel to England but does not know about customs declaration forms. What happens?

6. Sit face to face and hold hands. Without using any words, B tries to express a need and A responds to it.

The aim in all of these exercises is for you to become aware of the contribution of nonverbal communication. After each exercise, talk with your partner about your feelings during the exercises: how each differs from the last, what was most difficult, where communication broke down. When A was hearing-impaired, was he or she treated as if old and foolish? Which of the senses or means of communication would you most hate to be deprived of?

Hot Potato

Form a group of six to eight people. Each group sits in a circle and chooses a leader. Pass an object from person to person around the circle. It might be a soft hat, for example,—something that will not be damaged if dropped. This object is the "hot potato," and your objective is to get it out of your hands as quickly as possible by passing it to the next person. At any moment, your leader can point to whoever has the hot potato and call out a letter of the alphabet—for example, "C!" The person with the hot potato passes it on as usual, but must say six words which begin with "C" before the hot potato completes another circuit. If the hot potato returns before the six words are spoken, that person exchanges places with the leader, and the game begins again. If it turns out that completing six words is too easy, try eight or ten words. Remember that the game should be challenging but not impossible.

Peculiar Pencil

Your whole class sits in a circle. One person begins by taking a pencil and using it in such a way that shows that the pencil has become something else. The class must identify what the pencil has become. Then the pencil is passed to the next person in the circle who must use it in a different way. There can be no duplication, and the pencil should be passed around the circle several times.

Uncle Glug

Divide into groups of ten. Choose one person in each group to be Uncle Glug. Uncle Glug is a born storyteller. If you were to ask him the time of day, he would probably tell you about the winter it got so cold that all the clocks froze solid and how, to this day, clocks are still three months slow. Uncle Glug is the narrator in this game. The rest of you in the group are his imagination. Uncle Glug narrates a story, which you act out as he is telling it. As well as taking the parts of the story's human characters, you may join the action as animals or as pieces of scenery such as trees, rocks, or even a snowdrift.

At times you may choose to speak for yourself, either for emphasis or simply because it would seem more appropriate for a character (or even an object) to tell his or her (or its) own story at a certain point. The telling of the story might move between Uncle Glug's narration and the firsthand words of the actors.

At first, Uncle Glug may tell a well known story such as "Red Riding Hood" or "The Three Bears." The stories will be open-ended, developing as much by your actions as by Uncle Glug's narration. Remember that it is the improvisation which is an end in itself, rather than the performance of a planned scene. The purpose is for you to gain experience in supporting a group effort, whatever direction the effort may take.

The following thirteen exercises can be done in groups or as a class, with a leader reading the instructions. You can also read the instructions to yourself and then try some of these alone.

Transformations

1. With your hands, create a beachball. With great effort, gradually squeeze it to the size of a baseball. Feel the change of size and shape with your whole hand. Your entire body feels the exertion. Your face expresses it, too.

Stretch the baseball into a long cylinder. Tense and hold to maintain the two ends of the cylinder. Roll the cylinder between your hands, narrowing it into a long noodle. Twirl the noodle. Wiggle it. Gather the noodle into a mass. Smooth it into a flat disk. Roll it. Sail it like a frisbee. Fold the disk in half, in half again, and so on until it is a speck in the palm of your hand. Blow it away.

2. Repeat the above changes, making them in a series of abrupt exertions. Exaggerate the start and stop of each exertion. It may take three stages to get from beachball to baseball.

Stuck!

Bump into someone or something as if it were sticky. At the point of contact, push while the rest of your body appears to pull away, struggling to get unstuck.

Flying

Poised on the ball of one foot, rotate your body freely in all directions. Move your head, shoulders, hips, knees. Dip, sway, change feet, use both feet. Glide with your arms out to the side.

Tightrope Wobbling

As you inch your way across an illusory tightrope, flex your knees to indicate the spring of the rope. Transfer your weight carefully from foot to foot. Try bending your knees further still. Try walking backwards!

Butterfly

With one hand you can make a butterfly. Keep your fingers straight as you flutter them, moving your hands up, down, and in circles through the air. As the butterfly comes to rest on your finger, your shoulder, or someone's nose, your fingers stop fluttering and start undulating together in a slow rhythm. As the butterfly flies off, jiggle your head slightly as you follow its fluttering, circular flight.

Snake Charmer

Your undulating arm is the snake. Begin with it hidden behind your back. Have it slowly wriggle out. Your hand—the snake's head—vibrates for a hiss.

Alter Egos

Begin as a short person. Turn to your left and look up into the face of an illusory tall person. Slowly turn back to your right. When you turn, you grow tall. As the tall person, lower your gaze to look down into the face of the short person you just were. As you alternate characters, be sure you look up or down to the same point in space each time. Now revolve completely around as you switch characters. Change your facial expression. Experiment with basic opposites— happy and sad, menacing and frightened, angry and apologetic.

Buried Alive!

Create two characters. One of them, weak and helpless, is trapped below ground. The other, strong and adventuresome, will come to the rescue. The strong character is walking above ground and hears a cry for help. Where is it coming from? Listen intently.

The weak character is crouched in a hole, calling out in the hope that someone will hear. Strong puts ear to the ground, then starts digging furiously. Weak extends hand; Strong keeps digging. Each time you change characters, revolve once to clearly indicate the switch. The moment of rescue: Strong reaches down and, keeping hand in the same spot, revolves to become the weak character being pulled up to safety. (The success of the illusion depends on your maintaining a sense of the vertical separation between the two characters.)

The Gift

Create two characters. One will be the giver and the other the receiver. Begin as the giver. Create an object. Turn to your right and offer the object to your illusory receiver. Revolve to your right. Change your hand positions and facial expressions to become the receiver. Be sure to receive the same object that was offered and from the same place in space.

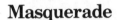

Masquerade

Visualize five masks, all lying on a table in front of you: Surprise, Anger, Arrogance, Tragedy, Comedy. Pick up Surprise and look it over. Put on Surprise, while your hands are in front of your face. Remove your hands, revealing the mask in place. Tense your face to maintain the expression as you turn your head left and right. Remove Surprise—changing your face back to neutral behind your hands—and return it to the table. Select Anger and put it on. Return it and try Arrogance. Try on Tragedy and Comedy alternately. See how quickly you can switch the two. Have one mask get stuck on your face. Try pulling it off. Insert your finger tips behind the edge of the mask to pry it off. Keeping your head and hands in place, move your shoulders and arms forward, your chest back as you pry.

Erase a Face

1. Assume a neutral face. Hold your hand next to your face, close but not touching. Slowly draw your hand across your face, changing your expression to fear. Keep your eyes focused straight ahead, oblivious to your moving hand. Erase fear, slowly moving your hand back across your face. Return to neutral.

2. Repeat the hand movement, revealing a different expression each time your hand passes over. Make the changes complete and precise (no smirking or giggling in neutral). How quickly can you create and erase your face?

3. Try this with a partner, slowly passing your hand over his or her neutral face to change it.

Garbage Picker

Pick up a small box. Turn the combination dial or pick the lock. Anything inside? Put the box in the sack you are carrying to collect your finds.

Select a wide-mouthed jar with a lid. Tense your hand around the lid to maintain its shape as you turn it counterclockwise, moving from the wrist. Pheeew! What an odour. Screw the lid back on clockwise. Toss it away.

Pick up a bottle. It still has liquid in it. Pry off the cork. Select a glass from the pile, blow out the dust (cough), and pour. Indicate the filling of the glass by lowering it slightly. Finish pouring with a snap. Drink.

Pull out a soggy blanket. Grasp it a section at a time and twist your hands in opposite directions to wring it out. The blanket should feel a lot lighter when you're done. Fold it and drop it into your sack.

Continue your treasure hunt, until your sack is bulging full, then carry or drag it away.

Combination/ Transformation

Mime an inanimate object—not a character encountering an object, but the object itself. Select two or three totally unrelated objects and create a mime in which a character *logically* encounters them. Select two totally unrelated activities, events, or situations and create a mime which logically links the two into a cohesive plot.

Select a character, an object, and an animal. Create a mime in which all three are logically inter-related.

The next few exercises can be done in small groups.

Stationary Journey

1.   Move freely about the room and pay careful attention to the way your weight shifts from foot to foot in the process of walking. What do your feet, ankles, knees, hips, arms, shoulders, and eyes do? How do they move in relation to one another? Now stay in one place and experiment with "walking on the spot." Can you create the illusion of a fairly natural walk without leaving your place? (Hint: don't focus your eyes on your feet.) This is often called "the mime walk."

2.   Choose someone to be your leader, and stand where you can see the leader. Give yourselves sufficient space to do the mime walk freely.

3.   Follow the leader as he or she walks through a series of environments. The leader chooses any kind of walk or switches from one to another during the journey. He or she may change the pace from slow to fast to running. You are led through rain, mud, fog, over puddles, through snow drifts, across desert sands, up a dune, into the wind.

4.   Switch leaders. Move through more abstract environments such as feathers, honey, peanut butter, cobwebs, outer space.

Magic Box

With your group, create a large box. Stand around it in a circle. One of you open the box, and take out an object. Define it with your hands. Use it. Give it to someone else in the circle. The receiver stretches or squashes or pulls the gift into the shape of another object. A telescope can become a cane, a cane a trombone; a trombone can stretch into an accordion. In turn, each of you pass the transformed gifts on to someone else. If you prefer, you can return the gift to the magic box and take out a new object to use and pass on.

Movers

One person begins this activity and will gradually call the rest of the group in to help. Create a very big box and try to push it. Snap your hands flat against the side of the box, tense, and hold. Keeping your hands in place, straighten your elbows, pushing your shoulders and chest away from the box. Oof! It won't budge.

Push with your shoulder. Place your arm from shoulder to elbow flat against the box. As your arm and torso move toward the box, your hips move away from it. Still no luck.

Push with your bottom. Start with your pelvis shifted forward, buttocks tucked under. As you push, arch your back and pelvis back toward the box, and push your chest forward and up. The box still won't move! Call (silently) for some others to help.

Everyone push against the box. Use different parts of your bodies, watching each other to maintain the shape of the box. All together, one...two...three...puuuush! The box begins to move slowly, as do all of you together.

For the next two activities, which are really mime plays, it will probably work best if all of you participate as your teacher narrates.

The Polluted

In this mime story you will have the opportunity to explore animal movement. Think about some of the animals (birds included) you have observed, and consider the following:

– Which senses seem to be stronger and more important?
– How does the overall design of the body relate to the animal's movement?
– Where is the body weight centred?
– How is the animal equipped for protection from predators and natural elements?
– How are the sounds the animal makes created?

Pick one animal with which you are fairly familiar and try to picture how it moves when it is afraid, eating, hunting, courting, playing, and sleeping.

Find a space on the floor and lie on your side in a relaxed position. Imagine that you are a tiny bird, still inside your shell. It is time to begin working your way out.

The bird huddles in its shell in the centre of the stage. It hatches awkwardly, rests from the exertion, and opens its beak to gawp helplessly several times. The bird fluffs its feathers, pecks at and swallows some food, takes a deep strengthening breath, and discovers it owns a right wing which moves up and down. Moving the right wing very rapidly, the bird

succeeds in getting enough lift to tip itself over on its left side. After a couple of gawps bring no help, the bird discovers its left wing and flaps it enough to roll itself not only upright, but over onto its right side. It manages to push itself upright.

The bird fluffs its feathers, pecks at and swallows some food, takes a deep strengthening breath and tries flapping both wings at once. From tiny fluttering baby bird wings, the feathered appendages reach and unfold to become the great wings of an eagle. The bird grows in power and strength until finally it is able to defy the pull of gravity and achieve the miracle of flight. The bird flies high and proud; it soars to right and left; it takes its rightful place as king of the skies.

But now, in its flight, the bird encounters a hazy cloud of air which obscures vision, irritates its respiratory system and hurts its proud eyes. The bird lands but cannot escape the haze. It ruffles its grimy feathers, takes a deep coughing breath and pecks up some food only to find that it too is poisoned. The bird wipes its ugly-tasting beak with its wing and tries to walk away, only to discover that its leg is mired in oil-slick adhesive muck. In growing desperation, the bird pulls away from the muck but only succeeds in getting its other leg and ultimately its wings also befouled. And there it sits, its airborne majesty reduced to the gawping helplessness of its hatchling state; utterly, terminally, horribly, the polluted.

Mime-in-the-Box

You crouch inside a very small box. Cautiously, you explore your prison, hands touching sides, top, bottom. You push with your back, with your feet, with your hands. Push harder, push stronger. Tension. And release! The sides of the box fall away around you, and you're free. Free! Slowly you stand and step from your broken prison. A few tentative steps, a skip, then a stride. Jubilant. Your movements expand and grow carefree. You spin and run forward. Bam! Your hands flatten against the unexpected wall. Your body jerks taut at the impact. Bewildered. Slowly, hand after hand, you follow the wall, meet a corner and turn. Follow another wall to another corner. Moving frantically now, follow to another corner and another. Pound and push, desperately. Exhausted, you lean against the wall. And slowly it moves in toward you. Apprehensive, you run to another wall. It too is slowly moving inward. And the others. With your whole body, with all your strength, you try to hold them back. You are last seen crouched inside a very small box.

The Flight of Icarus

For this mime play, choose a partner and work together as your teacher narrates.

Daedalus and his son Icarus are trapped in the labyrinth, prey to the Minotaur. Side by side, father and son move through the maze, their hands sliding along myriad walls, following endless corners. There is no way out. Gazing up, Daedalus sees a bird in flight. A feather drifts down. Freedom! Father and son begin gathering feathers and fashioning wings. Icarus slips into his wings, tests them, rises a few inches off the ground, and discovers that he *can* fly. Impatiently, Icarus rejoins his father, who is still binding his wings to his arms. Daedalus looks ahead to the sun, then cautiously extends his wings. With outstretched arms, father and son begin to fly—slowly, fluidly. They leave the labyrinth below; above them, the sun. They begin to feel the sun's heat melting the wax holding their wings. Daedalus draws back, but Icarus is enraptured with the power of flight. Daedalus' pleas go unheeded as Icarus soars towards the sun. Ascension. Pain. His wings disintegrate. Icarus spirals to earth.

Black Death

You may find that you are able to start this piece in one role and stay with that character throughout. But each of you should be ready and alert in case, for the sake of the story, you have to alter your role, or even take on a new one altogether.

Work in two large groups or as a class while your teacher narrates the following story.

It is early morning in this mediaeval market-place; house-doors are opening and people pass by happily greeting one another as they pass. A woman is singing as she cleans her courtyard; a boy, also singing, goes to the well to fetch water and returns to his house. Some children are playing in a little group on the right. Presently there is the sound of a small drum-beat, and a young pedlar comes into view, beating a drum to attract attention to himself and the wares he has to sell. The children stop their game and crowd round him laughing gaily. The pedlar is generous and gives them some trinkets to play with. One of the boys has been given a pipe which he begins to play and some of the children find themselves dancing and gradually men and women come from their houses to watch and join in.

Buying and selling is at its height when the Burgomaster passes by. He is much respected by all the citizens and they give him a great welcome.

The scene is at its happiest when an old friar joins the crowd; as he comes among them the mood changes, for he brings news that in a neighbouring village there is plague and many people are dying. The children do not understand why their mothers and fathers suddenly look so serious and quiet, but the dancing comes to a standstill and the tune on the pipe has changed to a minor key; the day is clouding over and a shiver passes through the crowd. It seems as if there is a faint hissing sound in the air although the crowd seem to hear nothing. Now we see three weird figures creeping among the people like shadows. No one can see them, but we see that they hover as a hawk hovers before seizing its prey. One by one they find their victim and stand close by like a shadow and immediately the victims are stricken with plague and fall to the ground, contaminated; no one dares touch them, and terror runs through the crowd. The boy with the pipe is taken with plague and his father runs for the quack doctor, who quickly comes and performs various rites; but in the middle of the cure, one of the shadows crosses his path; the quack doctor too has the plague and terror grows to panic. Many of the crowd creep back to their homes. A few of the people stay with a nun who has remained quiet and tranquil throughout; her faith revives their fearful spirits. Plague is defeated, the three figures lose their power and pass on to the next village.

Slowly life returns to its normal round. It is as though a cloud has passed by; and the singing is resumed as before, but it is a different voice, for she who sang before was a victim of the plague; but life continues.

Drama Journal

Which ideas were best expressed without words? Which ideas were the most difficult to express without words?

A classical mime artist requires years of study and practice. What elements of mime could be useful to all drama work?

What do you feel you have learned from this type of movement work?

Does work in mime have to be shown to others to be effective?

Dance Drama

Our feelings, attitudes, and ideas are with us, no matter what we do. Movement gives form to our feelings, enabling us to identify and use feelings in personally rewarding and socially acceptable ways.

Nancy King
Giving Form to Feeling p. 17

So Brook's actors set off in the sacred forest, to seek the trunk of the tree, as it were. They gathered as birds and in sound and movement set off for about the tenth time that day. But the heat was so stifling the actors could scarcely move. Some bird-actors didn't even make the first valley of the imaginary journey: too exhausted. The real birds of the forest watched from the trees, scoffing. It wasn't going too well that day.

Suddenly, Lou Zeldis the flute player began to walk round the forest in a circle: the famous Walking Show. *He just walked round, expanding the circle little by little.*

And very slowly began to change into a bird.

As he walked, he transformed. And quickened in pace. And was a bird, absolutely. And flew. He flew! *I saw him do it. He became a bird and flew over the trees and up to the sky. Applause from the real birds watching from the trees! They knew they had seen a supreme moment of theatre. An actor, human they say, flew.*

Ah, but did his feet really leave the ground?

It was the hugest discovery for me! It doesn't matter! It doesn't matter a damn, provided you fly.

John Heilpern
Conference of the Birds p. 310

This chapter moves you further into drama by using movement combined with music and sound. By moving to music, by responding to the rhythm, tempo, and structure of music, you can become more aware of your senses and more sensitive to the mood that is being created. Dance drama activities also promote group understanding. As you work nonverbally within your group, you will find new ways to focus energy, to develop trust and to promote artistic feeling.

Dance drama does not require that you learn the technical aspects of dance. In dance drama, you blend the patterns of dance-like movement with the story being told in the drama. Sometimes dance drama is used within the drama itself to convey the conflict of the story, to show an event from the past, or to picture a dream.

Some very powerful work can be done in dance drama using myth, legend, and rituals. Because these kinds of stories tell so much with so few details, there is room for you to elaborate upon the few facts given to create a wonderful story. Feel free to use make-up, masks, costumes, and chanting to add to the power of your interpretation. When these elements of theatre are added to your drama, you are truly creating meaning through art.

On the next page a cartoon demonstrates one possible use of dance drama.

Workshop

Starting with Music

As a class, listen to a selection of instrumental music, and visualize movements or actions that you think would go well with the music.

Now divide up into groups of six or eight and discuss the interpretations of each member of the group. What stories did you envision? Did the music convey a mood? Did the music convey a theme? Stand in a circle with your group. Play the piece a second time and during the playing, move, one at a time, to the centre of the circle, and assume a shape. Shapes should complement one another.

Starting with Words

Each of you read the following passage, and decide upon how you would interpret the actions represented in this story. When you are all finished reading, your teacher will read the story aloud, and you will each, all at the same time, act out your interpretation.

You are a traveller in a far-off land, the weather is very hot and you have been walking since seven o'clock in the morning. Now it is lunchtime and you lie down exhausted in the shade of a big plant with large green leaves...you are eating the sandwiches you have brought with you...you finish off the last bite of the last sandwich... and screw up the paper into a ball and put it back tidily in your knapsack...and now you begin to feel really sleepy...and you lean back against the stem of the plant with

your eyes half closed...and then, out of the corner of your eye, you notice that, although there is no wind, the branches of the plant are slowly waving in the air and coming nearer and nearer to you...and, too late, you realize it's a man-eating plant, and it's got you in its grasp...and you struggle against it...trying to fight off the branches...and you're getting weaker and weaker...but then the plant seems to give up the struggle, and its branches retreat...that was a close shave...but it's coming back again...and this time it finishes you off.

Starting with Feelings: Action and Reaction

1. Divide into groups of five or six people. Each of you develop one aspect of a nightmare, for example, running away, screaming, holding your hand over your face, or falling down, and decide how this makes you feel. Decide on the cause of this action, for example, "I want to get away," or "I want to yell for help." Each action should have a beginning and an end and include sound and movement.

2. Now each of you will show your work to the others in your group. Then your group must decide on what caused you to act this way. For example, suppose you choose to yell "Help!", while backing away from the group. This is your "reaction." The group must then decide what they will do to cause you to react in your chosen way. One choice would be to stalk you slowly as if to back you into a corner in preparation for an attack.

If this choice satisfies both you and the group then the group has completed one person's action and reaction. Each person in the group, one at a time, shares a reaction so that the group can make the stimulating action.

3. When all the actions and reactions have been developed so that the feelings involved are clear, your group should decide in which order the actions and reactions will be shown. Try to order the actions on the basis of what seems to fit where, and why. You may choose to start with an action that takes place at a low level and gradually work up to standing level. Or you might choose to start with a slow activity, change pace with a faster one, and so on.

When you have set the order, you must decide on how you will make the transition from one action/reaction to another. Each of you must know when one reaction is finished and the next action is beginning without everything stopping. A change shouldn't occur because of a verbal cue. The cues should be nonverbal and integrated into the rest of the activity.

Each group must also decide on a beginning and ending position for the entire sequence of actions/reactions. Make sure that you know how long the ending will be held before your group breaks up. Once you've got your work put together, repeat the entire sequence at least three times. This will allow your group a chance to develop an

appropriate sense of pace, dynamics, focus, and so on. If all the groups decide to show their work, make sure that each group's work is shown before discussing any one group's efforts. When and if the work is to be discussed, each of you should have a chance to offer personal observations but without naming names. All comments should begin with "I." Each group should have a chance to share any problems that were encountered and tell how these were solved. Finally, feelings, ideas, or questions should be shared.

Nightmares

Each of you think of a nightmare that you have had, or take a situation from a movie that appeared nightmarish. Divide into groups of five or six. Each of you quickly relate the outline of your nightmare. The group chooses one on which to work. (The person whose nightmare you have chosen to use should not play his or her own part.) Each piece should have a beginning, middle, and end. Level, focus, pace, and all the other elements should be checked to make sure that they have been considered.

The who, what, where, when, and why of the situation should also be actively explored. Attention should be paid to the feelings of the person whose nightmare it is and to sharing these feelings with those involved. If there is easy access to props, levels, lights, tape-player, or record player, these may be used as needed. But consideration should be paid to why they are used and how they affect the work.

40

Fantasies

Each of you think of a fantasy that you have. It might be winning a lottery or the ability to fly. Think of what feelings your fantasy instills in you—the thrill of being rich, the freedom of flying. Now divide into groups of about six, and each of you share your fantasy and your feelings about it with the members of your group. When you have all shared, discuss how each fantasy might be physicalized. For example, the fantasy of floating in space might be achieved by having the person rest on the arms of the others, who gently throw him or her up and down as they move about the room.

After all of your fantasies are worked out, your group should order the fantasies so that, using transitions, you can go from one to the next without stopping. Repeat your sequence several times to develop pace and flow. Each group then shares the work with the other groups. After all the work is shown, there should be a brief discussion about the give and take within the groups. Whose ideas were used? Whose were not and why? How do each of you feel about the way both your group and the other groups responded to your personal fantasy?

The Dance of the Thirteen Skeletons

Read the poem silently to yourself.

THE DANCE OF THE
THIRTEEN SKELETONS

In a snow-enshrouded graveyard
gripped by winter's bitter chill,
not a single soul is stirring,
all is silent, all is still
till a distant bell tolls midnight
and the spirits work their will.

For emerging from their coffins
buried deep beneath the snow,
thirteen bony apparitions
now commence their spectral show,
and they gather in the moonlight
undulating as they go.

    And they'll dance in their bones,
    in their bare bare bones,
    with the click and the clack
    and the chitter and the chack
    and the clatter and the chatter
    of their bare bare bones.

They shake their flimsy shoulders
and they flex their fleshless knees
and they nod their skulls in greeting
in the penetrating breeze
as they form an eerie circle
near the gnarled and twisted trees.

They link their spindly fingers
as they promenade around
casting otherworldly shadows
on the silver-mantled ground
and their footfalls in the snowdrift
make a soft and susurrous sound.

    And they dance in their bones,
    in their bare bare bones,
    with the click and the clack
    and the chitter and the chack
    and the clatter and the chatter
    of their bare bare bones.

The thirteen grinning skeletons
continue on their way
as to strains of soundless music

they begin to swing and sway
and they circle ever faster
in their ghastly roundelay.

Faster, faster ever faster
and yet faster now they race,
winding, whirling, ever swirling
in the frenzy of their pace
and they shimmer in the moonlight
as they spin themselves through
    space.

    And they dance in their bones
    in their bare bare bones,
    with the click and the clack
    and the chitter and the chack
    and the clatter and the chatter
    of their bare bare bones.

Then as quickly as it started
their nocturnal dance is done
for the bell that is their signal
loudly tolls the hour of one
and they bow to one another
in their bony unison.

Then they vanish to their coffins
by their ghostly thoroughfare
and the emptiness of silence
once more fills the frosted air
and the snows that mask their
    footprints
show no sign that they were there.

    But they danced in their bones,
    in their bare bare bones,
    with the click and the clack
    and the chitter and the chack
    and the clatter and the chatter
    of their bare bare bones.

1. Divide into groups of five or six. Decide on five scenes from this poem that could be re-created as frozen tableaux or pictures. Using each member of the group, create a series of tableaux that you feel would best represent the images in "The Dance of the Thirteen Skeletons." Remember that you must have a beginning and a concluding tableau, plus three additional tableaux in the middle. One of these middle three should present a sense of tension—the "conflict" of your drama. Remember, too, that you must have transitions, that is, something that will move you from one frozen tableau to the next.

2. The poem can easily be separated into four sections, each section ending with the lines, "and the clatter and the chatter of their bare bare bones." Divide into four groups—A, B, C, D. Group A is assigned the first three stanzas of the poem, group B the next three stanzas, and so on. As a group, develop movements to accompany the lines that you have been assigned. Although you should avoid using the actual words from the poem, you can add sounds and music to your work. You may wish to begin and end your section with a tableau.

3. After each group has worked out its section, get the four groups back together to show all four sections. When you've seen all the work, have a discussion about how each group's work could be linked. Can each group find a way to incorporate the other three groups— that is, the audience—into its dance drama? Are there any parts in any of the four sections that could be done with the whole group?

The Ash Tree

Read the following myth silently to yourself.

THE ASH TREE

The entire world is an ash tree of prodigious dimensions. The foliage is always green. It has three roots and its mighty boughs soar into the sky. Near the first root, which plunges into the underworld, gushes a fountain, the bubbling source of all primitive rivers. Beside the second root, which penetrates the land of the giants covered with frost and ice floes, is the fountain from which all wisdom springs. Finally, next to the third root—which according to one tradition emerges from the earth to sweep up into the very heavens—is the fountain of the wisest of the Norns. Everyday the Norns draw water from the well with which they sprinkle the ash tree so that it will not wither and rot away.

In its highest branches perches a golden rooster. He surveys the horizon and warns the gods, who dwell round the tree, whenever their ancient enemies, the giants, are preparing to attack. Under the ash tree lies a trumpet which one day will announce the final battle. At the foot of the tree is consecrated ground where the gods meet to render justice.

Demons continually scheme to destroy the tree. A cunning monster lurks under the third root and gnaws ceaselessly at it. Four stags wander among the foliage and nibble off young buds.

However, because of the tireless attention of the Norns, the tree continues to put forth green shoots and rear its indestructible trunk from the centre of the Earth.

In Scandinavian mythology, the giant ash tree represents all living nature, connecting heaven, earth, and hell. As a class, you will have to make several decisions about how you can bring this myth to life.

At first glance there may not seem to be much potential for dance-drama in this piece because nothing much seems to be *happening*. But notice all the action verbs in it. (There are more than you might think!)

- Will you begin by having everyone creating the ash tree?
- Will you divide into groups and have each group be responsible for one aspect of the myth?
- Will you use music or sound?

Choose a point in the myth that you think offers the best potential for your dance drama to explode into conflict. How might the rest of your improvisation contrast with this?

The Creation of the World

Read the following story to yourself.

Kabezya-Mpungu, the highest god, had created the sky and the earth and two human beings, a man and a woman, endowed with Reason. However, these two human beings did not, as yet, possess Mutima, or Heart.

Kabezya-Mpungu had four children, the Sun, the Moon, Darkness, and Rain. He called them all together and said to them, "I want to withdraw now, so that Man can no longer see me. I will send down Mutima in my place, but before I take leave I want to know what you, Rain, are going to do." "Oh,"

replied Rain, "I think I'll pour down without cease and put everything under water." "No," answered the god, "don't do that! Look at these two," and he pointed to the man and the woman; "do you think they can live under water? You'd better take turns with the Sun. After you have sufficiently watered the earth, let the Sun go to work and dry it.

"And how are you going to conduct yourself?" the god asked the Sun. "I intend to shine hotly and burn everything under me," said his second child.

"No," replied Kabezya-Mpungu. "That cannot be. How do you expect the people whom I created to get food? When you have warmed the earth for a while, give Rain a chance to refresh it and make the fruit grow.

"And you, Darkness, what are your plans?"

"I intend to rule forever!" was the answer.

"Have pity," cried the god. "Do you want to condemn my creatures, the lions, the tigers, and the serpents, to see nothing of the world I made? Listen to me: give the Moon time to shine on the earth, and when you see the Moon in its last quarter, then you may again rule. But I have lingered too long; now I must go." And he disappeared.

Somewhat later, Mutima, Heart, came along, in a small container no bigger than a hand.

Heart was crying, and asked Sun, Moon, Darkness, and Rain, "Where is Kabezya-Mpungu, our father?"

"Father is gone," they said, "and we do not know where."

"Oh, how great is my desire," replied Heart, "to commune with him. But since I cannot find him I will enter into Man, and through him I will seek God from generation to generation."

And that is what happened. Ever since, all children born of Man contain Mutima, a longing for God.

This creation myth, which comes from Uganda, gives you an opportunity to work both in groups and as a class. The groups could each work on roles like Sun, Moon, Darkness, Rain, Mutima, and all the creatures. All the groups could come together at the beginning to play Kabezya-Mpungu, and again at the end to play "all the children born of Man." You might have one group narrate the story, or create background sound effects.

Celebration

All over the world there are rituals, handed down through time, which observe the changing of the seasons. In spring the cycle begins again and creation celebrates its rebirth. This poem is a modern celebration of spring rituals.

in Just-

in Just-
spring   when the world is mud-
luscious the little
lame balloonman

whistles   far   and wee

and eddieandbill come
running from marbles and
piracies and it's
spring

when the world is puddle-wonderful

the queer
old balloonman whistles
far   and   wee
and bettyandisbel come dancing

from hop-scotch and jump-rope and

it's
spring
and
    the
      goat-footed

balloonMan   whistles
far
and
wee

e.e. cummings

This poem can be the basis for a final creation in dance drama. You should read it by yourself, and then have several people in your group or class read it aloud. Close your eyes while someone else is reading and let your imagination take you wherever the words and rhythm lead.

Share with your group:
– What are some of the springtime celebration rituals of children suggested by the poem?
– What actions, rhythms, songs, sights, and sounds do you associate with these activities?
– Where might your improvisation take place? In the street? In a schoolyard? An alley? What kind of a day is it?

Bring your own and your group's shared feelings and experiences out to play as you explore this dance drama.

Drama Journal

What elements of drama were you expressing through dance?

How does dance drama differ from mime and other movement activities?

How do these types of activities develop group skills in the drama class?

Does dance drama need music or sound to be effective?

What dance drama activities have you observed in music shows and rock videos?

Working in Groups

A group has a personality of its own. No two groups will be alike. If you introduce just one new member, you will alter the personality of the group.

Brian Clark
Group Theatre p. 48

...group development reduces the level of threat in the classroom, making students more comfortable with one another and less defensive. Threat—whether it be fear of embarrassment or ridicule, fear of a low grade, or concern about gaining the teacher's approval—causes students to defend themselves psychologically, and the most common defense is to close themselves off. Students who are defending themselves against threat are not open to learning. It's only when they feel comfortable enough to let down their protective shields that they can interact freely and constructively with new stimuli.

Gene Stanford
Developing Effective Classroom Groups p. 34

This section of the book is about working *in role* with other people. Role-playing is a very "safe" way of learning about yourself. Here, because you will be working in role with various partners, with small groups, and with the whole class, you will have the opportunity to see yourself in a variety of group situations.

The drama situations in this section all grow out of your interaction with your fellow participants. These spontaneous group activities give you the opportunity to speak and listen: to give and take at appropriate times and to lead and follow in significant ways. You will learn to offer ideas and to respect the ideas of others. Remember that it is the shared responsibility of all the role-players to develop the drama. You should be prepared to adjust your actions in order to help move the drama along in a way that is satisfactory for everyone. By listening and responding to the others in the group, you can actually create the drama moment-to-moment, responding spontaneously to the challenges that are presented.

Activities like the ones here develop trust and encourage participation. Through them you will build both the group *and* the drama, and they can be returned to again and again, as the need arises.

Working in Role

The techniques of drama centre on transformation: how people can turn into other people or other beings in order to create a there-and-then story in a here-and-now place.

Richard Scheckner & Mady Schuman
Introduction to:
Ritual, Play and Performance p. xv

A prominent film actress, whom I was once helping with a role, was thrown by the fact that her part was just an ordinary woman like herself—same age, background, schooling, emotional problems, etc. She felt she had nothing "to act." Her previous orientation to acting consisted of finding a mask to hide behind. She believed that the outer dressing of the part—age difference, historic difference, national difference—contained the real essence of acting. For her, acting was only a craft when it was miles away from her, and when it was used to illustrate something totally different from herself. She knew so little of herself and her own behaviour that she was unable to make any use of her SELF, to strip to her soul. She had only one wish: to put on a mask, to disguise herself.

Uta Hagen
Respect for Acting p. 27

Workshop

The activities in this chapter move you into role-playing, giving you a sense of what role-playing is. The activities are basically "role games," rather than true dramas. By working through these activities in role, you will learn the elements that make up role-playing, adopt roles different from your own, and learn to put your "self" back into the role you are playing.

Role is made up of two parts: your "self" and the "other person" that you become. This "other person" half of the role gives you the safety of exploring ideas and situations quite different from your own life. The "self" half of the role allows you to use your values and responses in the drama situation to understand what has happened. When you can balance the "other" part of the role—what you are given to work with—with the "self" part of the role, you can believe in the role that you are playing. Find the heart of your role, and you have created drama.

The role games in this chapter will help you listen to and observe each other closely. "Playing" in role enables you to join in, to learn by experimenting, to take on different attitudes, and to see how others respond. Role-playing is the basis of all drama, and these games will help you learn to role-play without tension or threat of an audience. The chapters that follow will focus on using these role-playing skills to build drama.

Who Am I?

Choose a partner. One of you decide secretly who you will be (for example, Santa Claus) and who the other person will be (for example, Santa's helper). Then you begin to talk to your partner in the role that you have selected without revealing what that role is. (For example, "Is everything ready for tonight?") Your partner answers back as well as possible. The game ends when your partner guesses the role that you are playing.

Famous People

1. Everyone write the names of four famous people—real (Joan of Arc) or fictional (Superman)—on four separate pieces of paper. Put all the names into a hat or bag, and get your teacher to pin or tape one name to each person's back.

Walk around and try to find out who you are by asking yes-or-no questions of everyone else. When you know who you are, pin the paper on your front and continue to help others.

2. Play the game again. This time, try it nonverbally.

3. Play the game a third time. Everyone is only allowed to make statements about who they think they are. For example, you can make the statement "I am a woman," but you cannot ask the question "Am I a woman?" The others answer only "yes" or "no."

Happy Families

Mark a number of small cards (depending on the number of people in your class) with family names and positions. Each family has four members (and four cards), for instance "Father Johnson," "Mother Johnson," "Daughter Johnson," and "Son Johnson." (Extra people in the class can be added in as grandparents.) Mix the cards up and have your teacher distribute them, one to each of you. When your teacher gives the command, move about the room trading cards with other players. At another sign from your teacher, all the members of each family must find each other and sit down on one chair. The family that is last to sit down is eliminated. Communications may be verbal or nonverbal.

Here's Where I Come In

The objective of the following game is for each of you to create your own role and then to bring all the roles together, or into contact with one another, during the story. The role you choose may be of either sex, older or younger than you, from history, fiction, film or TV, invented by you, or someone known to you.

Begin by sitting in a circle in small groups of four or six. (There is no preliminary discussion about what roles you may create or what the story is.) In turn, each of you announces your role and offers some description of appearance, age, health, job and so on, as necessary. The rest of you may ask for any further information until you have a clear picture of the role.

Work round the group until there is a complete set of roles. Some of these roles may be related to one another because there is nothing to prevent any of you from declaring a relationship with any of the roles announced so far. You may claim to be related as an aunt, cousin, grandparent to any one else's role, whether historical or fictional; you may claim to be a friend or neighbour; and, of course, you may not "know" any of the other players at all.

Someone may be willing to start the story going, or, if not, simply work round the group. It is usually better if each of you comes into the story when you see the right opportunity. The first player may begin in any way. He or she may simply get up, have breakfast and go to work on the local bus.

Each of you finds a way of linking with one or more of the other players and of helping to develop the story. You need to be constantly aware of the whole range of other players and to make or allow "openings" for them to enter the story.

The story does not have to be rounded off. The game is complete once each of you has entered the story and carried it forward in some way. As soon as there is a clear story or situation, you can either proceed to an improvised ending, or stop and discuss your work before completing it.

Waiting Room

Get into groups of four or five. Each of you imagines a stereotypical role—a hobo, playboy, business executive, drop-out, etc., and some reason why that person should be waiting somewhere—such as waiting for a dentist, for a train to arrive, a baby to be born, a dog or cat to be vetted, car to be cleaned or repaired, and so on. You then assume that each person in your group is there for the same reason that you are. The aim is to keep a straight face and make one of the others laugh without giving away too obviously why you are waiting. You can each ask questions of the others and react however you wish to whatever they say.

Persuasion

Work with a partner. Explore each of the following situations. Make sure you switch roles for each situation.

- Persuade your parent to turn the TV over to a program that you want to watch.
- Persuade your brother/sister to lend you the thing he/she treasures most.
- Persuade your busy friend to stand for the job of secretary of your recreation centre.
- Persuade your father to increase your allowance to cope with inflation.
- Persuade the cafeteria helper to give you a big helping of the pudding you like most.
- Persuade your grandmother /father who lives with you to go away for the weekend at the same time as your parents are away, so that you can have a party.
- Persuade your teacher to sponsor you generously at the Charity School Walk.
- Persuade the bus driver to let you travel home on the bus even though you have no money.

A Day in the Life of...

Work with a partner. In each exercise, one of you will take the central role, and the other will take the changing role part. At the end of each exercise, switch roles and repeat. As you work through each exercise, notice how you remain consistent in the single role, and how you must adapt as you play the whole range of roles.

Student

- with a parent at breakfast time
- with brother or sister who wants to borrow some of your clothes
- with your teacher who wants to see you about your work
- with your friend to plan what you will do tonight
- with the principal who has called you into his or her office because of reports of lateness and laziness
- with the youth leader who wants you to represent the club in an activity you are keen on

Mother

- with son/daughter at breakfast time
- with store clerk who overcharges
- with a workmate while working
- with a rare visitor (religious leader, disliked relative)
- with your husband over the evening dinner
- with your close friend who calls in to see you

Father

- with wife at breakfast time
- with a workmate while working
- with your boss whom you are asking for a favour
- with your best friend who is sharing your hobby
- with your child's teacher on parents' day at school
- with your son/daughter coming home late

In Others' Shoes

1. Get into groups of four and label yourselves A, B, C, D. A now interviews B and C interviews D. Do this in some depth and spend at least 10 minutes over it, asking about background, biography, beliefs, interests, etc.

2. The next part is not as difficult to do as it is to explain! A, you are now going to imagine—having interviewed B—that you actually are B, and C will do likewise with D. Now D is going to interview A (who is pretending to be B), and B is going to interview C (who is pretending to be D). Everything you say as imaginary B and D must be either what you have been told or what you imagine that B and D would do or say. Not only are the attitudes and information important, but all the nonverbal communication too—how they would sit, or use their hands or the facial expressions they would use. You must do your best really to be the other person using whatever cues and clues you have gleaned. When your teacher declares time up, A and C go back to your original partners to see how close some of your invented replies were to the truth. Reverse the exercise with B and D undertaking the initial interviewing.

Conflict!

Choose a partner, and then decide who will play which role from the columns below. Start the dialogue with the one line given, and then continue until the conflict is resolved. (Do not use physical violence to resolve the conflict.)

Son or Daughter
Mom (Dad) can I have the car tonight? It's really important.

Parent
I need the car tonight.

Boyfriend
I insist we split the cheque for dinner.

Girlfriend
Let me pay for it. After all, I make more money.

Boss
You'll have to work overtime tonight. It's an emergency.

Worker
I have to go home. It's my daughter's birthday.

Landlord
Pay the rent! You're two months behind.

Tenant
I won't pay the rent until you repair the kitchen sink.

Customer
I want to return this defective toaster.

Store Clerk
This store has a "no returns" policy.

Student
I can't write the test because I'm on the basketball team.

Teacher
You must write the test. Basketball is not important.

Company president
If you go on strike I'll have to close the plant—forever.

Union leader
The employees can't survive on the wages you are paying them.

What Should I Do?

Choose a partner, and work on as many of the following situations as possible.

- The husband/father's work is taking up too much time. His wife/children need the money but now see far too little of him. Similar situation with a working mother.
- A police officer making an arrest for stealing, or vandalism, or attacks on immigrant groups discovers that his or her own son/daughter is in the gang.
- A manager's family cannot cope with financial problems while his or her firm/factory is out on unofficial strike.
- A teacher's son/daughter is a pupil in the school; the teacher is having great problems maintaining discipline.
- The factory worker who is a pacifist discovers the factory's insecticides are being used in weapons for germ warfare.
- The social worker feels that he or she cannot desert the clients and strike, yet is called to do so by the union.
- The factory supervisor has to discipline and/or dismiss an employee who is a great friend.
- The innocent school pupil is accused of a theft that will spoil his or her record; he or she knows that a friend stole the money.
- The student minister is also a part-time factory worker and is made aware of the firm's shady practices.

Mood Swings

1. Choose a partner, and label yourselves A and B. A takes up a certain mood quite strongly—cheerful, sad, irritable, angry, friendly, fed-up—and imagines what has sparked the mood off. B picks up A's mood and then echos it, so B also becomes sad, cheerful, etc.

2. B now takes up a mood strongly. A tries to discover the mood and takes on the opposite mood.

3. A thinks of a strong feeling like fear, courage, loyalty, devotion, hate, tenderness, joy and imagines a problem with B. A does everything possible to push the feeling onto B so that he or she becomes fearful, courageous, loyal or whatever.

4. B decides on some kind of minor practical problem that he or she has (something is broken, lost something important, ripped something, cut hand, etc.) and praises and flatters A for his or her help. A feels fed up and gives the help reluctantly.

As you finish each of the above situations, make sure you discuss your feelings with your partner.

Broken Roles

1. These situations can be taken at a fun level or can lead into interactions that can become quite serious. In the following situations a problem is posed where the role of one of the players is not what we usually expect. Choose a partner.

Work through the situations making sure that you each take on some of the "broken" roles:
- a father/mother who needs to borrow money from a teenage son/daughter
- a teacher is found cheating on a public examination
- a police officer who breaks down and cries in the middle of an arrest
- a sea captain who is seasick
- a judge caught stealing in a supermarket
- a soldier who refuses to fight
- a doctor who is always complaining that something is wrong with him/her
- a school pupil who knows far more than his or her teacher.

2. In small groups, work through these same situations, adding roles to fill out the scenes.

Viewpoints

In drama, as in real life, there are usually several points of view to every problem. In the following activity you are presented with four situations, and each situation gives you several aspects of the problem.

1. A highway to be built: how might the following react—two farmers, two shopkeepers, two unemployed workers, two keen conservationists, two garage mechanics, two councillors, two to-be evicted tenants, two local porcupines?

2. A war is to be declared in 1812: how might the following react—two young sons of a parliamentarian, two elderly king's men, two beggars, two scholars?

3. The king has just been murdered while visiting the castle of an important lord; how might these react—two of the king's bodyguards, two ambitious warrior lords, two of the host's servants, two competing town criers, a local coven of witches, the sons of the host, the gate-keeper and his dog.

4. Trouble at the factory: the company is losing money rapidly. What happens in the following cases—boss firing an old worker, employee asking for more money, new employee being shown around, employee being offered promotion, initiation ceremony being planned for new apprentices, workers trying to draw up list of improvements?

Get into groups of six or eight and read through the first situation. Each of you must take on each role for thirty seconds. It doesn't matter if, at this point, your responses feel stereotypical or superficial. This work is only to prepare you for a deeper exploration.

When you have finished, write each role on a piece of paper and each of you draw one out of the pile. Now, with all of you in a "permanent" role, spend about ten minutes working through the problem. Notice if you are more alert to the wider issues, having spent some time with the other roles.

Continue on with the other situations.

2. When you have finished all the situations (or after each one, whichever your group prefers), discuss how each of you reacted to the problem. Did looking at the other roles help you?

Drama
Journal

How is role-playing different from acting?

Why do actors spend time in their training learning to role-play?

What roles do you find yourself playing in "real life"?

How much "self" did you find in the roles you played?

Do you prefer to be involved in the role-playing or to watch others role-play?

CHAPTER

7

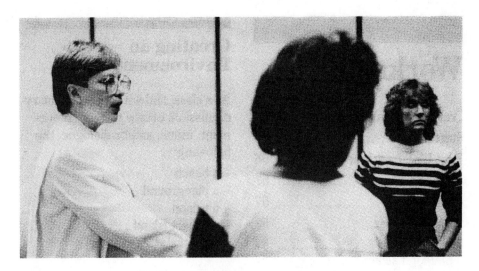

Improvising in Drama

The theatre has one special characteristic: it is always possible to start again. In life, this is a myth; we ourselves can never go back on anything. In the theatre the slate is wiped clean all the time.

Peter Brook
The Empty Space p. 157

This chapter is about *spontaneous* improvisation. In the activities, you are given information for beginning the drama, but you, as group members, are responsible for the direction your drama takes. There are no answers provided, nor are there right or wrong endings. You can find clues in the starting points given, but you must suggest directions and build on the ideas of others. The action in spontaneous improvisation is open-ended. It is the process of improvising that helps develop drama skills, not the product that you create.

Once the drama begins, your group has the responsibility for maintaining the improvisation. You will explore situations in a game-like atmosphere, learning the give and take of improvisation, free from a critical audience. You will be concerned with maintaining the improvisation, solving problems, and making decisions. This is the excitement of working in improvised drama—you initiate the action, develop the drama spontaneously, and then face the consequences of your own actions.

To experience what drama is, you *must* spend time in role, actually improvising. Working with audiences will be dealt with as we go. But this chapter gives you the opportunity, while you explore the concept of improvising, to focus on your own growth and development.

Workshop

Creating an Environment

As a class, and without preliminary discussion, create through movement, mime, and/or dialogue, the following:

– a beach
– a playground
– a prison
– a desert island
– a central train station
– an airport
– a supermarket
– a sports stadium
– a fairground
– a circus
– a café
– a hospital

Divide your class into two groups. A few people from each group go outside the room while the others decide on new locations to create. Bring the observers back into the room and keep secret from them your choice of location. The observers should be able to tell if the environment is hot, cold, dark, light, etc. as well as guess what the new environment is.

Starters

Choose a partner. One of you will begin by saying one of the following lines. (Or make one up yourself.)

– "Is he still breathing?"
– "Sorry. No foreigners."
– "Why don't you get your hair cut?"
– "Has it got two heads or is that three?"
– "They're a menace; it's time someone did something about them."
– "Now we're done for. I forgot to bring it with me."
– "Where on earth has my wooden leg gone?"

Your partner must respond *immediately* to you. Continue on to create a scene.

First Line/Last Line

1. Divide into small groups. Choose one of the following sentences around which to build an improvisation. The line must be used by one of you either as the opening or closing line.

– "Pass the salt."
– "I wonder if I dare ask my boss for a raise?"
– "He loses his temper so easily."
– "Nobody in this house ever listens to me."
– "Why can't you get home on time?"
– "I don't want you out on the streets after dark."
– "I spent the whole afternoon cooking dinner and none of you has eaten a thing."
– "Hey, darling, I've some bad news for you."
– "I've been hearing things about you."
– "I always knew that would happen."

Proverbs

Divide into small groups. Each group take one proverb as a starter for an improvisation. Your improvisation can be literal or developed in a symbolic way. It can be done as a mime or with words.

A bird in the hand is worth two in the bush.

A drowning man will clutch at a stone.

A friend in need is a friend indeed.

A rolling stone gathers no moss.

A stitch in time saves nine.

Absence makes the heart grow fonder.

Actions speak louder than words.

All that glitters is not gold.

All's fair in love and war.

Better late than never.

Birds of a feather flock together.

Blood is thicker than water.

Charity begins at home.

Discretion is the better part of valour.

Don't count your chickens before they're hatched.

Don't put all your eggs in one basket.

Don't tell tales out of school.

Empty vessels make the most noise.

Every cloud has a silver lining.

Forewarned is forearmed.

It never rains but it pours.

It's an ill wind that blows nobody any good.

Look before you leap.

Make hay while the sun shines.

Many hands make light work.

Necessity is the mother of invention.

Jumbled Jobs

Get into groups of six. Each of you write down three occupations (doctor, bricklayer, etc.), one occupation per piece of paper. Put all of the papers into a bag. Now each of you draw out one slip. With your group, improvise a scene using all of the occupations drawn.

Treasure Chest

1.   Your teacher will pick five or six objects—a book, a ruler, etc.—and show them to the whole class. You will discuss each object as to its possible or projected uses. Anyone can step forward and show how the object might be used.

2.   Now divide into five or six groups. Each group gets one of the objects and builds an improvisation around it. If your group's piece really clicks, show it.

Travel Agent

Divide into groups of three or four. One person is the travel agent and the others are customers. Develop your role by thinking about your age, sex, appearance, occupation, problems. Improvise a scene in a travel bureau. The agent might be advertising time travel or space travel, as well as "normal" trips.

The Plot Thickens

1.   Divide into groups of five or six. Each group member takes a number. The two of you who are numbered "one" and "two" start an improvisation on anything at all. The rest of you may only enter the improvisation in number order.

2.   After the improvisation is well-established, one of you may change the direction of the improvisation. For example, if the improvisation has become "feeding time at the zoo," the new participant could enter as:

- a film director who asks for a replay of the same scene with a different emotion, or who asks for the final scene of the film to be played out;
- a teacher who walks in to find out what is happening in the room.

Changes

Choose a partner, and agree on which of you will start the game. Stand face to face within touching distance of each other, in whatever pose occurs to each of you—arms folded and one arm raised, for example.

Let's say the person with the raised arm initiates the action. The aim is to create an activity out of these as yet unrelated postures. Take a moment to study them. Ask yourself, "Why might we be in such positions; what might we be doing here together?" Perhaps one of you is a parent with a child, and you are trying to persuade the child to go into the house and practise the bagpipes.

You begin to act out the situation. Perhaps you take your partner's arm as if to manoeuvre him or her to the house. Your partner, of course, does not remain passive during all this. Though he or she might not yet understand what the action means, he or she attempts to participate and respond to you and actively go along with the situation until catching on to your idea.

This first action might have taken only a few seconds to establish and your partner might immediately transform the scene into something new. For example, when you grasp your partner's arm the response might be "Ouch! That's the spot, Doc!" Thus, the original parent-child relationship has been abruptly changed to a doctor-patient one. This new situation might then develop for a few moments until one of you, with a single gesture, creates yet a third situation with an entirely different environment.

There is no way of predicting when the changes will occur. One action might last only a few seconds before it is transformed into a new one. Another might develop for a while before one of you senses a good point at which to change it. In the course of a few minutes of playing, you might find yourself successively in a hospital, on a safari, on a bus, in a ballroom, and wading through a swamp. You might become a child, a tree, a chair, a dog, a nurse, and a rich grandfather. Some actions will develop in silence, others will be verbal. There should be no breaks. The actions should flow together, each continuing until a new one develops from it. Accept whatever changes your partner initiates and find a way to participate. Even for bizarre or bewildering actions there's usually something that the two of you can figure out together.

Advertising Agency

In groups of eight, choose six people to be an advertising committee, a sort of idea group or "think tank." The other two, the "clients" make up, and give to the committee, a name for an imaginary product. The committee is not told what the product is, how it looks or what its function is. The product's name might be Toptads, The Fermit, Formula Seven, or any name you think of that gives no specific information about the product's appearance or use. The committee then proceeds to develop a design or a sales campaign for the product.

As a member of the committee, your object is to discuss the product in such a way that if someone were

to come unexpectedly into the room, he or she would not be able to tell that you actually know nothing about the product. Suppose, for instance, that the committee has been asked to design and market a product called Toptads. One of you might begin the discussion by saying, "Since they are green, I think each Toptad should be shaped like a watermelon." Someone else might continue, "...Yes, and be about an inch long." "That way," someone might add, "a person can carry a day's supply in his or her pocket." "That means about six Toptads per package," a fourth might remark, at which a fifth might add, "And there should be a message on the package about how to use them in an emergency"...and so on. The committee might go on to discuss billboard advertisements for Toptads, radio and television commercials, or perhaps a way to interest elderly people in Toptads.

You might have the discussion go around the "table," with each of you speaking in turn. Or, after some practice, the committee might prefer to have an open discussion, with all of you speaking in no special order. Always attempt to add to and develop the previous speaker's statement. Avoid negative statements. Your contribution should be an asset to the design idea or sales campaign. It should be met with an attitude of "Yes, and..." rather than "No, but...."

The two clients listen carefully to the discussion, making mental notes of as many of the suggestions as they can remember. At the end of the discussion, they must give a summary description of the product to the committee. The description must include divulging what the product actually was.

Trans-Siberian Express

This activity can be done either in two groups or with the entire class, depending upon the number of people involved.

Two-thirds of the group are passengers on the Trans-Siberian Express. You are travelling on a long journey across Northern Europe in the winter. The trip has already taken days. You are each to assume an identity and a reason for your trip, and you must fill in identification papers. Before you do so, however, your teacher will hand a folded slip of paper to each of you. One slip is marked with an X. Whoever gets the X is a spy. If you are the spy, take extra care creating your identity.

The other third of the group are train crew and security personnel who believe that there is a spy on the train, and are going to question each traveller. Be thorough and quick. Anyone whose story sounds false or whose behaviour is unconvincing should be suspect. Start rounding up the passengers.

The improvisation continues in whatever way you choose.

Mixed Doubles

Divide into groups of four. Two of you are A and B, and the other two are A and B's partners. The partners will speak A and B's thoughts. The partners sit slightly behind A and B. A and B agree on a situation—for example, a teenager trying to express a problem to a parent. A begins the improvisation and then one of three things might happen: A's partner may express A's thoughts; B may speak right away; B's partner may express B's thought before B speaks. Here is an example:

A: Mom, I have to talk to you.
A's partner: She never listens to me.
B's partner: Oh no! Now what?
B: Yes dear, what is it?

When you have finished a scene to your satisfaction, discuss how accurate your "inner thoughts" were. Then switch roles.

Drama Journal

What skills are you developing as you improvise in drama?

Do you agree with the statement: "Improvising is more listening than speaking"?

How important is your belief in the imaginary situation when you are improvising?

Is a prepared improvisation truly an improvisation?

Why is improvisation essential in the training of professional actors?

Small Group Improvisations

In any one lesson, students should experience working together as a class, in large and small groups, and individually.

Chris Day
Drama for Middle and Upper Schools p. 142

A classroom full of people is not necessarily a group. The individuals may have no sense of group identity. If they are not comfortable with one another, they hesitate to contribute much for fear of ridicule or embarrassment. Usually they compete with one another fiercely. When they can be induced to cooperate, their efforts are frequently ineffective because they lack the skills necessary for working together cooperatively.

To become a group this classroom of individuals must undergo certain changes. It must, in effect, mature. Sometimes a class develops into a group with a minimum of intervention from the teacher. Sometimes this evolution takes place smoothly and effortlessly; almost magically a class becomes an effective working unit.

Gene Stanford
Developing Effective Classroom Groups p. 3

Working in small groups is an excellent way of developing your drama skills. It lets you be part of the group process—sharing ideas and feelings, perhaps changing your opinions or getting other people to change theirs, and finally coming to an agreement. The learning that happens in drama most often takes place during group exploration, and small groups can cover more ground than large groups can.

In small group improvisation, your group should be made up of three to five people. This will give all of you a chance to take part and to get to know one another's strengths. You should also work with different people at different times, so that you have the experience of building your role in different situations. As you move from group to group, you may sometimes encounter leadership difficulties—who is to decide a course of action, or who plays which role. Remember that each individual must feel part of the group. By negotiating with the members of each group that you work with, you can all be part of the action of the drama.

The freedom to explore a situation in drama fully, without the pressure of being watched, leads eventually to good theatre, and is the basis of all good drama. It is while you are exploring the drama and interacting with each other that learning takes place. Once your group has understood its own improvised drama, then perhaps the drama can be polished and re-worked for another group to watch.

It is important that your group not feel pressured by time to complete a task solely for presentation to an audience, but there are many good reasons for wanting to share your work. If each group's work is part of a theme that the whole class is exploring, it helps to see the interpretation that others have developed on the same topic. Or, groups may be exploring a single situation from different viewpoints. (For example, one group might show a situation from a parent's point of view; another group from a teenager's point of view; another from the peer group's and so on.) You may wish, in presenting a scene, to use the rest of the class in role. For example, you are town councillors addressing the townsfolk.

Perhaps the most important time for sharing the work you are doing is when it might be the beginning of a drama that the whole class could explore. So if your audience is already in role, you eliminate a lot of discussion time, and gain a lot of extra practice in keeping yourself in role.

In order to strengthen the group work suggested here, your teacher may provide you with an overall structure for the drama, giving more information, changing the focus, or deepening the thinking. As well, he or she may wish to provide a change of pace, or alter what is happening in the drama. You should be alert and ready to adapt to changes. Earlier chapters provided you with a range of ways of working in role. In this chapter, you will see how some of these techniques come together to allow in-depth exploration of a theme.

The selections in this chapter are about growing older and the changes in life that old age brings. These sources will be the *basis* for your small group improvisation.

Workshop

Broken Telephone

Have your class sit in a straight line. The two people at either end decide on a phrase, saying, or simple sentence which they write on a piece of paper without anyone else seeing. This information is then passed down the line—from both ends at the same time—whispered from person to person. When the messages reach the opposite ends of the line they are written down. Compare both versions.

Old People

Get into groups of five and read the following poem, either silently to yourselves or one person aloud.

OLD PEOPLE

It beats me. The way
They sit there talking
Day after day.

Mrs. Lotts was married twice.
Her first husband lives in Sioux City.
Remember John Coleman?
He doesn't have a nickel.
My, your new dress looks nice!
That young Hodges girl is pretty.
Ruth gave me a recipe for a new kind of pickle.

(And heaven knows what all—)
Irma got sick. The Johnstones moved away.
Teddy is coming to visit. Lucille put new carpet in her hall.
Louise called the doctor three times yesterday.

It beats me. The way
They sit there talking
Day after day.
Arms folded, ankles crossed,
Talking and talking and talking and talking and talking.

Myra Cohn Livingston

1. Read the first three lines of the poem. Decide who is speaking and to whom. Using these lines as the opening of a scene improvise the remainder of the conversation.

2. The title indicates that this poem is about senior citizens. Choose another title and using the opening three lines of the poem improvise the remainder of the conversation.

3. Form new groups of five people. Take one complete statement from the central section of the poem. What characters and events are suggested by that statement? Improvise the background story.

4. If you feel confident with this step, present your work to another group so that they can have the opportunity of directing your improvisation and/or redirecting their own. Try out any alternatives suggested.

5. Form groups of eight or ten people. Half of you are social workers making a public service film for high school audiences about the concerns and problems faced by elderly people. The rest of you are the people who are in the film, directed by the social workers. When all the groups are satisfied with their films, move around and look at each others' work. As you

watch, comment upon, and discuss the other scenes, remember that you are still in your roles as either social workers or actors.

The Chinese Checker Players

Get into groups of six, and read the following poem, either silently or aloud.

THE CHINESE CHECKER PLAYERS

When I was six years old

I played Chinese checkers
    with a woman
who was ninety-three years old.

She lived by herself

In an apartment down the hall
    from ours.
We played Chinese checkers
every Monday and Thursday nights.
While we played she usually talked
    about her husband
who had been dead for seventy years,
and we drank tea and ate cookies
    and cheated.

Richard Brautigan

Write labels for the following characters: Mother, Father, older brother or sister, the young person, and the ninety-three-year-old friend. Fix the labels on five chairs placed in a circle. Each of you take a seat and the role assigned by the chair's label. The sixth person is the "controller" and sits on a chair behind the mother. In this improvisation, the young person's family is moving away. The situation is a farewell supper to which the old person has been invited. During the course of the meeting, the young person's intention is to suggest that the family take the elderly friend with them. The moment at which the news is broken is crucial to your drama.

Once the improvisation is under way the controller can signal the group to change roles. The controller takes the mother's chair, the person to the left of the mother becomes the controller, and everyone else moves one chair to the right. Continue with the drama. Roles remain with the chairs, not individuals. Keep working until everyone has taken on every role.

An Old Man's Lark

1. Stand in a circle, facing inwards. One or more of you volunteer to go into the centre of the circle, and the rest of you forming the circle link arms. Those inside have to convince the others to allow them out by using persuasive arguments (*not* force). After the game, discuss which strategies worked best.

2. Get into groups of six. Read the following poem, either silently or aloud.

AN OLD MAN'S LARK

From the fine nursing home
unnoticed one afternoon
with saved-up spending money
from his children far away

he bolted across the lawn,
caught a streetcar downtown,
had two cheeseburgers, a malt,
and watched a double feature.

His money all gone, he spent
the summer night on a park bench,
was found there the next morning
by his helpers young and hurt.

Donald Jones

3. Prepare an improvisation that involves the following people:

- an old person
- the son or daughter of the old person
- someone from the nursing home who finds the old person on a park bench
- the administrator of the nursing home
- a person who is thinking of putting his or her parent into the home
- an activist who is anxious about conditions in local nursing homes.

4. In new groups of five, improvise a scene which might occur when the old person returns to the nursing home and describes the adventure to others in the home. Pay attention to the way in which the others would respond to the story, particularly if they had always wanted to do something like it.

5. Join up with another group of five. Improvise a scene in which the old person leads a delegation of

63

people in the nursing home to the office of the director of the home in order to demand a regularly scheduled trip downtown. The director of the home is reluctant to agree because of the cost of the trip and the responsibility of the home for the safety of its elderly inhabitants.

Volunteers

You are going to make up a play about old people. You will know only how the play will start but nothing beyond this, so everyone will have to take some responsibility for creating this play.

1.   Think about old people whom you know. In what ways do they most need help? Are your grandparents still alive? What are their particular problems? Did you learn anything new about the elderly from the last three poems you worked on?

2.   To start this improvisation, your teacher will read out the following:

"Welcome to the first meeting of our newly established voluntary agency for helping the elderly. I have been appointed director of this agency. I understand that you have all seen our newspaper advertisement seeking volunteers—'Who will go out into the community and help the elderly in their own homes?'.

"Exact details of the nature of help needed are not yet known. This is your job: to determine what can be done by this agency.

"Come up with your own plans for projects. I will be in my office when you have ideas to discuss."

3.   Now divide up into groups of four to six, and discuss ways of helping the elderly. For example:

– home-visiting and helping to carry out tasks that the aged might find difficult;
– fund raising schemes (sponsored walks, a yard sale, a part-time job).

Meet with your teacher, and present your ideas. Your teacher—as the Director—will challenge you about the particulars of ideas.

4.   Each member of your group is responsible for preparing the case history of an elderly person. You must create a name, personal history, financial status, health report, and so on. (This sometimes works best as an evening's homework.)

5.   The drama starts again when your group arrives at its second meeting. At this meeting the "director" hears some of the case histories, and questions you about your facts. You then have to consider some of the problems posed. For example, how would you deal with an old person found lying on the floor too weak to move? How would you make the person comfortable? In groups of four or five, practise what you would do in such an emergency. Take turns observing the other groups and see that the right amount of care is taken. Each group must be able to prove its concern and ability to deal with the situation.

6.   The final problem that you must tackle (probably in a third meeting), will again be posed by the director. "It may be necessary at some time that some of you will have to persuade an old person to move into a Home. This is a very

difficult subject to tackle; does anyone feel capable of so doing? Those who feel capable can show the group how they would do this." Now someone will role-play an elderly person and those of you volunteering must break the news, tactfully, to him or her. The rest of you observe the action.

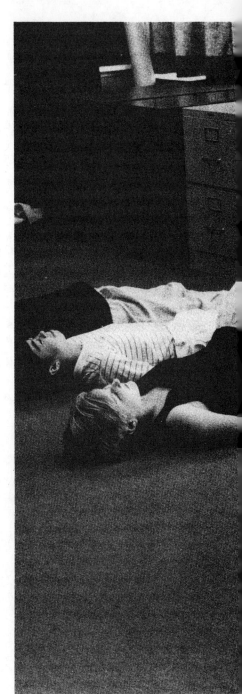

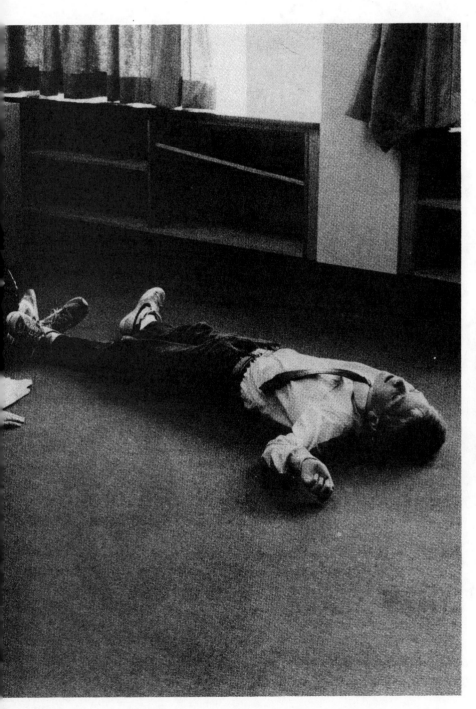

Drama Journal

What types of behaviour block successful group improvisation?

What are the benefits of all groups working at the same time?

Which activity developed your drama skills most: watching other groups, or working in your own group?

At what moment did your group "believe" in the drama?

When did you feel that you were helping the group maintain the drama?

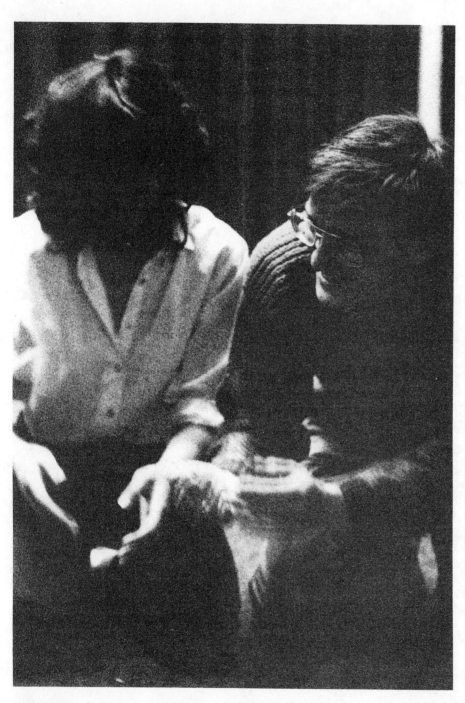

Whole Class Improvisations

A whole class working upon a drama situation will bring, receive and face totally different experiences than when working in pairs.

Dorothy Heathcote
Collected Writings p. 65

The crowd stare at the boots. The actors stare at the boots. Everyone in the place is staring at a pair of army boots. It was as if we were all seeing them for the first time. Then Katsulas, who must have been having a little think, approached the boots. What luck! To find a pair of boots in the middle of nowhere. So he put them on, for he hadn't a pair of his own. Then he's in those great boots, and he's feeling really good, and he's strutting around that carpet a new man, a powerful man, a giant of a man! Sometimes the boots won't walk where he wants them to. They kick and fight him. But Yoshi Oida decides he wants the boots, confronts the giant, grows frightened, hides in the crowd. Uproar! The giant goes after him, but grabs a child instead. Everyone's laughing now, except the child who's really scared. So the giant, who's a gentle giant, takes off one of the boots and gives it to him. The child doesn't know what to do. 'Blow,' mimes the giant. Marthouret is on the carpet now, blowing into the boot for the child. No sound. Blow harder: no sound. Harder! The boot makes the sound of a conch. Swados is blowing her brains out on the conch at the edge of the carpet, and everyone knows this but it doesn't matter. The child's eyes are wide. The giant asks him to try. He blows and blows, and the sound comes. The child just looked at the boot and he looked at the sky, and he couldn't say a word.

Enter Ayansola on one leg. Goggles over the bedsheet round his head, tartan socks tucked into his natty Italian shoes, a terrific sight. Ayansola gets that claw working hard on his talking drum as he hops about on one leg for extra effect. The crowd loves this showmanship and cheers him. SCLEEAAAAH! Katsulas is in there now, screaming, seizing the moment, cartwheeling across the carpet to the surprise and delight of the crowd. Others join him, running, diving, tumbling—acrobatics of a sort, which create their own energy and excitement. A dance begins to drums. Those actors were really enjoying themselves. With all its limitations the show had gradually become an ideal theatre performance. It was an event.

John Heilpern
Conference of the Birds p. 71-72

In this chapter, the whole class takes part in a single improvisation. New kinds of learning will happen. You will still be asking questions, making decisions, sharing ideas, and negotiating with each other, but there will be much more for you to listen and respond to, and, of course, there will be much more feedback for your work. The large number of people participating will add to the excitement and the tension of the drama.

After reading the selection in this chapter, you and your classmates decide on the most important or most interesting point of the story. This then becomes the first focus of your drama. This focus will change constantly as the situation in the drama changes and as you make choices and decisions as a class. New possibilities will open up as you and your classmates participate and contribute. By exploring and expanding the ideas and suggestions, your class can build the drama cooperatively.

Sometimes, even in whole group improvisation, you will need to work in pairs or in small groups in order to complete a task, before the whole class drama can continue. For example, there may be several sides to a particular issue. Your class may want to stop the drama and explore various interpretations of the problem. Each pair or small group can present its idea, and the class can choose the one most suitable with which to continue. Or, the group might decide to include the thoughts of several small groups and redirect the whole drama. There may be times when you have to negotiate the problems that have arisen out-of-role, and then continue the drama when the members have accepted the compromise. And there may be times when the disagreement between the groups is a more interesting idea for the drama than finding a single solution.

Because there are so many participants, your teacher may have to act as a moderator or director, and guide the drama along. In order to focus and extend your ideas, your teacher may present other options to the group. At times, your teacher may even assume a role in the drama, questioning you, asking you to clarify your actions, forcing you to make decisions. By working inside the drama, your teacher can constantly assist the group in building powerful drama. This type of ensemble work has group dynamics as its "mind" and theatre as its "heart."

Workshop

It Only Comes Out at Night

1. Everyone sit on chairs or stools in a large circle. The greater the diameter of the circle, the greater fun the game will be. The success of the game depends on total silence and stillness from the onlookers.

Select two people, one as the Hunter and the other as the Beast. Two helpers blindfold both and take them to opposite sides of the circle. Turn each player round three times. The helpers then return to their places. The game starts when there is complete quiet, and a leader (or your teacher) says (to build up the feeling of ceremony), "Night has fallen." The Hunter and Beast then start to move. The Hunter should be encouraged to listen for the whereabouts of the Beast so that the Beast can more easily be caught. They must both keep moving while the game is in progress, and it is the duty of the rest of the group to steer the players gently back into the circle if they move towards the edges. The drama can be increased by suggesting that the Hunter utters a huge roar on catching the Beast.

2. As your group becomes proficient you can develop the game in various ways. Four people can play—two Hunters and two Beasts. All four are selected from the group when everyone has their eyes closed, so that none of the four has any idea who they are seeking or avoiding. If one Hunter manages to catch another Hunter, they must tie themselves together by one leg and proceed with this "handicap." The Beasts who are being hunted may choose to reverse things at this point; one of them could decide to ambush the Hunters, uttering a ferocious roar as he or she catches them.

3. When everyone has had a chance to be inside the circle, discuss the experience with the whole group. How did you feel when you were being hunted? When you were the hunter? Were your emotions and feelings part of the role? When in your own life can you identify with these two roles? Are these two aspects part of everyone's make-up?

Escape from the Walled Town

1. Divide your class into pairs—Rescuers and Relatives. One pair will begin as guards. The Rescuers move to one half of the room, and the Relatives to the other. Build a "wall" out of chairs, thus dividing the two sections but leaving a gap in the middle of the wall. The Relatives build a set in their space representing the town near the wall. They might use a large table to represent a radio station, a high box or cupboard to be the secret code centre, and two chairs to be a bridge over a river. They then select spies who act as look-outs to see that the Guards do not approach their coding centre, and who watch for approaching Rescuers. The Rescuers set up a temporary encampment on their side of the wall. They might use a table as an infirmary tent, a round waste basket as a campfire, and coats or sweaters for sleeping bags.

2. When the set has been arranged, your teacher blindfolds the Guards and turns them around three times, positioning them by the gap in the wall. Then one set of partners is selected as the first rescue/escape team. The Relative, is blindfolded, and the Rescuer has to make his or her way deftly past the blindfolded guards to the other side of the wall and bring B back through the gap to safety. The Guards must try to catch the pair. They can only achieve this by listening to the sound of feet moving. The whole group must be absolutely silent. If a pair is caught, that pair becomes Guards.

Underwater World

Your teacher will narrate the action of the next activity, and you will react through mime and movement. You may wish to use music, to help create atmosphere.

Narrator: Find a space, and stand with your feet apart. Stretch up, reach for a point on the ceiling. Hold the stretch...relax. Stretch up again and relax slowly, letting go from your finger tips...through your arms...let your shoulders, head drop forward...let your spine curl forward...and bend your knees. Stretch up, reach for a point on the ceiling. Hold the stretch... ...relax. Stretch up again and relax slowly, letting go from your finger tips....through your arms...let your shoulders, head drop forward...let your spine curl forward...and bend your knees. Bring your feet together, gradually uncurl, until you are standing upright. Step forward on your right foot...stretch your arms forward...and reach your whole body forward. Hold your position. Relax your arms back to your body, and bring your left foot up to your right foot. Step forward on your left foot...stretch your arms forward...and reach your whole body forward. Hold your position. Now move around the space in this same way to the drum rhythm: slow step, stretch, relax; slow step, stretch, relax. Now lie down. Stretch right out. Close your eyes. Relax.

Now you are lying at the bottom of the sea in the soft green water... there are rocks on the sea bed... look at them, see their shape. There is a fish, swimming around the rocks...watch it move...it is moving away...getting smaller...

and smaller...it's gone...everything is quiet and still. Feel the sea around you. Slowly get up. At every movement feel the pressure of the water. Start to move about, slowly...slowly. Explore around the rocks. What can you see? Look...if you find anything, just examine it and put it back. Remember where it is.

Now you are on a boat ready to search for a ship, laden with treasure, which sank 300 years ago near these rocks. The islanders warn of dangers. What might these be? How can you avoid them? Choose a partner so that you can always dive in pairs....Because you are using oxygen cylinders, the mouthpiece makes it necessary to arrange a sign language for communicating with your partner. Each pair must decide what to take down: knife, rope, flashlight, harpoon, etc. You have two minutes to work out signs and equipment....Put on rubber suits, flippers, oxygen equipment....Test your mouthpiece.... Put on your mask....Switch on oxygen...and dive in. Remember to move slowly to avoid stirring up sand....Listen, underwater, for the sound of the drum to call you back aboard. The drum is a warning that sharks have been sighted. Don't panic, but come at once slowly to the surface. Stay with your partner....Keep breathing...ssh-ssh-ssh.

The Wild One

Read the following story to yourself.

A merman was caught at Orford in Suffolk during the reign of Henry II (1154–1189). He was imprisoned in the newly-built castle, did not recognise the Cross, did not talk despite torture, returned voluntarily into captivity having eluded three rows of nets, and then disappeared never to be seen again. That's what the chronicler Ralph of Coggeshall says in his 'Chronicon Anglicanum'.

Don't ask me my name. I've heard you have names. I have no name.

They say this is how I was born. A great wave bored down a river, and at the mouth of the river it ran up against a great wave of the sea. The coupled waves kicked like legs and whirled like arms and swayed like hips; sticks in the water snapped like bones and the seaweed bulged like gristle and muscle. In this way the waves rose. When they fell, I was there.

My home is water as your home is earth. I rise to the surface to breathe air, I glide down through the darkening rainbow. The water sleeks my hair as I swim. And when I stand on the sea-bed, the currents comb my waving hair; my whole body seems to ripple.

Each day I go to the land for food. I swim to the shore, I'm careful not to be seen. Small things, mice, shrews, moles, I like them to eat. I snuffle and grub through the growth and undergrowth and grab them, and squeeze the warm blood out of them, and chew them.

Always before sunset I'm back in the tugging, laughing, sobbing water. Then the blue darkness that comes down over the sea comes inside me too. I feel heavy until morning. If I stayed too long on the land I might be found, lying there, heavy, unable even to drag myself back to the water.

My friends are seals. They dive as I do, and swim as I do. Their hair is like my hair. I sing songs with their little ones. They've shown me their secret place, a dark grotto so deep that I howled for the pain of the water pressing round me there and rose to the surface, gasping for air. My friends are the skimming plaice and the flickering eel and the ticklish trout. My friends are all the fishes.

As I swam near the river mouth, something caught my legs and tugged at them. I tried to push it away with my hands and it caught my hands and my arms too. I kicked; I flailed; I couldn't escape. I was dragged through the water, up out of the darkness into the indigo, the purple, the pale blue. I was lifted into the air, the sunlight, and down into a floating thing.

I struggled and bit but I was caught in the web they had made. They took me to land and a great shoal gathered round me there. Then they carried me in that web to a great high place of stone and tipped me out into a gloomy grotto.

Others. There were others in it, others, others as I am. But their faces were not covered with hair. They had very little hair I could see except on their heads, but they were covered with animal skins and furs. When they saw me they were afraid and trembled and backed away and one fell into the water.

One of them stayed by me and kept making noises; I couldn't understand him. I could tell he was asking me things. I would have liked to ask him things. How were you born? Why do you have so little hair? Why do you live on land? I looked at him, I kept looking at him, and when the others came back, I looked at them: their hair-less hands, their legs, their shining eyes. There were so many of them almost like me, and I've never once seen anyone in the sea like me.

They brought me two crossed sticks. Why? What are they? They pushed them into my face, they howled at me. One of them smacked my face with his hand. Why was that? It hurt. Then another with long pale hair came and wept tears over me. I licked my lips; the tears tasted like the sea. Was this one like me? Did this one come from the sea? I put my arms round its waist but it shrieked and pushed me away.

They brought me fish to eat. I wouldn't eat fish. Later they brought me meat; I squeezed it until it was dry and then I ate it.

I was taken out into sunlight, down to the river mouth. The rippling, rippling water. It was pink and lilac and grey; I shivered with longing at the sight of it. I could see three rows of webs spread across the river from bank to bank. Then they let me go, they let me dive into the water. It coursed through my long hair. I laughed and passed under the first net and the second net and the third net. I was free. But why am I only free away from those who are like me, with those who are not like me? Why is the sea my home?

They were all shouting and waving their arms, and jumping up and down at the edge of the water. They were all calling out across the grey wavelets. Why? Did they want me to go back after all? Did they want me to be their friend?

I wanted to go back, I wanted them as friends. So I stroked back under the nets again and swam to the sandy shore. They fell on me then, and twisted my arms, and hurt me. I howled. I screamed. They tied long webs round me and more tightly round me, and carried me back to the place of stone, and threw me into the gloomy grotto.

I bit through the webs. I slipped through the window bars. It was almost night and the blue heaviness was coming into me. I staggered away, back to the water, the waiting dark water.

1. When you have all read the story, get into a circle. In role as villagers, begin to tell the story of the merman (or, if you feel adventurous, some other wild one) that you remember hearing your great grandparents talk about. Here are some ideas:

– you may talk about the story as if you didn't believe it, or you may be completely captured by the old tale;
– you may possess artefacts, which your family has had for generations, which prove that the merman existed;
– certain relatives of yours may have been there at the time (as a fisherman, priest, etc.), and have handed down stories.

When one of you is through, the next person can continue the story, adding new information, disagreeing with what has been said, or changing the mood.

2. In groups of five or six make a series of tableaux that depicts the story. Your class could create a sequence such as: the Merman in the Sea; the Fisherman; the Arrival in the Village; the Return of the Merman; or the Merman's Fate. What music would be suitable to play as you create the tableaux?

3. There is going to be a town meeting about the merman. Divide into groups of three or four. Each group is a family and must determine its views about the creature's capture.

- Should the merman be put back in the water?
- Is he "owned" by those who found him?
- How does your village feel about the fact that he was found in your harbour?
- How does your family earn a living?
- What impact will the merman have on your family?

Remember as you have your discussion to make your decisions in role.

4. All the families meet in the town square. How you will organize the meeting: who is the mayor? who are the council members? Here are some questions you must consider.

- What will be the merman's fate?
- Who will take responsibility?
- What will be told to the authorities from the castle?
- What does the church in the village have to say about this?
- What will be the outcome of the meeting?

Stranger and Stranger

1. There are many folk tales about people becoming "sea-people," lured to the sea by mermaids, mermen, selchies, or sealmen. Get into small groups, and read the following poem.

DOWN BELOW

There's a deep secret place, dark in the hold of this ship
A fine, private place, if one could get down there and hide
A whole crossword puzzle of ladder and corridor lies
Between that world and the white decks, the smooth wide
Expanse of holystone and elbowgrace and pride.

Could one get down there; but that's quite out of the question
I'll tell you why: clambering down to the door
Through those hot, narrow regions, you notice more and
    more strongly
A green growing odour seeping up through the floor
And the damp solid breath of mould, savagely pure.

That door can't be opened; it's blocked tight shut inside
Crammed against earth and greenery, all intertwined—
Roses, perhaps? The ship is listing, but skipper,
Though the hold should be cleared, is afraid of what
    we'd find,
He believes there's stowaways down there—but, good
    lord, what kind?

Joan Aiken

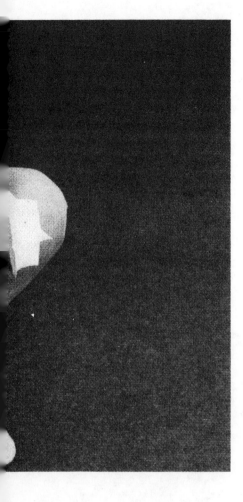

2. What type of stowaways you think would be found? What do you know about the legend of Atlantis? If you have time, do a bit of research about Atlantis.

3. Create, in slow motion, a movement drama that takes place underwater. Use music if you wish.

– Who are you?
– Why are you hiding under the sea?
– Do you ever surface?

When each group is ready, all the groups can demonstrate their movement drama at the same time.

– What interaction can take place among your groups?
– How can your group accommodate the involvement of others?
– What new dramas can you create as the groups merge?

4. In the same small group you now become a family. Your family must hide the fact that one of you is taking on the characteristics of someone from the sea.

– How was the secret discovered?
– What was the cause of the change?
  —Did he/she meet someone?
  —Was it a curse placed on the family?
– How will you try to hide the changes? Why?

Each family, in turn, can demonstrate how the situation originated and the family's method of hiding the problem.

5. When each group has presented its work, the class can choose which family's work to use as the basis for a drama. The family chosen is called to a meeting by the townspeople—the other groups—because this family represents a danger to the village. At the meeting (which should be run along the same lines as the one in the previous activity), explore the following.

– Does the problem represent a danger?
– What action will the village take?
– How does the family feel about the action taken?

6. Create a television program that shows the preparations being made for the arrival of the creature.

– How will it be housed?
– What would those who find it say in an interview?
– How would scientists explain its origin?
– What might descendents of those villagers who knew secrets about sea-people have to say about the merman?
– How had the creature managed to exist undiscovered until now?

Drama Journal

At what moment did you feel the entire energy of the whole class focus on the drama?

What must you do to maintain your involvement in whole class drama?

How does the teacher contribute to maintaining the focus of the drama?

How important is it to go out of role and discuss what is happening during the drama lesson?

What skills are you developing in whole class improvisation that an actor in a large company would find necessary?

Group Dynamics

A healthy group relationship demands a number of individuals working independently *to complete a given project.*

Viola Spolin
Improvisation for the Theatre p. 9

What happens when a competitive person joins a group made up of co-operative members? First, the co-operative members begin behaving in competitive ways. Second, the competitive person sees the former co-operative members as having *always* been competitive. Third, the co-operative members are aware that their behaviour is being determined by the other's competitive behaviour, but the competitive person is not aware of his or her impact upon the co-operators. Trust, openness of communication, liking for one another, and a problem-solving orientation are all easily destroyed by a competitive person. He or she uses the openness and trust of others to exploit them and take advantage of them. Without much question, a member who is co-operative with other group members runs the risk of being taken advantage of, and the result of such exploitation is usually anger and equally competitive behaviour. Therefore, because competitive behaviour dominates in groups, co-operative people will want to make sure that all members of their group are co-operatively oriented. They will also want to intervene when a member's competitive behaviour is subverting the co-operative goal structure of the group.

This chapter brings into sharp focus the methods of building group co-operation that have been explored throughout section B of this book. In the drama class, almost everything you do involves working with other people. Consequently, the way in which the group works together determines the quality of the work that the group does. Whether you are working with a partner, a small group, or the whole class, the behaviour of each individual affects the group. Drama demands co-operation in order that a single focus can be created. Some common problems of working in groups are: who is the group leader? How does a group make the best decision? has everyone had an opportunity to participate in the decision? While many aspects of group work are best learned in role, it is also useful from time to time to step back and look at the skills that the work is teaching.

In this chapter three aspects of group dynamics are examined: leadership; decision-making; and conflict and co-operation.

Workshop

Part 1: Leadership

Contrary to popular belief, the least effective group is the group in which one person gives the orders and the others do the tasks. The best group is the one with a leader who helps the group achieve its tasks *and* keeps or maintains the group working together in a co-operative way. Good leadership enables a group to:

1) set its goals;
2) proceed towards these goals;
3) find the necessary resources to accomplish these goals.

Any member of a group becomes a leader when he or she takes actions which help the group accomplish the above three items. At any given moment a *number* of group members will be performing different leadership functions in one of two vital areas:

1) helping the group achieve its *task*;
2) helping *maintain* the group as an effective whole.

Task Functions

1. *INFORMATION AND OPINION GIVER:* offering facts, opinions, ideas, suggestions, and relevant information to help group discussion.
2. *INFORMATION AND OPINION SEEKER:* asking for facts, information, opinions, ideas, and feelings from other members to help group discussion.
3. *STARTER:* suggesting goals and tasks to start action within the group.
4. *DIRECTION GIVER:* developing plans on how to proceed and focusing attention on the task to be done.
5. *SUMMARIZE:* pulling together related ideas or suggestions and restating or listing major points discussed.
6. *CO-ORDINATOR:* showing relationships among various ideas by pulling them together, and harmonizing activities of various subgroups and members.
7. *DIAGNOSER:* figuring out sources of difficulties the group has in working effectively, and identifying what is blocking the group from accomplishing its goals.
8. *ENERGIZER:* stimulating a higher quality of work in the group.
9. *REALITY TESTER:* examining the practicality and workability of ideas, evaluating alternative solutions, and applying the ideas and solutions to real situations to see how they will work.
10. *EVALUATOR:* comparing the group's actual decisions and accomplishments with the goals the group started out with.

Maintenance Functions

1. *ENCOURAGER OF PARTICIPATION*: encouraging everyone to participate, giving recognition for contributions, demonstrating acceptance and openness to the ideas of others, and being friendly and responsive to group members.
2. *HARMONIZER AND COMPROMISER*: persuading members to analyse constructively their differences of opinions, to search for common elements in conflicts, and to try to reconcile disagreements.
3. *TENSION RELIEVER*: easing tensions and increasing the enjoyment of group members by joking, suggesting breaks, and proposing fun approaches to group work.
4. *COMMUNICATION HELPER*: showing good communication skills, and making sure that each group member understands what other members are saying.
5. *EVALUATOR OF EMOTIONAL CLIMATE*: asking members how they feel about the way in which the group is working and about each other, and sharing your own feelings about both.
6. *PROCESS OBSERVER*: watching the process by which the group is working, and using your observations to help examine group effectiveness.

7. *STANDARD SETTER*: expressing the group's standards and goals in order to make members aware of the direction of the work and of the progress being made; also wanting to get open acceptance from everyone of the group's norms and procedures.

8. *ACTIVE LISTENER*: listening to other members, and being receptive to their ideas.

9. *TRUST BUILDER*: accepting and supporting openness; taking risks; and encouraging individuality.

10. *INTERPERSONAL PROBLEM SOLVER*: promoting open discussion of conflicts and increasing group togetherness.

These two lists aren't lists of instructions. They are descriptions of roles that can be observed in group work situations. The next exercise will increase your familiarity with these leadership functions and will give you practice in sharpening your observation skills as well.

Building a Tower

Divide up into groups with at least six people in each. Two people in each group are the observers. The remaining members of each group will "build the tower." Here are the steps to follow:

Each group gets an identical box of supplies, containing construction paper, newsprint, paper, tape, magazines, crayons, pipe cleaners, scissors, and glue. With a pre-set time limit, each group begins to build its tower. The groups work separately, but in sight of each other.

As the tower is being built, the observers should watch for and note the following information:

– how the group gets itself organized;
– how decisions are made by the group (are alternatives collected and tested? does the group arrive at a consensus? does one person railroad his or her ideas through?);

– whether participation and influence are consistent throughout the group or whether a few members dominate;
– which task and maintenance functions are not being provided;
– how the group members react to successes and failures as the tower grows.

As the group is building the tower, it should be aware of its:

– height,
– strength,
– beauty,
– ingenuity.

When the building is over, each group meets with its observers to discuss how the group functioned, and which leadership functions were fulfilled and which were lacking. Because all of you will remember how the tower went up you will, similarly, be able to reconstruct the event, from bottom to top. View the tower critically. Look for its strong points and its weak points. Discuss what leadership was taking place at all such points.

Part II: Decision-Making

The most effective group decision is the one made by consensus. Perfect consensus occurs when everyone in the group agrees on what the decision should be. This is very unusual. More often, consensus occurs when everyone feels that he or she had a fair chance to influence the decision, understands the decision, and is prepared to support it. Someone can disagree with or have doubts about the decision and yet still say publicly that he or she is willing to live with the group's decision.

Consensus takes time to achieve, but decision by consensus is usually of a higher quality than the individual decision of each group member working separately. To have a consensus, everyone must contribute to the process. Each person must listen carefully and communicate clearly.

Guidelines for Decision by Consensus

1. Avoid blindly arguing for your own individual judgments. Present your position as clearly and logically as possible. Then listen to other members' reactions, and consider these carefully before you press your point.

2. Avoid changing your mind only to reach agreement and avoid conflict. Support only those solutions with which you are at least somewhat able to agree. Yield only to positions that have objective and logically sound foundations.

3. Avoid "conflict-reducing" procedures such as majority vote, tossing a coin, averaging, or bargaining, in order to reach a decision.

4. *Seek out* differences of opinion. (Differences are natural and should be expected.) Try to involve everyone in the decision process. Disagreements can help your group's decision because disagreements allow for a wide range of information and opinions to be aired. This creates a better chance for your group to hit upon a more adequate solution.

5. Do not assume that someone must win and someone must lose when discussion reaches a stalemate. Instead, look for the next most acceptable alternative for all members.

6. Discuss underlying assumptions, listen carefully to one another, and encourage the participation of all members.

Parental Control

Divide into groups of six or seven members, and read through the following five points: "Parental Control for Older Teenagers." Discuss the points with your group, and then, using the Guidelines for Consensus, arrive at a group ranking for each point. This group ranking should be one that all of you can live with and support. In ranking the items, place a "1" before the statement that is deemed best, a "2" before the statement that is next best, and so on.

Parental Control for Older Teenagers

– Parents should not give much direction and guidance. Kids have to learn many things for themselves and should be left free to do so.

– The best thing a parent can do for their teenagers is to give responsibility with freedom as soon as they can handle it.

– Parents have a right and a duty to keep a firm hand on their children for as long as they are financially supporting them.

– Parental discretion and responsibility are necessary if we are to have a healthy society. Giving teenagers too much freedom is like giving a child matches to play with.

– Parents should give their children the freedom and encouragement to live their own lives. Giving direction and control will stunt creative self-expression.

After completing the exercise, answer these questions on your own.

1. How understood and listened to did you feel in the group?
   Not at all   1 : 2 : 3 : 4 : 5 : 6 : 7 : 8 : 9   Completely

2. How much influence do you feel you had on the group's decision?
   None   1 : 2 : 3 : 4 : 5 : 6 : 7 : 8 : 9   A great deal

3. How committed do you feel to the decision your group made?
   Very uncommitted   1 : 2 : 3 : 4 : 5 : 6 : 7 : 8 : 9   Very committed

4. How much responsibility do you feel for making the decision work?
   None   1 : 2 : 3 : 4 : 5 : 6 : 7 : 8 : 9   A great deal

5. How satisfied do you feel with the amount and quality of your participation in reaching the group's decision?
   Very dissatisfied   1 : 2 : 3 : 4 : 5 : 6 : 7 : 8 : 9   Very satisfied

6. Write one adjective that describes the group's atmosphere during the decision making.

(You may photocopy this page of the book.)

The Bean Jar Exercise

The purpose of this exercise is to investigate how the involvement of more and more people in a decision-making process affects the accuracy of that decision. The exercise can be done in an hour, and you will need a large jar full of beans. Only one person (perhaps your teacher) knows the number of beans in the jar. Here is the procedure:

1. A large jar of beans is placed in front of the class. You are each asked to estimate how many beans the jar contains.

2. Each person estimates the number of beans, working alone. Record your estimate.

3. Pick a partner and work out a system for estimating how many beans are in the jar. Record your estimate.

4. Join up with another twosome and estimate the number of beans. Record your estimate.

5. Now the four of you pick another foursome and, as an eight-member group, estimate the number of beans. Record your estimate.

6. Join another group of eight and, as a sixteen-member group, estimate the number of beans. Record your estimate, and, when called upon, announce it to the class.

7. Your teacher will now tell you the number of beans in the jar. Divide back up into groups of eight, and discuss your experience—how you felt during the decision making, and the way in which you operated in the groups. Finally, build a set of conclusions about the effect an increasing number of members had on the accuracy of the decision, and why the number of members influenced decision accuracy the way in which it did. Your conclusions can then be shared among all the participants and discussed.

Implementing a Personal Decision

This exercise provides a brief experience in implementing, and in *not* implementing, a personal decision. It is often used as a basis for forming new groups. The exercise can be done in less than a half hour. Here is the procedure.

1. Look around the room. In your mind select someone with whom you would like to pair up.

2. Now make a second choice.

3. Now choose a partner, and pair up with that person.

4. Take a moment to think about why the decisions you made did, and did not, get implemented. Are you with your first choice? Your second choice? Are you with either? What kinds of decisions did you make in order to be with the person of your final choice? As you think about your behaviour, is it typical of you in similar situations? Are you usually a "chooser" or a "choosee"? As a pair, which of you, do you think, exerted the most influence to bring the two of you together?

5. Discuss your answers to these questions with your partner.

6. Discuss the experience with others in the room. In the simple act of choosing a partner, people react differently. Many find they feel better being chosen than choosing; for them, being forced to choose one person over others is distasteful. Others feel better when they seek out someone and ask him or her to be a partner.

Part III: Competition and Co-operation

Competition is very useful in many aspects of life, but it often is misused in situations where co-operation would be a better approach. Even competitive sports require co-operative behaviour. For example, in a hockey game, members of one team have to co-operate with each other in order to be successful. Here's a chart comparing the effects of co-operation and competition in group work. The workshop exercise that follows it is even more convincing!

Co-operation	Competition
High effectiveness in solving complex problems	Low effectiveness in solving complex problems
Builds member skills in problem solving	Does not build problem-solving skills of members
Encourages acceptance of cultural and individual differences	Encourages rejection of cultural and individual differences
Encourages acceptance of differences of opinion and divergent thinking	Encourages rejection of differences of opinion and divergent thinking
Promotes positive attitudes toward the task and the group	Promotes negative attitudes toward the task and the group
Promotes group cohesion and liking among group members	Promotes dislike among group members and reduces group cohesion
Promotes positive self-attitudes	Promotes negative self-attitudes
Promotes co-operative attitudes and values	Promotes competitive attitudes and values
Promotes interpersonal skills	Does not promote interpersonal skills
Promotes group skills	Does not promote group skills
Promotes moderate anxiety about goal accomplishment	Promotes high anxiety about goal accomplishment
Promotes effective communication	Promotes ineffective communication
Promotes trust	Promotes distrust and suspicion
Promotes mutual influence	Decreases mutual influence
Promotes helping and sharing	Decreases helping and sharing
Increases emotional involvement in group goal accomplishment	Increases emotional involvement in individual goal accomplishment
Promotes co-ordination of effort and division of labour	Decreases co-ordination of effort and division of labour
Promotes creativity	Decreases creativity

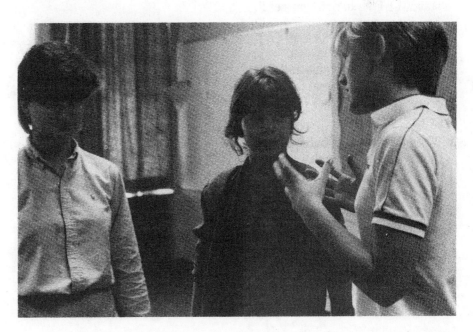

The Million Dollar Gift

This exercise focuses on co-operation and competition among three subgroups within a group. The exercise usually takes less than one hour, and involves the following role-playing situation. A national foundation wishes to award one million dollars to your school system on the condition that the entire system, which is made up of three subgroups, agrees on a project on which the million dollars will be spent.

The procedure for this exercise is as follows:

1. Divide your class into three subgroups of five or more members. You have fifteen minutes to meet one another, get acquainted, and to appoint a representative.

2. The three representatives move to the centre of the room and introduce themselves. The rest of you sit together in your subgroup, in a position where you can see your representative clearly. The representatives make certain that they understand the Foundation's proposal. The representatives then go back to the respective subgroups, and, within fifteen minutes, develop a million-dollar school project proposal to be presented to the other two subgroups.

3. When the fifteen minutes are up, the three representatives again meet in the centre of the room. They present their proposals and then reconfer with their subgroups for five minutes.

4. After the five minute meeting with subgroups, the representatives meet again and try to come to an agreement on the proposal that will be acceptable to all three subgroups. They meet for five minutes and then break for another five-minute meeting with their subgroups. During the representatives' meeting, you may communicate with your representative only through notes. This sequence is repeated three times, or until agreement is reached.

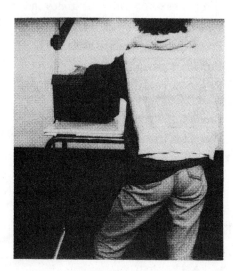

5. When an agreement is reached, the representatives state what they are feeling. Then those of you in the subgroups discuss how you feel. Everyone should pay particular attention to such issues as:
   - Did the entire group reach agreement on a common proposal? Was each subgroup too locked into its own position to compromise even when the prize was one million dollars?
   - Did the three subgroups tend to compete rather than co-operate? Did the degree of co-operation within each subgroup differ from one subgroup to another? If so, why?
   - What sorts of group pressures were felt by the representatives? How much power and freedom were given to each representative?
   - What were the goals of each subgroup in the negotiations? How did these goals affect the behaviour of the subgroup and its representative?
   - How were the decisions made within each subgroup? How were they made among the representatives?
   - Was participation and leadership behaviour distributed among subgroup members? What task and maintenance functions were present and absent?

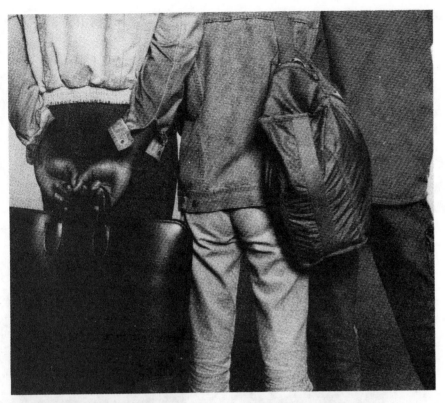

Drama Journal

List the group skills you must develop to be an effective group member.

Why are group skills essential for effective drama?

What new behaviour did you find yourself experimenting with because of group activities?

What behaviour in others helped you become a better group member?

Can a person be a "star" and still be an effective group member?

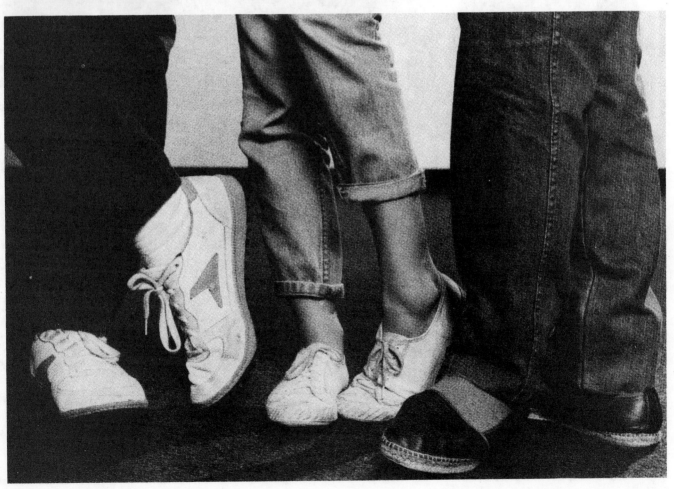

Finding the Drama

When the climate and structure of an improvisational drama class are sufficiently open, safe, accepting and stimulating, the students can be spontaneous and daring in responding to the unexpected challenges [of audiences].

George C. Mager
Liberating Education p. 34

But to arrive at the centre, the actors must undertake the most intense life of self-exploration. They must strip away their outward personalities, mannerisms, habits, vanity, neuroses, tricks, clichés and stock responses until a higher state of perception is found. To watch a piece of theatre performed truthfully is to see in a different way. Perhaps we awaken. We are shaken out of our everyday condition and we see life differently. Sometimes our lives are changed. But the actor must change first. He must shed useless skins like a snake. He must transform his whole being.

John Heilpern
The Conference of the Birds p. 157

All the chapters in this section take the kind of role-play explored in the first half of the book further—into drama itself. Basically, drama is an art form that examines problems in a special way. By working through the problems of a theme being explored in drama, you actually have the opportunity to see *all* of the issues concerned from inside the drama, feeling and thinking about a theme from the viewpoint of someone involved in the action as it happens. Everything you do or say affects the drama and affects all the participants' views on what is being examined. It is as if you are watching yourself in a play at the same time as the play is happening. You are physically and emotionally involved, and yet you are able to analyse what is going on.

As you saw in Section B, finding the drama usually happens after a great deal of exploration work. When your group is able to build on a single focus, when all the participants are fully in role, and when everyone is committed to making the drama happen, then finding the drama will be inevitable. Most of the work in drama concerns finding that moment when understanding strikes, when we learn about the situation and about ourselves. Once this kind of deep understanding has been reached in role, you can then reflect on your learning out of role. As well, you can begin to prepare your work for sharing with an audience, if this would be helpful in your drama growth.

The following chapters include drama work based on a *simulation game* (which presents almost a complete structure for you to follow), *problem solving* and *decision making* (which set up a conflict for you to solve through drama), and *ritual* (which uses centuries-old patterns for drama).

11

Simulation Games

The urge to communicate. We all have it. Simulation games harness the urge to communicate and structure it for the classroom.

Lynn Quitman Troyka
Taking Action p. VI

Simulation games take us one step beyond simple role-play. In a simulation game you role-play and make decisions as if this situation were actually real life. In fact, in simulation games the roles involved are taken from real life situations. As you will find out, the world is full of situations that are suitable for building simulation games.

Before the game begins, everyone is assigned a role. These roles are designed to create a conflict of interests within the simulation. In the situation you may well be asked to adopt an attitude which is different from your own real-life position. You are then given information that will be used to recreate the situation. Because the whole class is involved in the one game, you need to pay close attention to the description of the whole situation, and to the characteristics of each role.

The game begins with the class dividing up into groups. The different groups plan in role, as in most drama lessons. Then, all the participants come together in one large group to negotiate at an open meeting. Finally, the whole group is responsible for making one decision. This is further evidence of the need for healthy group dynamics in drama work.

Your goal is to become involved in the situation and to take part in speaking and listening to each other. Then, as you begin to examine the motives for people's behaviour, drama can be built out of the game. By examining other conditions around the situation, you can move the simulation game further into drama. You can begin to explore the motivation behind the roles and come to grips with why these roles have been specified in the situation. You can begin to place your "self" inside your "role."

In this chapter, the simulation game concerns sexism on the job. The activities will help you begin with the simulation game, and to turn the results into drama.

Workshop

Investigating...the Police

1. What do you think a police officer should be like? Decide on the ideal personality and disposition for a police officer and on what you see as a police officer's role in society. Now choose a partner, and take turns applying for a position with the police academy.

2. With your partner, interview several people outside your class about the police department in your community. You might ask, for example: What are the police doing that is good? How could this work become more effective? What difficulties do you believe are causing trouble in the community between the police and the young people?

3. In groups of three or four, create a tableau demonstrating a civil problem that the police have handled well. Will the police be male or female?

4. Get into groups of four. One of you is a woman who has applied for training as a police officer. Assume that you have passed the written entrance test and now must appear for an interview with a committee of three police admissions officers at the Police Academy. You know that the first question you will be asked is, "Why do you want to become a police officer?" Think about what you will say, and then role-play the situation. When you are through, discuss as a group the attitudes toward women that were or were not displayed.

Women on Patrol

As a class, choose someone (or ask your teacher) to read aloud the following "Situation Statement."

In a large Canadian city, the Chief of Police is facing a major confrontation with his male police officers. Last week, in response to a city-wide order from the mayor's office that there be no discrimination on the basis of sex, the Chief commanded that female police officers be assigned to patrol duty just as men are. Many male police officers reacted with anger and fear, for they felt that women could not be relied upon to be strong and forceful partners. The female police officers, on the other hand, were happy that the new order would finally give them a chance to participate in more than secretarial police work.

Although the union, called the Policemen's Brotherhood Association, has recently opened its membership to female police officers, it supports the male police officers' position, emphasizing that women might not be able to handle dangerous showdowns on the streets. In addition, several wives of the male police officers are very upset because they fear for their husbands' safety.

In an effort to resolve this highly sensitive problem, the Chief of Police's office has scheduled an open meeting to be attended by police captains, the male police officers, the female police officers, the male police officers' wives, the union, and representatives of the Foundation for Police Research. In preparation for this meeting, the Chief of Police requested that the Foundation for Police Research submit a summary report on women in police work. The outcome of the open meeting will unquestionably influence future actions of the Police Department concerning women on patrol duty.

There are six roles in this drama. Each role must be filled by at least one person—preferably by several people. The first step, then, is for each of you to read through the following descriptions of the roles and to choose one.

The Roles

a) *Police Captain*

You have a problem on your hands! You, along with the Chief of Police, are worried about the discontent in the Police Department ever since it was announced that female police officers would be assigned to patrol duty. You know that discrimination on the basis of sex is illegal. In addition, the personnel department has experienced some difficulty in recruiting qualified men. Yet you also know that most male police officers just wouldn't feel safe walking the beat or riding in a patrol car with a woman as a partner. It is up to you to conduct an open meeting so that all sides will get a chance to air their views. After someone has spoken from each group, you can allow a general discussion of the problem in which you may also participate. Try to get the entire group to work out a possible solution. Then you must make your final recommendations to the Chief of Police, your boss.

b) *Male Police Officer*

Oh no! You absolutely do not want female police officers to be assigned to patrol duty. They belong in secretarial jobs, at the switchboards, and sometimes at the questioning of female suspects. If you had a female police officer for a partner, what would happen if there were danger? She would probably freeze. Who would help you if you had to handcuff some unruly, husky guys? What would happen if it were necessary to chase on foot a robber or murderer? Women, you feel, are simply not strong or brave enough to do the job of a police officer. On the other hand, as worried as you are about all of the above problems, you do feel that women should be given a fair chance. Can you present this idea at the meeting? What if you are ridiculed by the other men? It is up to you to present your views—use whatever arguments you can think of, not only the ones given here—at an open meeting called to discuss the problem.

c) *Female Police Officer*

At last! Now you are going to have a chance to do the work you've always wanted to do: to help keep the peace and make greater contact with the public. You resent the restriction of all female police officers to desk jobs as secretaries, switchboard operators, or—if they are lucky—to the job of questioning female and/or juvenile suspects. You want female police officers to have an equal chance to walk a beat or work in a patrol car. You have had exactly the same training as men, including self-defence, and you feel that women make excellent patrol partners. It is up to you to present your views—use whatever arguments you can think of, not only the ones given here—at an open meeting called to discuss the problem.

d) *Wife of a Male Police Officer*

Female police officers on patrol duty? The idea may disturb you very much! You may not feel that your husband will be safe with a female police officer as a partner walking a beat or working in a patrol car. You may think that women should not consider themselves the physical equals of men. Also, some of you may be worried about your husband spending so much of his time with another woman, even if she is working with him. There are enough worries being the wife of a policeman without having a new worry added. On the other hand, you may feel that this is a huge step forward for women. It is up to you to present your views—use whatever arguments you can think of, not only the ones given here—at an open meeting called to discuss the problem.

e) *Representative of the Foundation for Police Research*

More and more research in the past few years has shown that female police officers are highly capable of doing all types of police work, including patrolling on foot and in police cars. Your foundation is a nonprofit group that has been set up to study various problems in all aspects of police work in Canada. You have been asked to attend the open meeting called by the Chief of Police's office so that you can bring the research information your foundation has gathered. Some of your major recent research findings concerning female police officers are summarized in the written report which you recently submitted to the Chief of Police. It is up to you to give evidence supporting the view that female police officers should be given patrol duty. As you speak at the open meeting, you can refer to your summary report and to whatever other arguments you can think of.

f) *Representative of the Policemen's Brotherhood Association*

The idea of using women on patrol is out of the question! Ever since your union was established over a hundred years ago, it has fought for the rights and the well-being of the policemen it represents. You feel that equal rights and laws against sex discrimination simply do not apply here. Female police officers should stay at the desk jobs, even if their chances for advancement within the Police Department are limited. Being practical, your union has decided to open its membership to female police officers. You want to keep the girls happy, but you think they should stay in their place and not make trouble. It is up to you to present your views—use whatever arguments you can think of, not only the ones given here—at an open meeting called to discuss the problem.

When you have chosen your role, write your role-title on a name tag, and pin it on your chest. Find all the other members of your role-group, and discuss why you each chose the role. See if anyone in your group has chosen the opposite point of view presented within the role description. How will you deal with this situation?

In your group, read the following "Summary Report From the Foundation for Police Research."

Background

In Canada, women have been involved in police work for many years.

Locations Where Women Are Given Police Patrol Duty

Foreign Countries: Europe (since 1966) and Israel (since 1960).

United States: More than eighty communities, including large cities such as Washington, D.C., San Francisco, and Dallas; and small communities such as Salinas, Kansas, and Bogalusa, Louisiana.

Evaluations in North America So Far

Study of the effectiveness of women on patrol has only begun. The majority of reports are favorable, but based on limited information.

... In Vancouver, a female police officer arrested one of the R.C.M.P.'s ten most wanted fugitives.

... In Montreal, an observer in a police station reported that the appearance of female police officers at a riot or domestic argument provokes less violent reactions than the appearance of male police officers when called upon.

... In Toronto, a probationary female police officer became so flustered during a violent confrontation that she was unable to radio for assistance, and her driver, a male officer, was roughed up.

... In Halifax, inexperienced female police officers were judged to be less effective than inexperienced male police officers when it came to arrests and traffic violations. Once they gained experience, however, the female police officers had records similar to those of experienced male police officers. It was also observed that female police officers were more likely to take a subordinate role in an incident than were the male police officers. (A three-month study)

... In St. John's, three nights after she first went on patrol, a female police officer gave chase to one of three holdup men and captured him at gunpoint while her two male colleagues were holding the others against a wall.

Discuss this information, and plan what you will say at the open meeting. At this point each role-group must choose a leader who will represent it at the meeting.

Now everyone is called together by the police captain role-group. At this open meeting, you can all dramatize what you think would go on. At the end of the meeting, a decision must be reached.

Drama Journal

How did you make the simulation move beyond game into drama?

How difficult is it to play a role you didn't choose?

What are the benefits of having a role assigned rather than choosing it?

What skills are important in order to role-play with honesty a person of a different sex, age, and character from yourself?

How is a scripted play like a simulation game?

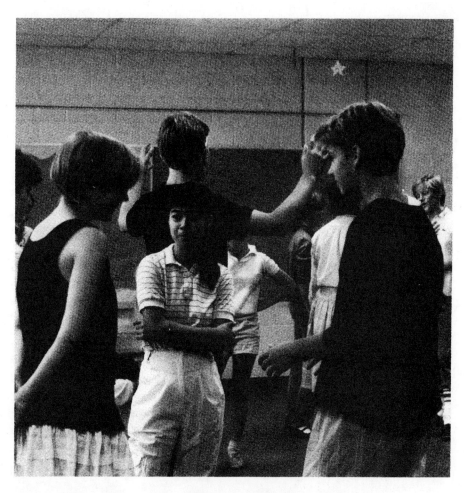

CHAPTER 12

Solving Problems

Although identification with role and place is vitally important, I have always found that it is the problem that is the main determining factor in successful drama. If you have a focus which really holds everyone's interest, the rest will take care of itself.

Geoff Davies
Practical Primary Drama p. 19

Once we are on the track of self-discovery in terms of an enlargement of our sense of identity, and we now try to apply this knowledge to an identification with the character in the play, we must make this transference, this finding of the character within ourselves, through a continuing and overlapping series of substitutions from our own experiences and remembrances, through the use of imaginative extension of realities, and put them in the place of the fiction in the play.

Uta Hagen
Respect for Acting p. 34

Chapter 10, the conclusion of section B, dealt with group dynamics—that is, the ways in which a group works. It looked at the problems of competition and the importance of co-operation, and explored effective ways of setting and reaching group goals. You were also presented with problems that had to be solved, and you became aware of the tensions that can exist in life when members of a group try to reach an agreement.

Drama also is about solving problems. In drama, the problem is called the conflict. It is the struggle to solve the conflict that gives drama its power. In this sense, conflict is the core of drama. Conflict is not necessarily a physical struggle, such as a swordfight between enemies. It may be what happens in a situation where a consensus has to be established within a group. It may be what happens between two groups as each group struggles to hold on to what it believes and values. Or, it may be an individual's inner struggle as he or she tries to determine a direction that should be taken, or a goal that should be achieved.

In this chapter you will practise group dynamics *in role* within a group. You will be presented with a source, and, in role, you will make decisions about how to develop the ideas of the group. In role you will give and accept leadership, and contribute and discuss suggestions for building the drama. Your decisions are important to the development of the drama, and you and your classmates will be responsible for the effects of those decisions. In this way, your group will actually be creating the different aspects of the conflict that it will then work to solve.

Problems or difficulties arising during the drama work can sometimes be worked through in role without stopping the action. At other times, the drama will have to be stopped and the difficulties sorted out through discussion. It is important that the group always work at focusing and directing the action, so that the drama can be a spontaneous response to these challenges.

In this chapter, you will be working with a source from science fiction. The problems you encounter are, nevertheless, human struggles which have their counterparts in our own everyday lives.

Workshop

Timely Expedition

1. You have been given a chance to travel through time. Working on your own, write down:
 – your means of travelling through time;
 – the five people—because of their occupations—that you would take with you on a time-travel expedition (for example, a medical doctor);
 – any unusual items that you would take on a time-travel journey;
 – any dangers that might challenge you.

2. Find a partner and discuss what you have written down. Feel free to change, adapt, or drop ideas as you talk about them.

3. Form groups of four or five and decide on one list of five people. With your group, discuss whether you would actually *want* to travel in time, and whether you'd prefer to travel forward or backward in time.

As the Stars Disappear

The teacher will narrate the action of the next activity as you work in mime.

Teacher: Find a space. . . .Stand with your feet apart, weight equally balanced. . . .Hunch your shoulders right up to your ears. . .let your shoulders drop. Again pull right up. . .and drop right down. . . .And again. . . .Shake-out your shoulders. . . .Let your head drop forward onto your chest. . . .Close your eyes. . . .Roll your head to rest on your right shoulder. . . .Roll your head onto your left shoulder. . .and then forward onto your chest. . . . Lift your head up, keeping your eyes closed. . . .Drop your head onto your chest again. . . .Roll your head onto your left shoulder. . . . Roll your head onto your right shoulder. . .and then forward onto your chest. . . .Your head should feel very, very heavy. . . .

On the sound of the drum lift your head up. . . .Start moving about the drama space, walking slowly and keeping as far away from everyone else as possible. . . .The space is getting smaller, move about again. . .and smaller. . .and smaller. Make the area as small as possible. . . .You are in a huge elevator. It is going up, steady yourself waiting for it to stop. . . .As you step out you have a feeling of weightlessness. . .so light. Move about the space. . .feel so light. . .so free. . . almost floating. . . .Lie down gently. . .close your eyes. . .relax. Lying in a soft cushion of air, quite safe. . .floating. . .look at the stars in the distance, up in the dark sky. See the patterns they make. . .just softly glowing. . .and now fading away as the sky gets lighter. . . . Concentrate on them as they disappear.

Stand up and look around you. . . . This is a space-ship, the start of a journey to an unexplored planet. . . . Hear the take-off engines? How long has the journey lasted so far? Nobody has been to this planet before. What is it like? What precautions must you take to avoid accidents?

Divide into groups of five or six for exploration upon arrival. . . . Appoint a leader. . . .Will space suits be necessary? (Scientific research by unmanned satellites suggests that there is oxygen.) Each group must decide what particular study it will make. . .rocks?. . .ground structure?. . .plant or animal life?. . . minerals?. . .water?. . .

Your landing is imminent. . . .Lie down to avoid impact damage. . . . Put on your space suits if needed. . . .Open the hatches. . . .

The Choice

Read the following science fiction story silently to yourself.

THE CHOICE

Before Williams went into the future, he bought a camera and a tape-recording machine and learned shorthand. That night, when all was ready, we made coffee and put out brandy and glasses against his return.

"Goodbye," I said. "Don't stay too long."

"I won't," he answered.

I watched him carefully and he hardly flickered. He must have made a perfect landing on the very second he had taken off from. He seemed not a day older; we had expected he might spend several years away.

"Well?"

"Well," said he, "let's have some coffee."

I poured it out, hardly able to contain my impatience. As I gave it to him I said again, "Well?"

"Well, the thing is, I can't remember."

"Can't remember? Not a thing?"

He thought for a moment and answered sadly, "Not a thing."

"But your notes? The camera? The recording machine?"

The notebook was empty, the indicator of the camera rested at "1" where we had set it, and the tape was not even loaded in the recording machine.

"But good heavens," I protested. "Why? How did it happen? Can you remember nothing at all?"

"I can remember only one thing."

"What was that?"

"I was shown everything, and I was given the choice whether I should remember it or not after I got back."

"And you chose not to? But what an extraordinary thing to. . ."

"Isn't it?" he said. "One can't help wondering why."

Wayland Young

1. Decide why Williams, with an opportunity to achieve fame and glory, might have chosen to forget what life on earth would be like in the future.

Share your ideas with a partner. Make sure you question each other about the ideas being presented.

2. In small groups, create a time-machine using your bodies. You may add movement and sound to your machine to show how it works.

Instruct another group in how to create your machine—how it looks, works, and sounds.

3. With the whole class, one person begin a simple, repeatable movement as part of a time machine. Then, one at a time, the rest of you join in to create a large time-travelling device.

4. Choose a partner. One of you will be Williams, the other takes on the role of a reporter. Before the interview begins, the reporter should take time to write down some of the questions that he or she wants to ask Williams. At the same time, Williams can be thinking about the details of his life: his background, upbringing, personality, and attitudes.

Conduct the interview in-role, every set of partners in the class working all at once.

When you are satisfied with your interviews, volunteers can share their work with the class. The rest of you can make notes of the type of questions asked—factual, opinion, value—and of the amount of thought given to the answers.

5. The entire class will role-play reporters and stand in a circle around one of you who will role-play Williams. The group will question Williams, progressing from factual questions (full name, age), to value questions (don't you feel you were wrong to volunteer since you did not bring any information back?).

During the interview, some of the "reporters" can change roles and role-play Williams' parents, best friend, employer, etc.

6. By yourself, decide what the society was like that met Williams in the future.

– What year did Williams travel to?
– What did the inhabitants look like?
– How did they communicate?
– What did they show Williams that made him choose to forget?
– What would the opposite choice have meant to Williams?

In groups of four or five, compare your individual responses. Decide which of your societies you would like to represent, perhaps combining your ideas. Discuss your chosen society's culture and history, making certain that you are prepared for a meeting with Williams.

One group will now volunteer to disband. Each member will go to another group and role-play Williams. Each of the remaining groups will act out the meeting between their society and the space traveller Williams.

Worlds Apart

Divide the class into two groups. Each group will be responsible for setting up a society that they think might exist in one hundred years. It is important that each group has a clear sense, both mentally and physically, of the society being portrayed. If it will aid you, your group may use symbolic properties, settings, and costumes. For example, each member of your society may wear a make-up mark on the forehead through which he or she (or it) receives extra-sensory communications.

When the groups are ready, begin a play about the meeting of two societies. *Only one group* will role-play the society it just created. The second group will be time-travellers from *today's* world. During the course of your play, decisions will have to be made that are appropriate to the context of the play. The consequences of these decisions must be accepted by both groups. You will have to decide, among other things:

– How will the travellers be met?
– Where will they be taken?
– What will they be shown?
– What will the future society want to know about the time-travellers?
– How long will the visitors be allowed to stay?
– Will any information, places, or customs be withheld from the visitors?

As your play progresses, the travellers must remember that they are guests and privileged to be received on their mission.

When the play is over, reverse groups, if you wish, and create a second play.

Drama Journal

Why is the definition of drama as "Man in a mess" appropriate to the work in this chapter?

Can there be drama if there is no problem to be solved?

Could the drama be successful even though the problem was not solved satisfactorily?

When was your class working "as a group" to solve the drama problem?

How much frustration did you feel about the problem to be solved in drama? How tempting was it to come to a simple solution?

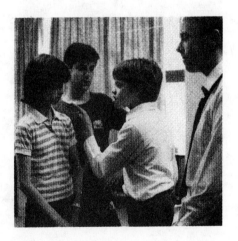

From Ritual into Drama

By re-playing his experience, the human re-cognizes it—in other words, re-creates it so that it is given genuine meaning both personally and culturally. Thus, in the final analysis, "we" are responsible for human existence.

Richard Courtney
Re-play p. 42

A ritual is an action or an activity that is done in exactly the same way each time it is performed. This is because a ritual is believed to have special power, and the *way* in which the ritual is performed takes on great symbolic significance.

The rituals of primitive societies were very important in these people's lives. These rituals brought individuals together with one main purpose. All thoughts and energy would be focused on one single activity. Everyone behaved in the same way and worked toward the same goal. In this way, ritual taught a people what was expected of them. This allowed the group to maintain control and structure. As well, through ritual, the knowledge and beliefs of the society were passed on to future generations. The group experience took over and an understanding was created that was shared by all.

In a ritual, members of a society enacted their hopes and fears, for they believed that ritual would influence nature and the gods. For example, before a bear hunt, the warriors might act out the killing of the bear, with one hunter being the bear, and other hunters the attackers. The people felt that this would make the gods sympathetic to their cause and help in the killing of the bear.

Rituals were very different from one society to another. For example, some clans or tribes used magic, dancing, masks, or costumes to enhance the power of the ritual. Naturally, all these things would help make each ritual seem unique.

Ritual is very important to students of drama. For one thing, early primitive rituals were the beginning of formal theatre. (The duties of the priest and other participants in the ritual gradually became roles taken on by actors. The other members of the group went from being worshippers to being an audience.) As well, for students of drama, rituals offer a tremendous source of material for creative work. By re-enacting formal rituals that are found throughout the world, you gain an understanding of the people with whom the rituals began. You can create your own rituals, and use these as part of a drama you are creating, or as the beginning or ending of your drama.

But most important, you should recognize that the drama lesson itself often resembles ritual. In the lesson, you co-operate with each other, work towards a single focus, and strive for an emotional joining-in of all involved.

The first three exercises are a warm-up for the improvisations you will explore in this chapter. Some of the exercises from other chapters might also be helpful—here are some suggestions: *Introducing...!* in Chapter 1; *Just a Squeeze* in Chapter 2; *Mirror Images* and *Following a Leader* in Chapter 3.

Workshop

Gathering

Sit in one large circle. Anyone in the circle can start the activity. Go around the circle to the right.

- Each person in your class has a turn saying his or her name aloud (Stephen, Susan,...).
- Repeat the first activity adding the word "and" before your name. Try to establish a rhythm in calling out the names (Stephen and Susan and...).
- Call out a number to replace your name and establish a rhythmical pattern (one and two and...).
- Establish a rhythm with sound; for example, beating on the floor—right hand, left hand, right hand.
- Assemble the above activities together (Stephen, one, beat, beat, beat, Susan, two, beat, beat, beat...). Aim to get back to the starting person without anyone breaking the rhythmic sequence.
- Substitute nonsense words for names but keep the number and beat (Kar-too, one, beat, beat, beat, Is-bic, two, beat, beat, beat...).
- Try any variations of the above, including new ways of keeping rhythm.

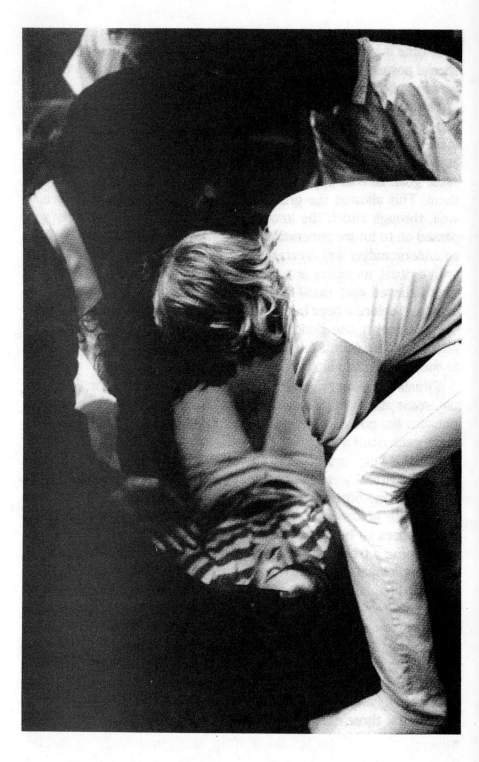

Patterning

1. Form a large circle. Every second person step forward to make an inner circle. The circles move in opposite directions with rhythmic movement of feet—one-two-three-stop, one-two-three-stop,...Count aloud.

Using selected nonsense words that the group has agreed upon, change the counting to chanting.

Add a movement, such as lifting your arm up on one set of beats, lowering it on the next set. Both circles can perform the movement together, or one circle can raise arms as the other circle lowers arms. Gradually speed up the rhythm, perhaps to the beat of a drum played by your teacher. Finish on a "freeze."

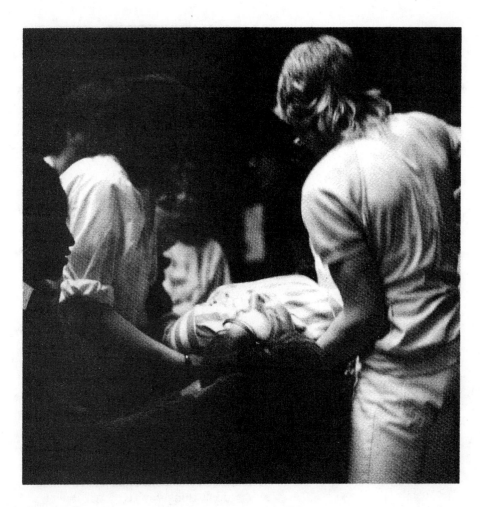

Greet to Meet You!

Stand in a large circle, leaving plenty of space in the centre for action. Whoever wishes to go first advances to the centre making a sound and performing a movement, and then freezes. The second person moves in and, on reaching the centre, is greeted by the first person who "unfreezes" and uses the movement and sound that he or she has invented. The second person greets in reply. They are joined by a third person, and the ritual pattern of greeting is repeated. It is important to keep to the order of greeting when first playing the game; gradually, as more people come into the circle, an interesting pattern of sounds and movements emerges from the various reactions to the "greetings."

After working through your entire class, you can adapt the rules as reactions spontaneously trigger off other variations. For example, a number of people may make the first move into the centre, and greet each other. If the group is slow to move, the centre players can invite others from the circle into the gathering. Use plenty of contrasting sounds and variations of sound level and speed of movement so that the patterns in the centre constantly change. You can also use home-made percussion instruments and masks.

When the exercise is working smoothly, your teacher can call "freeze," and ask the watching players to consider what the frozen group might represent. From the various suggestions, the players in the centre can bring the scene realistically to life using words. The character each adopts should be related vocally and physically to the sound and movements of his or her original greeting.

The Way to Start a Day

Read the following story.

The way to start a day
is this—

Go outside
and face the east
and greet the sun
with some kind of
blessing
or chant
or song
that you made yourself
and keep for
early morning.

The way to make the song
is this—

Don't try to think
what words to use
until
you're standing there
alone.

When you feel the sun
you'll feel
the song too.

Just sing it.

But
don't think you're
the only one
who ever worked
that magic.

Your caveman brothers
knew what to do.
Your cavewoman sisters
knew too.
They sang
to help the sun
come up
and lifted their hands
to its power.

A morning
needs
to be sung to.
A new day
needs
to be honored.

People
have always
known that.

Didn't they chant
at dawn
in the sun temples
of Peru?

And leap and sway
to Aztec flutes
in Mexico?

And drum
sunrise songs
in the Congo?

And ring
a thousand
small gold bells
in China?

Didn't the pharaohs
of Egypt
say
the only
sound
at dawn
should be
the sound of
songs
that please
the morning sun?

They knew
what songs
to sing.

People
always
seemed to know.

And
everywhere
they knew
what gifts
the sun
wanted.

In some places
they gave
gold.
In some places
they gave
flowers.
In some places,
sacred smoke
blown to the four
directions.
Some places,
feathers
and good thoughts.
Some places,
fire.

But
everywhere
they knew
to give
something.

And
everywhere
they knew
to turn
their faces
eastward
as the sun
came up.

Some people
still
know.

When the first
pale
streak of light
cuts
through the
darkness,
wherever they are,
those people
make offerings
and send
strong
mysterious
songs
to the sun.

They know
exactly
how to start
a day.

Their blessings
float
on the wind
over
Pueblo cornfields
in New Mexico,
and
you hear
their
morning songs
in villages
in Africa,
and
they salute
the sunrise
ceremonially
in the high
cold mountains
in Peru.

Today
long before dawn
they were
already waiting
in Japan
with prayers
and they were
gathering
at little shrines
in India
with marigolds
in their hands.
They were
bathing
in the sacred
Ganges river
as the sun
came up.

And
high
on a mesa edge
in Arizona
they were holding
a baby
toward the sun.

They were
speaking
the child's
new name
so the sun
would
hear
and know
that child.

It had to be
sunrise.
And it had to be
that
first
sudden movement.
That's
when all
the power of
life
is in the
sky.

Some people
say
there is
a new sun
every day,
that it
begins
its life
at dawn
and lives
for one day
only.

They say
you have to
welcome it.
You have to
make the sun
happy.
You have to
make
a good day
for it.

You have to
make
a good
world
for it
to live
its
one-day
life in.

And the way to start,
they say,
is just by
looking
east
at dawn.

When they look
east
tomorrow,

you can too.

Your song
will be
an offering—

and you'll be
one more person
in one more place
at one more
time
in the world
saying
hello to the sun,
letting it know you
    are there.

If the sky turns
    a color
sky never was before

just watch it.

That's part of the
    magic.
That's the way
to start
a day.

1. Get into groups of six or eight. Discuss ways of celebrating the rising of the sun.

2. You are members of a primitive society. With your group, and using suggestions from the source, try to create a ritual using sound and movement which will honour the start of a day. Be sure to include some of the components of rituals: movement, gesture, dance, voice, chant, and song. Eventually include accessories: instruments, props, costumes, mask, make-up, lighting. Here are some elements to consider:

– Is there repetition of verbal and nonverbal actions?
– Is there a symbol being used, and, if so, is there a conscious understanding of its significance?
– Is there a dominant sense of order so that actions are clearly framed within a structure?

When your group has worked out its ritual, consider how you can include the rest of the class in your work. For example, is there a place where others can join in the chanting or in the movement?

The Sun Dance

Read the following story about one Canadian tribe and its preparations for the great annual Sun Dance festival.

When the "moon of ripening berries" came, Chief Running Wolf sent a message to the bands: "The time for the Sun Dance Festival draws near. Prepare to move to the Sun Dance site. Go to the big bowl at the foot of the great mountain where the waters run swiftly."

Then the camps were filled with excitement, for this was the greatest festival of the year.

As the time for the Sun Dance arrived, there were many things to do. First, there was the buffalo hunt to get the sacred tongues, which were to be eaten during the festival. They had to be dried in the sun and put into bags for safe keeping. All the tipis were taken down, and travois made of the poles. Great bundles were piled on the travois, for there must be enough food to last for several days.

Each person carried his new clothes in a decorated skin bag to wear when he arrived. Crow Child's grandmother had found time to make him a new bag, all his own, to hold the beautiful new suit. He wrapped his necklace of bears' claws that Swift Runner had given him in the folds of the suit. He looked forward eagerly to the festival.

When all the bands arrived at the site, quickly their tipis were put in place, and their belongings stored inside. Then the making of the great lodge began. They all dressed in their new clothes, and singing together, went to choose the Tree of Life. The most beautiful cotton-wood that they could find was chosen to honour the Great Spirit in his Sun Dance Lodge. High up on its trunk was a fork that would make a nest.

Chief Running Wolf spoke to the tree saying, "You are the most beautiful of all the trees we see in the forest. Proudly you lift your head to the blue sky. Soon we shall cut you down and then great honour will be yours. You will be the centre of the lodge and will carry our prayers up to the Great Spirit."

When the tree had been cut down, strong strips of buffalo skin were tied to it, so that it could be pulled to its place. Every man and woman and child helped, and as they pulled they sang:

'O tall tree,
With your beautiful green
    branches,
We have laid you low,
We have laid you low;

Soon you will be lifted again;
Soon you will be lifted again;
With your head high
Above all the others.'

When they brought it to the site all the lower branches were cut off, leaving only those at the top of the tree. Quickly green twigs were entwined above the fork so that it looked like the sacred eagle's nest.

Red Cloud, the Medicine Man, stood reverently at the tip of the tree as it lay on the ground.

He said to the people, "Bring now your gifts to offer to the Great Spirit that we may ask his forgiveness and his blessing."

At once the people brought their treasures to be fastened to the top-most branches. Over these gifts the people had worked long hours to be able to give something beautiful as their offering. Crow Child slowly unfastened his necklace of bears' claws and hung his precious gift on one of the highest boughs, praying as he did so, "Make me a brave hunter for my people."

Then carefully the tree was raised and put into its place. During this time, Red Cloud stood beside the tree, chanting and praying. In his hands he held huge eagle's wings which he lifted slowly toward the blue sky. When the tree was at last firmly fixed into the ground he burst into a song of reverence. The Tree of Life carried the prayers of the tribe to the Great Spirit.

Around the tree the Sun Dance Lodge was now built. Poles were arranged in a large circle with an opening toward the east. Then some of the people went into the forest once more. This time they returned carrying green branches of the poplar trees before them. Happily they chanted a song:

'Here we come in peace.
Here we come in peace.
Hi ye hi ye hi ye!
Hi hi ye ha hi ye!
We come in peace!'

Over the poles were fastened the poplar boughs to make a roof. At the end of the lodge, opposite the entrance, places were made for the Sun Dance Woman, the Medicine Man, and the dancers, behind a hedge of woven willow branches. In the centre of the lodge the sacred fire was kept burning. At the four corners of the tree were small stones with a little hollow in each to hold tobacco. All the days of the festival this tobacco burned as an offering to the Great Spirit. Facing the opening to the east, the holy buffalo skull rested at the foot of the tree. Everything was ready for the festival, and the Sun Dance began.

Everyone had a part in the festival. The drummers beat out the songs of the people and the music for the dancers. Often the skins of the drums became loose. Then they were tossed to someone near the fire at the entrance.

The heat made the skins tight once more, and the drums were tossed back to the players. Once Crow Child caught a drum. He held it carefully over the fire and then threw it back to its owner.

Red Cloud and Sweet Grass, the Sun Dance Woman, fasted all the days of the festival. Red Cloud sang his songs and offered prayers to the Great Spirit. Sweet Grass prayed for blessings upon herself and the tribe.

The people joined in the songs, raising their voices in chorus, while drummers kept time to the singing:

'O hai ya hai ya ya hai!
O may he take pity on us,
Father Sun, O my father,
O hai ya ya ha.
Yo ha hi on a ha hu hu!'

After four days the festival ended. The tipis were taken down and packed on the travois. The food and many of the gifts were given to those who needed them. Then the homeward journey began. As he walked away, Crow Child looked back again and again to the great lodge. He saw the tree holding its head proudly toward the sky. He saw his gift among its branches, and it twinkled as the tree swayed in the slight breeze. The necklace seemed to carry a message to him, which said, "You will be a brave hunter for your people!"

Divide into four groups. Each group is responsible for creating an activity that will contribute to the presentation of this particular Sun Dance ritual.

Group #1: Movement

– How will your group be seated?
– Which levels will you use?
– Which actions will you repeat?
– Will you mirror the actions; that is, will you follow a leader?
– What rhythm will you use?
– How will you begin the ceremony?
– How will you end the ceremony?

Group #2: Chanting and Words

– When will you use "real" language?
– When will you use invented language?
– When will you speak loudly? softly?
– When will words or phrases be repeated?
– Will any words be echoed?
– Will the call and response technique be used?
– Will any parts be said solo? in pairs? in small groups? whole groups?

Group #3: Sound and Song

– What rhythm will you use?
– What choral techniques will you use: solos, duets, small and large groups?
– Will you use real instruments?
– Will you use invented instruments?
– Will you use any recorded music?
– Will your use of sound and song be constant?
– How can you help create a mood?

Group #4: Environment

– Will you create a main symbol to focus upon?
– What props will you use?
– What costumes will you use?
– Will you use masks? make-up?
– How will you create and use space?
– Will you use any special lighting?
– What mood do you wish to create and how can you artistically assist in creating this mood?

After the individual groups have arrived at decisions on how to implement their tasks, discuss ways to assemble all the elements. Present the ritual with the whole class working together.

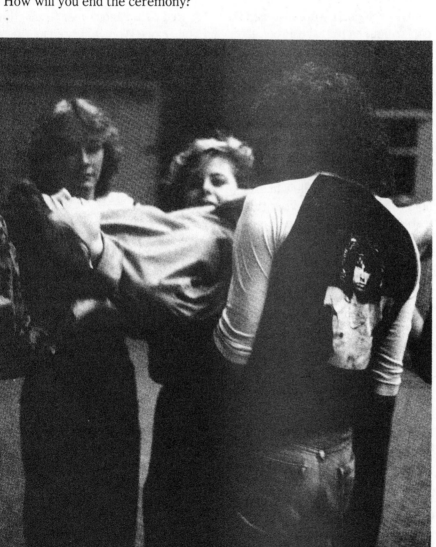

Hunting the Bear

Read the following story about how a primitive tribe created a ritualistic ceremony for the hunting of a bear.

The primitive men are hungry and search unsuccessfully for food. A medicine man places a bear's head over that of one of the hunter's. The hunter growls, uses his hands as though they are paws and lumbers about. He has become the bear. The other men imitate him, prowl and dance around him, and "hunt" him. They pretend to thrust spears into the bear, who then falls to the ground. The medicine man pretends to cut off the head. With a shout, the head is speared and held high. The medicine man leads the hunters in a dance of triumph. The dancers believe that they make such strong magic during the dance that they will more easily be able to hunt and find food.

In two or three groups (depending upon the size of your class), prepare the ritual of the bear hunt. The ritual should start slowly and gather momentum as the hunters move in to "kill" the bear. Here are some suggested elements to consider in preparing the drama.

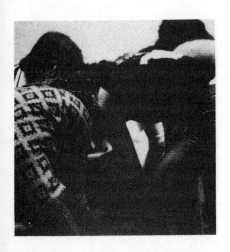

– How will you communicate the feeling of extreme hunger?
– How will you represent the searching of food?
– Will the bear be represented by a single person, a pair, a small group?
– How will the bear move? What will it sound like?
– How will the medicine man be portrayed?
– What are some other roles that the participants could take?
– Will there be standing? crouching? leaping? prowling?
– Will there be dancing?
– Will you imitate the bear's actions?
– How will the space be used? a circle? a line?
– How will the hunters approach the bear? close in on the bear? capture the bear?
– Will you use a drum or any other instrument to beat a rhythm?
– Will any props, costumes, or makeup be used to enhance the ritual?
– Can you create masks for the ceremony?
– How can you create the fierceness and bravery of the hunters?
– What nonverbal sounds will you use? grunts? growls? moans? humming?
– Will you use any words?
– Will there be places of silence? rest?
– Will the ritual include the killing of the bear? If so, how will it be handled?
– Will there be some group work done that will then be made part of the whole in presenting the ritual?
– How will you end? quietly? with a yell? fading out? or building up? with music or chant?

Why do you think the rituals of primitive society were the beginning of drama?

What drama techniques did you use to create your ritual?

What rituals have you observed in today's society?

Explain the techniques by which your group involved those watching in your ritual enactment.

How important were group skills in the development of your ritual enactments?

Building Belief in Drama

Another kind of artificiality is from students who are trained to imitate emotion—a demonstration of weeping in grief where the only feeling is one of simulating or pretending grief. None of these activities can lead to change in understanding.

Gavin Bolton
Towards a Theory of Drama in Education

I have played one and the same part in a Chekhov play hundreds of times and yet I cannot remember a single performance in which completely new sensations did not arise in my soul and during which I did not discover in the play itself new depths of which I was never aware before.

Stanislavsky quoted in
David Magarshack's
Stanislavsky on the Art of the Stage p. 225

Chapter 6 was about learning how to role-play. In this chapter, you will learn to refine your role-playing skills and to sustain your role over a period of time. Both of these abilities will help you create a more powerful drama situation.

Drama operates in a fictional setting, and it is sometimes difficult to believe in what you are doing. Yet, drama must never be done in a "pretend" way, or the feelings that you express will not be truly felt. The more honestly you can respond to the situation, the more you will be drawn into the role—thinking, feeling, and interacting within the drama. In this way, you discover your role from *inside* the drama activity. Your role will grow from within; it will not be something put on from the outside, like a costume. Being part of a role that has been created in this way will help you believe in the drama and help you remain committed to its development. In this way, the drama can be built up over a series of lessons so that your commitment to the work will grow as well.

As you work with your role in this chapter, it is important that you avoid clichés and stereotypes. Clichés are pre-set responses to dramatic situations. For example: suppose you received a letter containing very bad news. The dramatic cliché would be to gasp, clasp your forehead, and move about in a distraught manner. However, in real life, different people would react in different ways to this same situation. In drama, you are asked to find the appropriate response for the role that you are playing, one that is thoughtful and one that allows you to express your own responses to such situations. You are asked to go beyond the superficial and to discover the human qualities of the role that you are playing. By listening and responding to others in the group, and by taking the time to work through the problems of building belief in your role, you will create a piece of powerful drama. By working from inside yourself to find your role, you will also understand how to build a character in drama. And remember, no one watching is going to believe what you are doing, if you don't believe it yourself.

In the first part of this chapter, you'll be working with developing individual characters. The second part of the chapter could be a separate exercise, but could also be a meeting place for the people you create in part one!

Workshop

Through Their Eyes

An actor saying lines written by someone else must try to speak as if the lines were being created on the spot. This improvised quality that good actors bring to their work helps the audience understand the character of the speaker and to believe in what is happening.

An actor must explore the lines many times before their meaning can be truly exposed, and improvisation is an excellent means of achieving this understanding. As you work around the words, under the words, and between them, you will give yourself a context and a base on which to build your characterization.

As you find in yourself the attitudes that your character is expressing, you will believe yourself in the drama. Then an audience may also find meaning in your work.

The script excerpts selected have lots of room for characterization. However, because the excerpts are very brief, you will have to develop a more complete role for the speakers as you work "through their eyes."

1. Choose one of the following monologues:
   - Read it silently by yourself.
   - Read it aloud several times alone.
   - If there are words or passages you are unclear about, consult with a classmate or a dictionary.
   - Find a place to sit by yourself. Close your eyes, relax and try to imagine you are watching your character from some hidden spot, following his or her actions.

2. If you know that someone else has chosen the same character, compare observations when each of you has finished.

3. Decide on some specific physical actions you can do with the situation your character is in and improvise the words of the speech as much as possible. Don't worry that you won't be word-perfect. Work on your own without an audience.

4. At some point, share your scene with the group members. After all the members have presented their work, discuss similarities and differences in the various roles. Carry on the discussion in role, so that you are talking about yourself as "I" as you speak.

Connecting

With a partner, you are going to use your monologue as the basis for a continued improvised drama. Person A can begin with the monologue and person B can continue improvising dialogue based on the character and the situation:

- Use the information in the monologue to build upon.
- If person B is not sure of what to say, he/she can ask questions of person A.
- Remember to add physical activity to your scene.
- Redo the scene, and this time, person B can choose a new role as a response to the monologue.
- Person B can then give his/her monologue and person A can respond.
- Do the scene again, but have person A respond only with physical activity—mime, gesture, movement.

Second Self

With a new partner, person A can give the monologue to person B who will be a mirror physically and, as well, will repeat the words of person A. Try this again, but this time, person B will act as the alter-ego of person A and will try to express what person A is really thinking. Person A should feel free to argue with person B (in role) in case he/she feels her/his thoughts have not been portrayed accurately. In this way, a dialogue will emerge about one character based on the one minimal scene.

Person B can then give the monologue and person A can act as the alter-ego.

Out In the World

Creating a drama from a monologue can then be handled in small groups of four or five. One person can give the monologue, and the other members of the group can respond in role: they can interview the speaker, they can be family or friends, they can be at a group gathering, they can be strangers, meeting at a crossroads.

Each group member can then give a monologue. The other members should try different roles as they build the drama.

Coming Together

In new groups of four or five, the monologues can *all* be presented within a drama situation. You will have to work your monologue into the action wherever it fits. The goal of this work is to use improvised dialogue until you can legitimately include your monologue:

– Each person can present his/her monologue to the group. Be sure to maintain the character role that you have developed.
– Discuss a frame that could be used to include all of the speeches OR
– Begin by incorporating the monologues and see if the connecting frame happens naturally.

Once your group has found a way of including all of the monologues, you can present your polished scenes to the class.

Your class might try having everyone attempt to be a part of one monologue that is presented.

– How will you work everyone in?
– What frame will emerge to structure the work?
– Will the group be able to maintain the idea of the original script?
– Is the character of the speaker developed by what is happening in the improvisation?

1. More Socks

I go to the laundromat to do a wash. Included in the wash are 8 pairs of socks. Out of the wash come 6 pairs of socks plus 1 gray sock and 1 blue sock. A week later I go to the laundromat to do a wash. Included in the wash are 6 pairs of socks. Out of the wash comes 4 pairs of socks plus 1 black sock and 1 green sock. A week later I go to the laundromat to do a wash. Included in the wash are 4 pairs of socks. Out of the wash come 2 pairs of socks. The other socks never show up. The next day I go to the laundromat. As an experiment I put nothing but my last 2 pairs of socks in the wash. Out of the wash comes a body stocking. In the body stocking I find a note. The note says: "Quit trifling with the laws of nature and bring the machine more socks."

2. Bread Crumbs

So I'm going out with this girl for the first time and we're going to the movies and, as usual, I'm throwing out my bread crumbs. And she asks me what is it that I'm doing and I tell her that I'm throwing out bread crumbs so I can find my way home because I have this bad sense of direction. So she laughs like it's a big joke and I say I don't see why my personal troubles should make such a big joke. And she said, "Look—don't worry—I'll take you home!" So I got mad. I said, "Look—we each have our own way of finding ourselves. Who is to say yours is better than mine?" And she said, "You can't make a whole life's philosophy out of bread crumbs." So right out on the street we had a fight. And I got so mad I walked away and I completely forgot to follow my bread crumbs. And an amazing thing happened—I had no trouble getting home. It seems to make my whole past life invalid.

3. Cottage Cheese

You have cottage cheese on your chin. Why don't you ever wipe your chin after you eat? You're thirty-one years old. You're old enough to learn to use a napkin. You're thirty-one years old, you've started to get wrinkles. It doesn't help when there's cottage cheese along with the wrinkles. And if it's not cottage cheese, it's egg. And if it's not egg, it's tuna fish. And if it's not on your chin, it's on your nose. And if it's not on your nose, it's in your hair. How do you manage to get it in your hair? I'm sorry but I can't take it anymore. A supposedly mature woman with all that cottage cheese, egg, and tuna fish on your chin and your nose and your hair. I want a divorce.

4. I Talk Too Much

I talk too much. I'm quite bright, so it's interesting, but nevertheless, I talk too much. You see, already I'm saying more than I should. Men hate it for a woman to blurt out, "I'm bright." They think she's really saying, "I'm brighter than you are." As a matter of fact, that is what I'm saying. I'm brighter than even the brightest men I know. That's why it's a mistake to talk too much. Men fall behind and feel challenged and grow hostile. So when I'm very attracted to a man I make it a point to talk more slowly than I would to one of my woman friends. And because I guide him along gently from insight to insight he ends up being terribly impressed with his own brilliance. And with mine for being able to keep up with him. And he tells me I'm the first woman he's ever met who's as interesting as one of his boy friends. That's love.

5. Standing Alone

I never used to go out on the street. I was always afraid I'd get beat up. I knew it was a stupid fear. I knew it was unrealistic. I looked up statistics on people who got beat up when they went out on the street. It's surprisingly small. But still—I had my food delivered. I had my newspapers delivered. All my dates were at my house. And as long as I didn't go out on the street I seemed to be fine. Until—one day—I was sitting comfortably in my living room when suddenly it came to me that I did not *dare* go into the kitchen—that if I went into the kitchen—I'd get beat up. So I sat through all four late shows thinking my problem out. And at five in the morning I finally concluded that it wasn't anybody on the *outside* I was afraid of. It was *me* I was afraid of! That actually the only person who regularly beat me up was *myself*! So I arose without fear and went into the kitchen. And nobody beat me up. And I put on my coat without fear and went into the street. And nobody beat me up. For the first time in years I felt *alive*! I knew I would never be afraid again! I felt so good that the first couple of people I saw I beat up.

112

6. Joey Wants To Scream

It started when I was a little kid and I was playing ball and I was in a tight spot—so inside my head I began announcing my way through the ball game:—"O.K. The count is three and two. Joey steps off the mound. Digs a toe into the dirt. O.K.—He's back in now. He checks the runners. He's into the windup. And here's the pitch—" From that point on, inside my head I announced my way through everything! School for instance:—"The old second hand is ticking away, three minutes to go in the history exam. Joey can't seem to come up with an answer to Question 5. He looks out the window. He picks at a nail. He looks over at the other kids—and wait a minute—is he? Yes, he is! He picks up his pen!" And even after I got out of school:—"The supervisor is looking over Joey's shoulder. Joey pretends to be busy. The supervisor has found a mistake. Joey can't seem to listen. The supervisor asks Joey if he understands. Joey says he does. Joey stares out the window. The supervisor moves on—" I even announced my way through my marriage:—"Joey has nothing to say. Joey's wife has nothing to say: Joey's father-in-law says isn't it time you were making serious plans, Joey? Joey digs a toe into the carpet and stares out the window. Joey's little boy says, 'Fix it, Daddy'." And so it goes. From early morning to late at night. Even when I'm in bed:—"Joey pounds his pillow. He closes one eye. He closes the other. He feels sleep coming. It's coming—. Joey's wide awake. Joey sneaks downstairs and makes himself a drink—Joey wants to scream."

7. Worst Moment

I used to wonder how I'd stand up to the worst moment in my life. I stood up to the depression but I didn't think it was the worst moment of my life. I stood up to my parents' death but I didn't think it was the worst moment in my life. I stood up to my husband cheating on me but I didn't think it was the worst moment of my life. I stood up to my children deserting me but I didn't think it was the worst moment in my life. The worst moment in my life is when I realized: This is my life. I don't know if I can stand up to it.

8. A Little Too Verbal

WOMAN. I'm just this regular person, and I'm pretty much happy. I've been to college and I lasted all the way through and even managed to be engaged by my junior year, first semester, and we were married the June I graduated. My gown was off-white because I figured I could get to wear it again sometime. I never did. We had four bridesmaids: my sister, my roommate, my best friend from high school and my cousin, because my mother insisted. And we had four ushers: my brother, Gary's two brothers and Gary's father's partner's son, because his father said we had to. The wedding was sort of big, but we had no leftovers. We flew to Europe right after the reception. I was sick on the plane. So was Gary. We were divorced right after he graduated from dental school. That was rough, but okay. I think now it really was much harder on my mother than on me. She gained about eight pounds after we separated and rejoined Weight Watchers after the divorce. Jennifer, my daughter, was born in Boston where Tuft's dental is. She is a constant joy, and I find myself depending on her more and more. That's kind of odd, because I didn't know that could happen this early...but it does and it did. I have a semi-interesting job. I mean, I like it fine but I figure it's probably not worth the college education I got for it. I mean, for the job I have now, I could've gone to a state school and used my Regents' scholarship. But oh no. I had to go to Wisconsin. Well, I don't mean to say it like that because I did have to go to Wisconsin. Everyone went there my year. I probably wouldn't have Jennifer now if I hadn't gone to Madison and met Gary. Oh, I can't even imagine that. Of course, I guess I probably would've met somebody at Albany and gotten married and had Jennifer anyway, and even if the marriage hadn't worked out, I'd be no worse off than I am now. But the thing is, where does selling clothes at Peck and Peck lead to? I like talking to people; it's kind of my thing; but I'm having a hard time staying interested in the things I'm saying. So three weekends ago, my parents took Jennifer and I went to Chateau de Vie for the weekend. I'd never done a singles weekend before, but I figured why not—sort of my own "Last Tango." I could be anyone I wanted. No history, no ties, no truth. But see, I can't lie. I can't pretend like that. I found someone up there truly okay looking. Not great, but like my mother always said, "Who am I to complain?" And he liked me fine although he didn't talk much, and we spent Friday night together and most of Saturday day until I burst and told him we shouldn't pair up so fast 'cause it was wrecking our chances of finding someone to be with. (Pause.) He couldn't understand that and I didn't know how to explain. But he left me alone and I packed and drove back to the city and I still had a quarter of a tank. I didn't call my parents for Jennifer until Sunday night because I knew how they'd be and I couldn't face it. So, I spent Sunday alone in the apartment and that was a rare treat. Well, the weekend ended, and Jennifer came back with more toys to trip over and lipstick-stained forever. Really, I have so much—Jennifer, the Literary Guild, Saturday night on CBS and Pampers. Kimbies are not the same. And somehow through the last couple of years, I have inadvertently discovered that I am no longer frantic about my life. Oh, I know I'd like it a lot if I came home and found Alan Alda sitting in the living room. But I figure that's probably not going to happen. I do know that I don't want to come home and find Gary there. Definitely not. So Jennifer and I will continue to watch Sesame Street and Mister Rogers and Zoom and the Electric Company, and one of these days we'll start thinking about toilet training and we'll be okay. I mean, everything for us really is going quite well. In fact, I can't think of anything *major* that I really want to change about my life...except that maybe I'm a little too verbal.

9. Artichoke

A girl's room is a very private place. It's where I keep my personal belongings. It's where I have my private thoughts. And even though we're not religious here, my room is, for me, almost like a chapel. Grampa and I adore each other—but that doesn't mean we could share a room. Nearly every night I sing myself to sleep. And it was Grampa who said, "Lily, you have a very interesting voice, but it is—untrained." And you must remember that Grampa snores and sometimes smells medicinal. In my old book of Emily Post she says that nothing must be spared the guest. She says he should have a good mattress and both a soft and a firm pillow. He should have a brand new cake of soap, mouthwash and a good clothes' brush. He should have a light at the head of his bed and two or three books should be provided. These books should be chosen more to *divert* than to *strain* the reader's attention. He should have an ashtray, a calendar, and a clock that works. In August even though there are screens, he should have a fly swatter.

Those things require a generosity of self. I could manage them, with grace, for two or three days. I could manage them with a chip on my shoulder for a week. I can't manage them at all for the whole summer. If there's any way to prevent it, I'd rather not leave my room.

Joanna M. Glass

10. Ground Zero

My name is Haley. William Haley. I...I live in an apartment in a big city. It doesn't matter which. Every night my apartment is very quiet and...very empty. Dead. Nothing except a few traffic sounds from the street below, maybe some background music on the radio. The clock.

My life is just as quiet, just as empty. Dead. And every night after I fall asleep I have a dream. The same dream, night after night.

The dream always begins with a large black-and-white map of the city. At the centre of the map is a heavy black X. Around the X are a number of concentric circles. And then a bright red dot appears in the middle of the X. It feels as if that tiny needlepoint of red light is connected to some secret part of my brain. The dot opens up and colour ripples out around it into a scale of colours that fade at the edges of the outermost circle.

It's always at this moment that I realize that this is the kind of map on which they chart the impact of nuclear explosion. I always feel hypnotized by it. I bend closer over the surface of the map. Closer and closer, and slowly the inner circle expands and grows until it surrounds me.

It surrounds me. Suddenly I find myself standing in the middle of a downtown street. A clear day, the middle of the afternoon. Windows glint in the sunlight. It's very quiet. There's no one else around. No cars in the street. Not a breath of wind. The city is empty except for me. I know—I always know at this precise moment—what is going to happen. I look down at the ground. There on the asphalt is a crude chalk circle drawn around my feet. The kind of circle a little girl might draw for a game. I know that this is ground zero. The bomb is going to fall. It's always the same and it's always a strange feeling to realize that I'm not afraid, not at all afraid. A great sense of joy wells up inside me. A desire to raise my arms to the heavens, to exercise all of my body in praise of this moment. Because only by being destroyed, only through the ultimate annihilation of a nuclear explosion brighter than a thousand suns can I finally lose myself, turn to pure energy, become one with the universe. I will be totally cleansed of my mediocre existence, reborn into the cosmos. I will be truly free.

And as I lift my arms and feel the ripple of muscles wash upwards, a great white light is slowly bursting outwards from where I stand. This is it. And then I realize what this is. I'm terrified. I know that it's too powerful for me. *This is no dream.* I'm gazing into the single eye of the fireball. I stare into that blank white eye, that tiny blinding point of light. It gazes back at me calmly, hypnotically. I'm frozen with fear. I know I'm going to die. I want to run somewhere, to hide. If only I were back in my apartment...I want to shout *no!*

Brian Shein

Faster Food

1. Stand back-to-back with a partner, and call yourselves A and B. A calls in a fast-food order for a party of 20 people to B. B tries to repeat the order when A finishes. Reverse the roles, and attempt the exercise again.

2. Find a partner and decide who is A and who is B. All the A people in the class stand in a line facing their partners in the B line. Team A are the customers calling in orders to Team B, the staff. Everyone in Team A speaks at the same time. Each person in Team B must concentrate on his/her Team A partner so that the order can be repeated.

3. Teams reverse roles. This time, the customers are in a rush, and the staff have a specific problem that will interfere with carrying out the order. How will the customer respond? Will the customer be co-operative? Will the order get filled?

Discuss with your partner the outcome of exercise 2. In real life, how would this situation have been resolved? Has anything like this happened to you? What difficulties happen in the work place?

Hamburger Heaven

The excerpt that follows is from the novel *Hamburger Heaven*, in which a young man, working at his first job, must decide between honesty and thievery. This source demands that you carefully explore the situations this person finds himself in, so that the drama will help you understand why he acted in such a way.

The first thing you will read is a description (a "blurb") of the novel, and then the excerpt itself.

Kenny Lapin would rather be out cruising on a warm summer night. He'd rather have a Harley than ride on the back seat of his friend's beat up old Honda. He'd rather have a girlfriend and some nice threads. He'd rather be rich. Then someone yells: "Run of Bens!" and it all starts again, the same routine, the same heat, the same bosses telling him what to do and how fast to do it—all for a measly $2.35 an hour in the kitchen of the Benny Burger Restaurant.

Kenny's first job is serving up hamburgers in the local burger joint where days are long, food is fast, and cash is slow. He knows there's got to be a better way to make money, so he decides that if he can't earn his dream his only choice is to take it.

• • •

"So this is your first day?" Greg said with a self-assured swivel in his chair. Kenny's head nodded like a springboard.

Big Greg Brewster leaned back with a sigh and flicked his Benny Burger tie clip. Kenny inhaled and looked around. The white-panelled walls reflected the fluorescent light making the walk-in refrigerator, directly behind Greg, shiny and hard edged. Beside it, the ice machine rumbled with freshly made cubes. The back sink lurked in the corner beyond the ice machine.

"Run of burgers," someone yelled from the kitchen.

"You have your black pants?" asked Greg.

Kenny raised the crumpled brown paper bag he held. "They are—" He hated the prospect of working in a hot kitchen all summer. "In here," he said.

Greg moved back and forth in his chair. His round face and blue eyes reminded Kenny of a Tiny Tears doll. "Everybody knows how hard the first day is." Greg brushed back his mane and continued in his matter-of-fact way. "Your shoes look all right." Kenny looked down at his black oxfords and then at Greg. "See if you can give them a polish."

"Sure," said Kenny realizing already that Greg would be giving him orders from now on.

Greg gazed down at Kenny's ankles and grinned at the way they winged out. Kenny pulled up his socks nervously. Greg felt sorry for this awkward kid.

"How many years of high school do you have?" he asked.

"I have another year." The rubber bands on his braces started hurting.

Greg played with a paper clip on the formica-topped desk. "What's your favorite subject?"

Kenny wondered why Greg was asking these questions. He glanced down at his wristwatch and wished it was time to leave. "Biology, I suppose." Kenny hated school as much as the next guy, and, in fact, had no favorite subject. But why not say Biology? It sounded as good as anything else.

"I like a man with direction," said Greg fiddling thoughtfully with his nose. He cocked his head and peered directly at Kenny. "Are you willing to work hard for us?" he asked with great concentration.

"Yes," said Kenny, knowing that was what he had better say. It was almost true: Kenny wanted to earn his own money and be his own man, but he wasn't looking forward to slaving at a place like Benny Burger. He had a friend who quit on his first day. "Yes," repeated Kenny, more to assure himself than Greg.

"Good," said Greg Brewster, "because that's what having a job is all about. We expect certain things of you. After all, we are buying your time." Then Greg grinned. He liked this kid, even if he did look like Bugs Bunny with braces. Greg was glad he had signed him up.

"Well, who knows," Greg went on. "You may be quick enough to be a good bun man." He eased out of the chair and stood six feet tall. He motioned for Kenny to follow him. As Kenny followed, he glanced into the kitchen. It was hot, steamy, and hectic. Everyone was in uniform doing the same endless chore. "Drop twenty pies," someone yelled. A fat kid who looked like he knew his business flipped three flimsy burgers at a time.

"This way," directed Greg as he strutted between the chrome walk-in freezer and the back sink that stretched along the wall. There Kenny got a whiff of an institutional-size dose of ammonia.

"You'll like working the late shift," commented Greg. Kenny shuddered. "It's not that bad." He smiled as he turned down the metal-tipped steps to the basement.

"I don't mind." Kenny crumpled his bag closer to his chest. "It's summer and I can sleep late." He

hadn't much choice in the matter. When he had applied for the job the only openings were in the night shift. "I don't care when I work. I need the money."

"Who doesn't?" Greg swaggered.

They came to the supply closet. Aluminum and painted gray. Greg took out his ring of keys.

"We need as many people as we can get with the Benny Bonanza coming up."

"You mean Benny's really coming to this store?" asked Kenny. "I thought he was just on the TV commercials."

"Well, he comes to the stores too." Greg had a quick little smile. "It's our busiest day." Greg opened the cabinet doors and sorted through shelves of neatly folded shirts. "What do you take? Small or medium? Let's say a medium." He pivoted around and handed Kenny a shirt.

The shirt was starched and made of crinkly material like a Halloween costume. A patch over the left pocket bore Benny's smiling face with his catsup lips and pickle nose. BENNY BURGER was written in navy blue. The shirt had Kenny in a spell.

"This shirt," said Greg, "is your responsibility. Take it home, wash it, and iron it every night."

Kenny gritted at another order. "All right," he said. Greg slapped him on the back. The bossier he acted the more cheerful he became and smiled until his dimples creased.

"Now go over there and change." Greg pointed to a door behind the round table in the crew dining room, a sealed-in space with a table heaping with crumpled wrapping papers and half-eaten food.

•　　•　　•

"I would like two Big Burgers with cheese," said the customer, staring at the menu overhead.

Kenny took his pen and scanned the grid of the menu ticket that lay on the computerized register, a low chrome slab welded to the counter. He found the cheese Big Burger line and pressed the appropriate space. PING. In red digital numbers, $1.80 appeared across the register's electronic window.

"And two large fries," said the customer, folding his arms and squeezing.

"Two large fries," echoed Kenny. PING. One dollar read in the window.

"And one small coke and one small root beer," the customer said.

PING, PING went the computer. Kenny looked up.

"That will be all," said the customer.

Kenny read down the left column to "Tax Total." His ball-point pen pressed down on the round red spot and completed the circuit: PING: The amount glowed in slanting red dashes—$4.32.

"Will that be here or to go?"

"Here," said the man, pointing up and down at the floor. His flabby cheeks parted into an accommodating smile.

Kenny raced to the far side of the counter and got a tray and a place mat. He glanced over to the bin. Good. Greg wasn't there. Kenny looked through the window to the kitchen. Mel was lecturing to Jeff and a new hire about dress procedures. Kenny didn't know where Greg was. And he didn't care as long as he wasn't around. Because Kenny was going to do it.

"Pi. . .picking up two Big cheese," said Kenny, swooping down to the warming bin and then on to the fry station, where he

picked up two large fries.

"That will be four dollars and thir. . .thirty-two cents," he said, moving the tray across the counter and in front of the computer window. The customer smacked his lips and inspected his order. The Big Burgers and large fries were hot and proud in their boxes.

"How about my drinks?"

"So. . .sorry, sir." Kenny stepped back and charged over to the soda station. He was nervous. He knew it was a matter of timing.

Kenny watched the kitchen as he jerked the two cups underneath the root-beer and coke spouts. Mel was blabbering and had made the V sign. He pointed to the pickles: only two pickles per Big Burger. As endlessly as Mel lectured, it was almost impossible to gauge when he would suddenly end his dissertations. Timing. Mel jabbed one finger in the air. Only one pickle per regular burger.

The foam from the soft drinks rushed over the edges of the cups. Kenny removed them from the spouts and put them down. He shook his hands dry and capped the sodas, then returned to his register.

"That will be. . .four dollars and thirty-two cents."

The customer put his hand in his pocket and his sleeveless shirt with blue sailboats and fishes creased over his belly. The pink flab that hung from his arms jiggled like Jello. He pulled out a billfold and gave Kenny a five-dollar bill.

Kenny took the pen and touched the five-dollar dot for "Amount Received." Kenny's pen hovered over "Change." He slyly moved his eyes both ways. Only Cathy and a pig were around. Why not? Why not? Kenny's throat stiffened in anticipation. He subtracted four dollars and thirty-two cents from

five dollars. Sixty-eight cents. He pressed "Cancel."

"Si. . .sixty-eight cents change," he said as he pressed for a small coke, tax total and then the exact change spot. PING. PING. PING. The cash drawer slid out from under the counter. "Si. . .sixty-eight cents change," repeated Kenny while thirty-two cents read in the window. He took the five-dollar bill and put it in the drawer. He gave the man his change but didn't close the drawer.

"It smells so good," said the customer, lifting up his nose. He turned and trudged over to his wife who was seated at a table.

No one was in line for Kenny's register. He peeked down at his drawer. One hundred seventy-five dollars and forty-three cents lay there in Kenny's grasp. All of it stacked and ordered in twenties, tens, fives, ones and change. Now. Now. Kenny flicked a quarter of his own money into the drawer. Now he could take a five-dollar bill and be only eight cents under.

His index finger and thumb snagged Abe Lincoln while his other three fingers crumpled the bill and pressed it to his palm. A wall of adrenalin crashed in his heart. He was doing it. His stomach was lifting his torso away from the rest of his body. He looked around quickly and slipped the bill into his pocket.

His cheeks rose uncontrollably and forced up a fierce little smile. Kenny wanted to laugh. How easy life can be. He was beating the system that was beating him. Everything was going to be all right. He looked over to Cathy. She smiled back. Everything was going to be all right, Kenny repeated to himself. He breathed in and pretended to relax.

James Trivers

1. Find a partner and discuss the pro's and con's of working in a hamburger restaurant. Decide what details make this story realistic. Discuss the dreams you think Kenny Lapin has about his success at the burger restaurant.

2. In small groups, mime a situation that demonstrates life in a fast food restaurant. How can you build reality and belief in your improvisation? What details can you use that paint a vivid picture of this situation?

3. a) As a class, arrange your chairs in a circle. Your teacher will be the owner of a chain of fast food restaurants. You can decide, as a class, on the food sold, the name of the chain and on an advertizing slogan.

   The owner, is running a training session for would-be managers at the chain of take-out restaurants. Divide into groups of five. One member of your group will be the owner's assistant, and the remaining four will be applicants for the position of manager. Your teacher will then meet with each group to discuss problems that arise when you work in fast-food stores. You can recount some of the events that occurred during the other improvisations.

   When these discussions are over, the assistant from each group will meet with the owner to decide on five criteria for hiring a manager. At the same time, the candidates for managerial positions can, in role, list on paper four or five experiences that they have had that would qualify them for the position.

   The interviews can take place in groups all at the same time. The three candidates waiting for their turn can be silent observers of the interview taking place between the fourth candidate and the owner's assistant in each group. As owner, the teacher can circulate around the groups, helping to focus the questions and support the interviewees.

   The class returns to the large circle. Each assistant discusses the qualities of the candidates and announces his or her choice for manager. The owner congratulates the managers who have been selected, and explains that with this job comes responsibility and the difficulties of leadership.

   Return to your group. The three employees create a situation of conflict that will require the new manager to handle the problem to the best of his or her leadership abilities. The situation of conflict may arise from work hours, pay, conditions, or unfair policies. The owner's assistant will be a silent observer.

   When each group is finished, return as a class to the circle. The owner will question the assistants about the running of the branch restaurant. Some questions might be:
   —how are the managers handling difficult situations?
   —what are the relationships like between the managers and the employees?
   —which managers will be promoted to assistants?

   The managers and employees should be prepared to discuss any disagreement they have with what they hear reported.

   b) Choose a partner from any group in the class. Begin to build up your role by discussing with your partner (in role) a problem that you are having at home that makes working difficult. This means that you will have to expand your role to include details about personal history, family background, etc. Since you will be in the role of an employee, a manager, or an assistant to the owner, you and your partner could be meeting over lunch, at a party, or during the work day.

c) One employee from each group must be let go because of declining profits. The assistant and the manager interview the employees one at a time in order to decide who should be retained. Each employee must present his or her case as honestly as possible according to the character he or she has created. For example, maybe you don't really care if you are the employee to be let go.

Then, the decisions of all the groups are announced to the owner, while the others look on. At the conclusion, your class can discuss:
—how the employee was told;
—why the situation was fair;
—whether anyone supported the employee.

d) Form new groups—still of five people—with one "fired" employee per group. The other four people are friends or family. Improvise a scene in which the employee discusses with these people what took place.

e) In a small inner circle, the employees who were let go meet to discuss the problems that arose. The rest of the class can sit as silent observers in an outer circle.

f) Return to your original groups of five people. Create a drama where another employee is wrongfully accused of improper behaviour. Decide on the situation. Then improvise the action that results. (The group member who role-played the first employee to be fired may take on a new role as an official sent by the labour board to handle the dispute.)

g) When each group is finished, return, as a class, to the circle. The owner chairs a meeting of all employees, managers, and assistants, and each scene of conflict is depicted in turn. The assistant, the manager, and the employees of each group discuss the problem, and the official from the labour board can be moderator.
—Will the employee be fired?
—Will the manager get to the bottom of the problem?

Drama Journal

Describe a moment during which you had full belief in your role and in the imaginary situation.

What do you have to do to communicate your role to others who are inside the drama?

What additional things must be done to communicate your role to others who are watching outside the drama?

Your role becomes a character when it is important to communicate a full picture of the role to the audience. How can drama help you develop a truthful characterization?

What character stereotypes must be avoided for these roles:
– an old person;
– a young child;
– a person not in full possession of his or her faculties; and
– a person of the opposite sex?

Situations for Drama

From the actor's viewpoint, it is his situation, not his character, which is dominant. This is true for one powerful reason: all people, and all characters in plays, think about their situation more than their own personality or character.

Robert Cohen
Acting Power p. 17

An actor must never follow the road of mere display and imitation. An actor's creative impulse dies in imitation...when his attention is concentrated on the external form, making him show outwardly what he does not feel inwardly.

Stanislavsky quoted in
David Magarshack's *Stanislavsky on the Art of the Stage* p. 225

A "minimal situation" is the smallest amount of information that you need to begin building a drama. Since there is so little to go on, your group must develop the action and the words through role-playing.

First, you have to make decisions about how the drama will proceed: is there enough information about what is happening? does everybody know where the scene is taking place? the time period? the locale? have you each decided on the role that you will play? It is not necessary that you develop all aspects of the drama or of your role before the drama begins. In fact, many of the details of the drama and much of the attitude that you will take on in role-playing will come from the responses of other group members. You will pick up clues from one another as to who you are and what is happening. But you will have to watch carefully the actions and words of the other people in the drama, and cue your own responses from theirs. You will be involved in a process of negotiation and sharing, where everyone's ideas are of equal worth.

Once you have established the basic idea, there are all kinds of ways that you can proceed with the drama. You may want the drama to go back in time and show what happened before the given situation began. You may wish to use a flash-forward, or a slow re-enactment of a dream sequence, or include a story that was told long ago. Sometimes you will be working alone as everyone works at his or her own pace on an aspect of the theme. At other times, you will be working with partners and with small groups. There will be times when you will all come together and the improvisation will include everyone in the class. Don't worry if at first you are easily distracted by what the others in the room are doing.

As the drama progresses, remember that you each have the responsibility of *maintaining* the imaginary circumstances and of *developing* the action. In order to do so you may, at times, have to stop the drama to clarify a point or to have the teacher give new input so that the drama can continue. If two conflicting themes begin to be developed in the drama, you will have to step out of role and have a brief discussion to determine which theme to follow. Or you can get your teacher to assist you by acting as a narrator in role, or as a storyteller. If your group loses interest or energy, you can stop the drama and set up new conditions by asking "What if...?" You can then make decisions that may revitalize your belief in the drama.

Although the introduction to this section mentioned the value of audience participation, showing your work too soon can also be disruptive. At the early stages a piece may be more successful if you concentrate on developing the drama and on exploring, in role, the different attitudes that people have. Demonstrate parts of your work, however, when you want to bring up issues and ideas that you would like other groups to reflect on. Indeed, you may wish, during this process of sharing, to encourage other groups to tackle your material so that they can offer you another perspective.

The minimal situations that you have been given to work with in this chapter are from a genre called "young adult novels." When authors write these novels they choose contemporary and important issues that allow the reader to identify with what is happening. So, although your life may be very different from the scenes presented here, you should be able to find something that you can relate to. Read through the excerpts, and decide which ones you would most like to work on.

Workshop

Z for Zachariah

Z for Zachariah is a novel about a future post-war situation. Ann Burden thinks that she is the last living person on earth until she sees the smoke of a campfire coming closer to her each day. One day she is greeted by a man called John R. Loomis wearing what he calls a safe-suit (which happens to be the only one in existence). Ann is glad to encounter another human being but is unsure if the meeting really is a good thing for her. Though Loomis seems pleasant enough, he says odd things in moments of delirium as he recovers from an unexpected attack of radiation sickness.

Now read the excerpt.

May 24

It is a man, one man alone.

This morning I went as I planned. I put on my good slacks, took the .22 and hung the binoculars around my neck. I climbed a tree and saw him coming up the road. I could not really see what he looks like, because he is dressed, entirely covered, in a sort of greenish plastic-looking suit. It even covers his head, and there is a glass mask for his eyes—like the wet suits skin divers wear in cold water, only looser and bulkier. Like skin divers, too, he has an air tank on his back. But I could tell it was a man, even though I could not see his face, by his size and the way he moves.

The reason he is coming so slowly is that he is pulling a wagon, a thing about the size of a big trunk mounted on two bicycle wheels. It is covered with the same green plastic as his suit. It is heavy, and he was having a hard time pulling it up Burden Hill. He stopped to rest every few minutes. He still has about a mile to go to reach the top.

I have to decide what to do.

Choose a partner and decide which role you will each take. There are several situations you can role-play with this scene. Here are some suggestions:

– Explore what happens when the two characters meet. Will he be trustworthy? Will he trust her?
– Tell each other what happened before the day—May 24—in the excerpt.
– Invent a new situation that is similar to the one in this scene.

The Cat Ate My Gymsuit

Read the following excerpt.

Mr. Stone exploded. "That's it! I've had it! Now you listen, young lady. You'll be very sorry some day. I've spent my whole life trying to keep America's ideals in mind, and this school a good place to educate young people. And then along comes a teacher who talks about feelings and being in touch with yourself and she doesn't believe in grades and argues at teachers' meetings and doesn't dress like a teacher and won't salute the flag. And I also have to deal with community pressure. Well, I just won't have it."

I got really scared. It's horrible to be yelled at. Then his phone rang. He picked it up, listened for a minute, and looked up and said, "Marcy, I hope that you understand that I only want the best for all of you. You may now return to class."

122

1. In groups of four, take on the following roles:

Person A:

You are an English teacher who believes in using new techniques for helping young people learn. The principal does not trust your strategies and has ordered you to stop using drama in the classroom.

Person B:

You are the principal of this high school and believe in high standards for your students. You are suspicious of radicals and teachers who encourage students to go on peace marches.

Person C:

You are a student who now loves taking English. You respond to the teacher's way of working and are becoming politically aware.

Person D:

You are the student's mother and you want to support your daughter and her teacher but your husband has forbidden you to interfere.

The situation is the school board meeting where the principal asks to have the teacher's contract terminated.

2. Other situations that you might explore:

- students drawing up a petition to help the teacher keep her job;
- the father explaining to the daughter why he has asked the mother not to interfere;
- the teacher talking to the students about their responsibility in this difficult situation;
- the mother taking a stand.

The White Mountains

Read the following excerpt.

"Another world?"

I was lost again. He said, "They teach you nothing about the stars in school, do they? That is something that perhaps makes the second story more likely to be the true one. You are not told that the stars at night—all the hundreds of thousands of them—are suns like our own sun, and that some may have planets circling them as our earth circles this sun."

I was confused, my head spinning with the idea. I said, "Is this true?"

"Quite true. And it may be that the Tripods came, in the first place, from one of those worlds. It may be that the Tripods themselves are only vehicles for creatures who travel inside them. We have never seen the inside of a Tripod, so we do not know."

"And the Caps?"

"Are the means by which they keep men docile and obedient to them."

At first thought it was incredible. Later it seemed incredible that I had not seen this before. But all my life Capping had been something I had taken for granted. All my elders were Capped, and contented to be so. It was the mark of the adult, the ceremony itself solemn and linked in one's mind with the holiday and the feast. Despite the few who suffered pain and became Vagrants, it was a day to which every child looked forward. Only lately, as one could begin to count the months remaining had there been any doubts in my mind; and the doubts had been ill-formed and difficult to sustain against the weight of adult assurance. Jack had

had doubts too, and then, with the Capping, they had gone.

I said, "They make men think the things the Tripods want them to think?"

"They control the brain. How, or to what extent, we are not sure. As you know, the metal is joined to the flesh, so that it cannot be removed. It seems that certain general orders are given when the Cap is put on. Later, specific orders can be given to specific people, but as far as the majority are concerned, they do not seem to bother."

"How do the Vagrants happen?"

"That again is something at which we can only guess. It may be that some minds are weak to start with and crumble under the strain. Or perhaps the reverse: too strong, so that they fight against domination until they break."

I thought of that and shuddered. A voice inside one's head, inescapable and irresistible. Anger burned in me, not only for the Vagrants but for all the others—my parents and elders. . . .

"You spoke of free men," I said. "Then the Tripods do not rule all the earth."

"Near enough all. There are no lands without them, if that's what you mean. Listen, when the Tripods first came—or when they revolted—there were terrible happenings. Cities were destroyed like anthills, and millions on millions were killed or starved to death.

"But in one place, at least, a few men escaped. Far to the south, across the sea, there are high mountains, so high that snow lies on them all the year round. The Tripods keep to low ground—perhaps because they travel over it more easily, or because they do not like the thin air higher up—and these are places which men who

123

are alert and free can defend against the Capped who live in the surrounding valleys. In fact, we raid their farms for our food."

1.   Choose a partner and work on the following situation.

Person A:

You are a young person about to be initiated into a world where your mind will be totally controlled by mechanical beings for the "perfect life." If you take part in the capping ceremony you will not be able to make any decisions of your own. You have decided to escape.

Person B:

You have discovered that Person A is going to leave home in order to avoid the mind-controlling capping ceremony. You want Person A to take you along so that you can be a free person, but Person A refuses because you will be a burden. You threaten to report the escape.

The scene is about Person A, trying to leave home during the night, who is discovered by Person B.

2.   Join another group, and decide who will be A and B, and who will take on the new roles of the parents of one of them. Role-play a scene where the parents, who believe fully in mind-control, try to prevent the escape because they feel it is wrong.

3.   In new groups of four or six improvise this scene: On the way to the White Mountains A and B are captured. They must convince the guards that they are on a mission and need to get through to their destination.

Listen for the Singing

Read the following excerpt.

Without another word, Mr. Lloyd opened the register and began to take roll call. There was no need to instruct them how to answer when he called their names.

"Barbara Abbott."
"Present, sir."
"Mark Ayre."
"Present, sir."
Anna listened as the names went by. None meant anything to her.
"Simon Dangerfield."
"Present, sir."
"Margaret de Vries."
"Present, sir. But I'm called Maggie."
Mr. Lloyd lowered the book and stared over Anna's head at the girl who had spoken out of turn.
"Your name is Margaret, Miss de Vries, is it not?"
"Yes, but...."
"There will be no use of nicknames in this class," Mr. Lloyd told her and went on.
Anna wished she dared look around and see the girl who had had courage enough almost to argue. She suddenly remembered hearing Maggie's voice before, as she and Gretchen were leaving the office. So there was a name she knew.
Thank goodness they don't call me Annie, she thought.
They were nearing the S's now. But she knew exactly what to do, after listening to so many others. Nothing could go wrong. Even if he did remember her brothers and sisters, he would not say anything about them at this point, surely.
"Carl Schmidt."
"Present, sir."
"Anna Solden."
"Present, sir."

Anna relaxed and waited for the next name to be called. Mr. Lloyd did not go on.
"Schmidt and Solden," he said slowly. "Where was your father born, Schmidt."
"Kitchener, Ontario, sir," Carl answered.
Anna had been to Kitchener just last spring to visit friends of the Schumachers. Many German people had settled there on coming to Canada. She remembered Dr. Schumacher telling Papa that the city had been called Berlin, after the city in Germany, until the 1914–1918 war.
"And your mother?"
There was a tiny pause as though maybe the boy had not heard the question.
"In Munich," Carl said, dropping the "sir."
Anna waited for Mr. Lloyd to yell at the boy but he was on another track and did not even notice.
"In Germany. Just as I thought," he said, his voice ominous though the words sounded harmless enough. "And you, Miss Solden? Where are your parents from?"
Unsure of what he was after but frightened all the same, Anna lapsed into the accent of her childhood.
"Papa came from Hamburg and Mama from Frankfurt but we lived in Frankfurt until we came to Canada," she said.
Only after it was out did she realize she had said more than she needed to say and played right into his hands.
"Well, well," Mr. Lloyd said, "so you really are a German yourself, Miss Solden? Are you proud of your Fatherland?"
Anna stared at him, feeling like a trapped bird. What did he want from her? How could she answer?

This was a thousand times worse than having him ask if she were Rudi's sister.

"Miss Solden, you are German, are you not?"

"*I* am, sir," a quick, breathless voice said, breaking the tension for a second and then adding to it. "I'm a real German. Well...half."

"What do you mean? Who...?"

"I'm Paula Kirsch. Mother's Scottish but my father's parents were German and, believe it or not, I was actually born in Austria in Braunau am Inn, the exact place where Herr Schicklgruber came from. He calls himself Adolf Hitler now. Is this a history lesson, sir?"

Anna could not believe her ears. Mr. Lloyd looked as if he might literally explode. She could see veins standing out on his forehead. She had never felt more afraid. How did that girl dare talk back to him like that?

"Aren't you going to finish taking the roll?" came another voice, a boy's this time. It sounded like the boy who had warned her not to sit up front. "My name's Weber, sir. You haven't got to me yet."

Mr. Lloyd snatched up the book from the desk where he had laid it after calling out Anna's name. The book shook in his hands.

He can't be afraid of us! Anna thought, not believing her eyes.

"Susan Sowerby," the teacher got out.

"Present, sir."

"Martin Tait."

"Present, sir."

The crisis was over.

1. Choose a partner, and work on the following scene:

Person A:

You are a teacher in Canada during the Second World War, and you resent the immigrants from Germany.

Person B:

You are a student whose parents emigrated from Germany during World War I and are now Canadians. It is the first day of high school, and you are confronted by the teacher because of your German name.

The situation is the teacher questioning the student about his or her background.

2. Improvise the following scenes:

– The student complains to the principal.
– The parents go for an interview with the teacher.
– Students in the lunchroom take sides about the issue.

Guy Lenny

Read the following excerpt.

By the time Guy got back from his route he was sweating. The sun was up and there was a white haze over the city. It was going to be a really hot day, a great day to be out of the city and on the river. He could almost feel that cool, cool water on his bare feet.

He stashed his bike under the stairwell and raced upstairs. As he pushed open the door he yelled, "Hey, Pop! Let's get going!"

"Shhhh! Your dad's still asleep," Emily appeared at the kitchen door, waving a spatula.

"What are you doing here?" Guy said.

Emily pulled at her orange shirt. "Good morning, Guy," she said, giving him a big smile. "How about some bacon and eggs? Your father wants you to have a good breakfast before we leave."

"We? Who said you're coming?"

She cracked two eggs into a pan. "I'm a good fisherman, Guy. I always went fishing with my brothers when I was growing up. Want to bet I catch a bigger fish than you?"

He took a bottle of milk out of the refrigerator and tipped it to his mouth. Why did she have to come along? His father and he couldn't really talk with her around. Not the way they used to. She ruined everything.

"Now don't sulk," Emily said, watching him, but not fussing the way she usually did when he drank from the bottle or dipped his hands into food. "The three of us are going to have lots of fun this weekend."

"If you go, I'm not," Guy said. He wiped his mouth across his shirtsleeve.

"Guy!" Emily shook her head. "What have you got against me?"

"Women are bad luck," he said. It was a dumb thing to say—but he'd said it. He went to the table for a piece of bread. Everything about Emily made him mad. She had long stringy arms and legs, and the way she looked at his father with that eager, possessive shine in her eyes infuriated him. He didn't know what his father saw in her.

For about six months she'd been coming around, making suppers during the week and cleaning up on weekends. Guy and his father used to do all those house things together—shopping Friday night and laundry at the laundromat Saturday morning. If they felt like it, that is, and if it wasn't a perfect day to do something else like fishing, or going to the races, or just getting outside. But now Emily always seemed to be there, butting into their lives and messing things up.

More than once Guy tried to set her straight. "Pop and me have everything figured out. Housework, cooking, everything. The two of us get along perfect. And we never iron shirts or underwear in this house. We don't need that stuff." What he meant was we don't need you.

But Emily was a stubborn sort. Working on an overhead crane in an air-conditioning factory had given her wiry arms and a lot of will power. No matter what Guy said, she just smiled and went on doing things exactly the way she wanted.

One time, before he caught on to her, she brought him up to the overhead crane with her. Up a long skinny ladder to a little boxcar, just under the sooty ceiling of the factory. Guy saw everything down below through a smoky blue haze. Shouting over the crashing noise of the machines, Emily showed him how to work the levers. Then she got her arms around him and there was no way to wriggle out.

"How about a little kiss, Guy? Wouldn't you like me as your mother?"

"No!"

She laughed and held on to him. "Oh, you'll change your mind."

She was strong enough to hold him, but she wasn't strong enough to make him change his mind. About that, or anything else. Ever since that day in the overhead crane, when she had half suffocated him in her unwanted embrace, Guy had carried on a subterranean war with Emily. He didn't like her, and he didn't want to like her. He considered her an intrusion into his and his father's lives, and he was just waiting for the day Pop got fed up with her.

"I made you two nice eggs," Emily said.

"I don't feel like eggs." He got the peanut butter jar down from the cupboard, screwed off the cover, and took a big dip with his finger. Emily set down the plate of eggs on the table with an annoyed clatter. "Eat the eggs, Guy, before they get cold. You can't live on peanut butter. Sit down now! I'm going to wake up your dad."

Guy speared one of the eggs in the centre of its pale-yellow eye. Egg goo spurted all over the plate. Ugh. He went to the window and looked out, leaning his head against the screen. In the street below cars were kicking up a thick dry cloud of dust and smoke. Even the brass Indian at the corner looked miserable. Poor Chief Hiawatha! Almost every night some hotshot driver was sure to come wheeling down First doing about 150 miles an hour, not paying any attention to the signs, and never realizing, till it was too late, that First curved around Jefferson Park. Up in their apartment the television might be on full blast, but Guy would still hear the brakes squealing like stuck pigs, and then, Crash! Smash! Bop! Splat! Another car went plowing into the cement pedestal.

His father came into the kitchen wearing a pair of khaki shorts. His father had thick shoulders and hard hands calloused from handling all that steel at the Iron Works. He leaned on the table, scratching and yawning. "You all ready, Guy? Got your gear all packed?"

"Yeah, I'm packed," Guy said, "But I'm not going. Not with her along."

"What do you mean? Last night you said fine."

"Last night there was just the two of us." The injustice of it made it hard for him to talk.

"I told you," Emily said. "He says if I go, he won't."

"Now, Son," his father said, yawning again, "don't be a mule. Sure Emily's coming with us. With three of us fishing we'll really pull them in. Hey!" He winked at Guy. "We'll have someone to cook the fish. Who knows, maybe we can get her to clean them, too."

Emily leaned on his father's shoulder and smiled at Guy. "That's right—if you're real nice to me—"

"Come on now, Son," his father coaxed. "You know we'll have a great time fishing."

Guy chewed the inside of his lip. Why did his father have to talk in front of her all the time? Why couldn't they just for once be by themselves again? If he was alone with his father for a few minutes, maybe he could tell him how much he wanted this weekend just for the two of them. But lately he felt his father was going out of his way not to be alone with him. Almost as if he didn't want to talk to Guy at all. It was a scary thought.

"How about it, fella?" his father said. "We don't want to leave Emily behind, do we?"

His father had a look on his face that made Guy really want to say yes. He hated disappointing him. But the way Emily was leaning against his father, so smug and sure of herself, kept him shaking his head no.

"Don't beg him, Al," Emily said. "You don't have to humble yourself on my account. I don't care. You and the kid go. I don't know why he hates me so, but I don't want to spend all weekend with him if he's going to be like that!"

Good, Guy thought. Stay behind! That's where I want you to be!

His father sighed and rubbed his bare shoulders. "I'm not going without you, Emily. You're part of this group. I'd sooner call it off. We'll just forget it. Maybe another time, when Guy's feeling a little more big-hearted."

Guy scratched at a scab at the back of his hand. His father was mad now. He was afraid to look at his father's face. Now he felt punky, for sure. His father went into the bathroom and he heard the water running. He kept picking at the sore.

"Little jackass," Emily hissed, passing by him. "See how you ruin things for everybody!" She put away the carton of eggs and slammed the refrigerator door.

A few minutes later his father called from the bathroom, "Hey, Em. We'll take a ride, okay?"

"Sure, Al," she called back. "That sounds great, honey."

Guy's throat felt thick. Of course he wouldn't go with her, but at least his father could have asked him.

1. In groups of three, work on the following situation.

Person A:

Your father has a girlfriend who you do not get along with. She is a crane operator for a building firm, and you resent the fact that your father loves a woman who does this kind of work.

Person B:

You have promised to take your son or daughter on a camping trip but now you have asked your girlfriend along with you. You feel that it is important that you all go on this camping trip together so that you can all get to know one another.

Person C:

You want to marry this man but feel that his child does not like you. You are uncomfortable about going on the camping trip because you don't want to hurt either person's feelings.

Improvise a scene in which the father, his girlfriend, and his son or daughter are discussing plans to go on a camping trip together.

2. Improvise the following scenes with a partner. Change partners for each situation.

- The child talks to his or her mother on the telephone about the problem.
- The girlfriend talks to her boss about the child's resentment of her and her work.
- The father discusses with the boy or girl's teacher the difficulties he's having with his child.

Hold Fast

Read the following excerpt.

"Now, as far as the school is concerned, we must take steps to see that this type of incident does not happen again. We cannot have these things going on inside the school building.

"You say it was an accident. It may be possible that it was, but that remains to be proven. Two facts, however, are very clear to me, as they must be to you—you were fighting on school property and someone was seriously hurt because of your actions. I have no choice but to take measures to see that such a thing is not repeated.

"Stand up, please."

He waited till I did.

"Starting this afternoon, you are expelled from this school for a period of two weeks. You are not to return to classes until after that time. If there is any further trouble with you when you do return, then I may have to recommend to your parents that you be removed permanently from this school. You may leave now. You are excused."

Like someone hit in the head and knocked senseless, I turned and went slowly through the office door. It was so much of a shock that I didn't know what else I could be doing.

I was out in the corridor and half-way to my locker before it came to me that I should never a been out there, that I should still be inside his office, telling him that he was all wrong. There was no reason to be kicking me outa school. I didn't do anything!

I turned around and started to go back. I went straight to the office door again and opened it. I broke in on them talking like I done before.

Sellers looked at me, waited to hear me say something. He had his bloody arms folded again. I stood there. I could hardly get it out. Cripes, there I was again, trying to push words out of my mouth.

"Sir," I said when I finally got started, "you needs to read your stupid records. You couldn't recommend a lousy thing to my parents. Both of them are dead."

With a partner, work on the following situation.

Person A:

Like the character in the story, you are a person who lives with your aunt and uncle in a city far from your home because your parents have died. You have had difficulty adjusting to your new surroundings and have just been suspended for fighting in school, accidentally causing serious injuries to the other student.

Person B:

You are the uncle who is struggling to rule with an iron hand. You are very upset about the fighting and are determined that rules should be obeyed.

Improvise the scene in which Person A and uncle meet, and the uncle hears of the suspension.

2. With different partners, work on the following scenes.

– Person A tries to convince his or her cousin to run away from home with him or her.
– Person A tries to tell the aunt his or her feelings about living in the house.
– Person A goes to the hospital and attempts to apologize to the person injured.

It's Too Late for Sorry

Read the following excerpt.

By this time Harold had joined our little group and was jumping nervously from one foot to another.

"I think you are the most disgusting person I've ever known," Rachel said.

I sighed. "Is that all? I expected a better come-back than that."

"Kenny, you be nice to Rachel. Be nice," Harold pleaded.

"Are you going to let a retard tell you what to do?" Phil laughed.

"Good point, Phil." I nodded to him and turned to Harold. "Keep your mouth shut, retard. One more word out of you..." I laughed and made a fist and pretended that I was going to punch him.

Harold pulled his head back and made this weird face that broke Phil and me up.

"Keep your hands to yourself!" Rachel screamed at me.

"What do you think? I was really gonna hit the retard?" I said to her, and then turned to Phil. "Rachel thought I was going to hit the retard!"

"I told you the retard's catching. And she's catching it." Phil laughed.

"Kenny!" Harold cried. "You and me friends. I like you!" And he held out his hand to me.

I pushed it away and said, "Yeah, you're just about the greatest pal I've ever had. And just for the record—I mean, just so we're absolutely clear on this matter of our friendship, retard, I want you to know that I think you're the ugliest, stupidest, most retarded retard I've ever known!"

"Good, Kenny, baby!" Phil shrieked. "I couldn't have done better myself."

"Thank you, thank you." I bowed to Rachel and Harold. "Thank you, one and all. . .for all the great times. . ."

"You're going to feel sorry for this!" Rachel threatened.

I laughed in her face. "Did you hear that, Phil? Rachel threatened me."

"I heard. I'll be your witness."

"I hate you, Kenny Shea!" she screamed, and lunged for me.

I caught her hands, in midair, and Harold came clawing after me, crying, "I like you, Kenny. Be nice to Rachel."

I let go of Rachel and pushed Harold away. I didn't mean to knock him down, but he fell.

1. In groups of four, choose from the following roles, and explore the situation.

Person A:

You are a student who is very popular in school and gets along well with others. You have been given the job each Saturday of helping a retarded boy who lives down the block, and you are pleased with the progress you are making.

Person B:

You are Person A's girlfriend and are taking an interest in the development of the retarded boy. You want the retarded boy to go to the school dance with you because you feel he will benefit from this kind of social experience. Your boyfriend is not interested in your plan because it will interfere with his image at the dance, and it may cause his friends to behave differently towards him.

Person C:

You are the retarded boy. You have been enjoying your new friendship,

and are pleased that you have friends your own age who treat you fairly. (This is a difficult role to play. It must be carefully thought out so that you demonstrate a clear understanding of the retarded boy's position.)

Person D:

You have no time for the retarded boy and you don't want your friend (Person A) to spend time with him.

2. Improvise the following scenes.

– The mother of the retarded boy and the girl have a discussion because the mother wants to protect her son from the difficulties of life.
– The boy talks with his mother about the fact that he doesn't want the retarded boy to interfere with everything he does in life. He wants to have a life of his own.

Drama Journal

How were you able to translate into dramatic form the information provided?

What skills did you use that you had learned previously?

How does a literary source help you create stronger roles and build deeper drama?

What difficulties arose from the types of roles you were presented with, particularly if you did not like the person you were playing?

How important was it to discuss each group member's interpretation of the scene before beginning the drama?

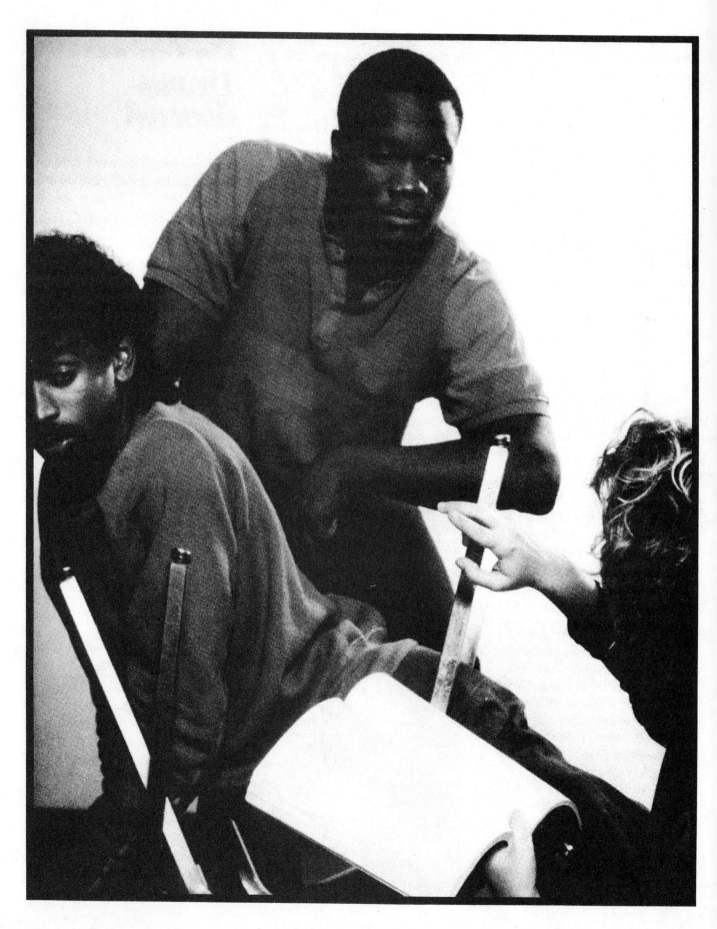

Building and Sharing

The "as if," "might," "could," and "maybe" are distinctively human modes. They are also theatrical modes, for theatre is the art of actualizing alternatives, if only temporarily, for fun.

Richard Sheckner & Mady Schuman
Ritual, Play & Performance p. 5

This section demonstrates several different ways for beginning the drama and then building it. Anything can be the starting point for drama. A "minimal situation"–perhaps only one or two details–can be enough to work with, if, as a group member, you bring the rest of the information to the drama from your own background. But sometimes, rather than being given a minimal situation to flesh out, you may be given a complete script or novel to work with. Then your group will have to find the best dramatic situations in that source. You may wish to pick several situations from the source, and link them together to create a theme.

The same starting situation for a drama becomes different things in the hands of different groups. It is very important, therefore, that you and your group take time to plan. Make sure you know where you want your drama to go. As your drama builds, your teacher can help you refocus if any difficulty arises. Your teacher can also help by questioning you while you are in role about the choices or decisions you must make. Your teacher can also point out the consequences to the whole drama of the individual actions within it. However, the decisions are yours and your group's to make.

As your group works through the process of building drama, you may want to test your work out on the rest of the class. Side-coaching from an understanding audience—provided it is done with sensitivity— can deepen the drama, help your group to sense when the work is focused, and provide ideas for refocusing when it is not.

If you run into problems that seem insurmountable, check out games and activities in earlier sections of this book that seem to relate to the problem area.

The chapters in this section—Building and Sharing—offer starting points for drama and suggest ways of building from these. It is important that you use the sources as jumping-off points and not feel trapped by them. They are here as a way into the drama. Once you and your group get going you can take the drama experience anywhere you wish.

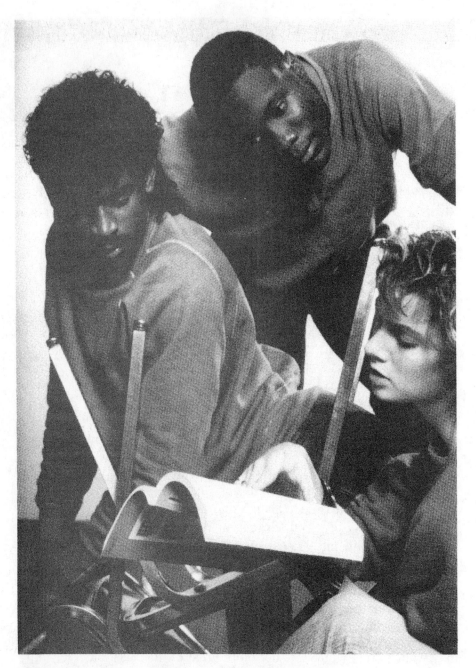

16

From Novel into Drama

Drama involves students in the playful aspects of literature, adding life, humour, pleasure, and intellectual excitement to a piece of literature.

James Hoetker
Dramatics and the Teaching of Literature p. 63

Stories provide many beginning points for drama. In order to introduce you to the wealth of material available in stories, this chapter is based on an excerpt from a novel—*The Machine-Gunners*. It is about young people in England who want to do their part to end World War II.

When you dramatize a story, you begin by discussing it in order to make sure that your class or group agrees on the main issues. Then you can decide which issues or parts you wish to dramatize, and how the action will begin. It is important that the dramatization be more than just a recreating of the plot and details of the story. Instead, use the issues, the themes, the characters, and the conflict as a *beginning* for your dramatic exploration. For example, the situation from the story as a starting point—you and your classmates might choose to begin the drama by using a *similar* situation, and then heading off in a different direction. You may decide to bring a new problem into the story in order to get a new perspective on what the story is about. You may want to explore the relationships of the characters in the story, and then improvise a drama using these roles. Sometimes the mood or atmosphere of the story will be enough to stimulate a whole new drama.

Dramatization of a story is a *new* telling of the story, often with very different results from the original. As you go back and forth between the original story and your improvised creation, you will learn how to bring more meaning and sensitivity to all that you read.

In the excerpt from *The Machine-Gunners*, the young people are considered too young to fight. By coincidence, they come across a weapon from an enemy plane that has been shot down, and decide to use this aircraft machine gun to fight their own war.

Workshop

Rag-Tag Army

Everyone in the class get into marching formation—several rows of four abreast, for example. Choose a leader to call out commands. March in formation about the room, following the commands of your leader. You need not know marching terminology: commands such as "Turn right!", "Left!", "In a circle!", "Stop!" will serve the purpose. After some practice, try marching without the commands of the leader, relying on each other's sense of the group's movements. Music might help to unify your actions during the experience. However, do not be too concerned if you cannot keep a perfect formation. Enjoy the group's flaws.

Battle Scenes Through the Ages

1.   The idea is for you to create still shots of battle scenes. To start with, your whole class gathers to one end of the room, and on a given signal from your teacher you attack an imaginary enemy at the other end of the room. Whenever your teacher claps, however, you freeze in whatever position you are in so that the "photographs" can be taken. This freezing technique will help you have more control and concentration in your work.

As you "advance and attack" think of storming old castles with battle axes, sword fights on ships, or infantry attacks with rifles and fixed bayonets. Experience different kinds of mood and atmosphere as you attack, from the secret, stealthy attacks of natives to the wild bravado of commandos. Some attacks can be fast and very loud, others slow, very controlled and quiet. Extend the scenes in length by making the still photograph a momentary pause in the action, which then continues on a given signal.

2.   Once you've had lots of practice in attacking, divide your class in half, one half at each end of the room. As you charge towards each other, pick out the person that you will meet in this imaginary fight. Each time you fight, choose a different imaginary weapon.

Try extending the scenes in length. Continue on with your fight after each freeze is over.

The Machine-Gunners

Chas McGill has the second-best collection of war souvenirs in Garmouth, and he desperately wants it to be the best. His chance comes when he finds a crashed German Heinkel, with a machine gun and all its ammunition intact. All he has to do is remove it from the plane. . . .

The police, the Home Guard, in fact everybody in authority in Garmouth, knows that the gun has been stolen. They are pretty sure the children have it, but where? And do the children realize that it could blow a hole through a wall at a quarter of a mile? It is essential to track it down before the children kill themselves or anybody else. And all the time other things keep disappearing too: cement, a telescope, tin hats, fire buckets, stirrup pumps, even an Anderson shelter!*

The bombing raids on Tyneside during the despairing winter of 1940–41 were appalling and relentless. The novel *The Machine-Gunners* is a tribute to the endurance, courage, and humour of ordinary people in extraordinary circumstances.

*An arched corrugated steel air-raid shelter, about the size of a large tent. Named after Home Secretary Sir John Anderson.

When Chas awakened, the air-raid shelter was silent. Gray winter light was creeping round the door-curtain. It could have been any time. His mother was gone, and the little brown attaché case with the insurance policies and bottle of brandy for emergencies. He could hear the milk-cart coming round the square. The all-clear must have gone.

He climbed out of the shelter scratching his head, and looked round carefully. Everything was just the same: same whistling milkman, same cart-horse. But there was too much milk on the cart and that was bad. Every extra bottle meant some family bombed-out during the night.

He trailed round to the kitchen door. His mother had the paraffin heater on and bread flying. It smelt safe. There were two more panes of glass out of the window, and his father had blocked the gaps with cardboard from a Nestle's Milk box. The lettering on the cardboard was the right way up. Father was fussy about things like that.

Father was sitting by the heater with his pint mug of tea. He looked weary, but still neat in his warden's uniform, with his beret tucked under his shoulder-strap.

"You remember that lass in the greengrocer's?"

"The ginger-haired one?" said his mother, still bending over the stove.

"Aye. A direct hit. They found half of her in the front garden and the other half right across the house."

"She didn't believe in going down the shelter. She was always frightened of being buried alive." From the way his mother hunched her shoulders, Chas could tell she was trying not to cry.

Chas's father turned to him.

"Your rabbits are all right.

Chinny had some glass in her straw, but I shifted it. But there's six panes out of the greenhouse. If it goes on this way, there'll be no chrysanthemums for Christmas."

"It won't be the same without chrysants," said his mother. Her lips were tight together, but shaking slightly. "Here's your breakfast."

Chas cheered up. Two whole slices of fried bread and a roll of pale pink sausage-meat. It tasted queer, not at all like sausage before the war. But he was starting to like the queerness. He ate silently, listening to his parents. If he shut up, they soon forgot he was there. You heard much more interesting things if you didn't butt in.

"I thought we were a gonner last night, I really did. That dive bomber...I thought it was going to land on top of the shelter...Mrs. Spalding had one of her turns."

"It wasn't a dive bomber," announced Father with authority. "It had two engines. He came down on the rooftops 'cos one of the RAF lads was after him. Right on his tail. You could see his guns firing. And he got him. Crashed on the old laundry at Chirton. Full bomb load. I felt the heat on me face a mile away." Mother's face froze.

"Nobody killed, love. That laundry's been empty for years. Just as well—there's not much left of it."

Chas finished his last carefully-cut dice of fried bread and looked hopefully at his father.

"Can I go and see it?"

"Aye, you can go and look. But you won't find nowt but bricks. Everything just went."

Mother looked doubtful. "D'you think he should?"

"Let him go, lass. There's nowt left."

"No unexploded bombs?"

"No, a quiet night really. Lots of

our fighters up. That's why you didn't hear any guns."

"Can I borrow your old shopping-basket?" said Chas.

"I suppose so. But don't lose it, and don't bring any of your old rubbish back in the house. Take it straight down to the greenhouse."

"What time's school?" said his father.

"Half-past ten. The raid went on after midnight."

War had its compensations.

Chas had the second-best collection of war souvenirs in Garmouth. It was all a matter of knowing where to look. Silly kids looked on the pavements or in the gutters; as if anything *there* wasn't picked up straight away. The best places to look were where no one else would dream, like in the dry soil under privet hedges. You often found machine-gun bullets there, turned into little metal mushrooms as they hit the ground. Fools thought nothing could fall through a hedge.

As he walked, Chas's eyes were everywhere. At the corner of Marston Road, the pavement was burnt into a white patch a yard across. Incendiary bomb! The tail-fin would be somewhere near—they normally bounced off hard when the bomb hit.

He retrieved the fin from a front garden and wiped it on his coat; a good one, not bent, the dark green paint not even chipped. But he had ten of those already.

Boddser Brown had fifteen. Boddser had the best collection of souvenirs in Garmouth. Everyone said so. There had been some doubt until Boddser found the nose-cone of a 3.7 inch anti-aircraft shell, and that settled it.

Chas sighed, and put the fin in his basket. A hundred tailfins couldn't equal a nose-cone.

1. When you have finished the excerpt, write a diary entry for one of the students of Tyneside that explains the frustration of not being able to help with the war effort when older family members are away fighting.

When you have finished your diary entry, come and sit in a circle with your class. Each of you tell what destruction can be seen as a result of bombing in the night by enemy planes.

2. Now divide up into groups of three. One of you must persuade the other two, who are an old couple, to leave their bombed-out home because their building is now totally unsafe, and to take temporary shelter.

3. In groups of three or four, you are going to plan a hiding place for a machine gun that your group has located. The following are some details for you to use:

– the year is 1942;
– you are about 15 years old;
– you cannot fight the enemy legally;
– you have located the downed enemy plane with the gun and ammunition;
– your hiding place must allow for the cementing of the gun to the floor.

When you have settled on your plan, use large sheets of newsprint and markers to make diagrams.

Each group must present its visual diagram to the whole class. Questions should be asked in order to clarify each group's presentation. At the conclusion of the sharing, the class must come to an agreement on the single best hiding place for the machine gun.

Your group must devise a plan to move the gun from the woods where the plane crashed to the new hiding place. Consider the following:

– how will you get the gun past the warden? (it is too heavy to carry);
– your group must not act suspiciously.

Each group can demonstrate to the rest of the class its idea for transporting the weapon. The teacher can role-play the warden.

When you have all presented your ideas, discuss, as a class, the problem of inexperienced people using a gun.

4. Choose a partner. You are teachers who have been asked by the authorities to find out what information the students in the school have about the gun. Consider these points:

– what scheme will you devise?
– will you be honest with the students?
– will you use psychological or propoganda techniques?

Each pair can enact its plan in front of the rest of the class with the class playing the students. As the teachers, you should attempt to be leaders who care about your students' lives. As the students, you must attempt to role-play within the situation, and refrain from stereotypical behaviour.

As a class, discuss the various situations that you experienced in the drama both as a teacher and as a student. Discuss the following:

– which methods seemed to work?
– what types of manipulating were being used by those role-playing the teachers?
– did those role-playing students maintain believable roles?

5. In the novel *The Machine-Gunners* the students are surprised by a wounded German soldier who has found their hiding place for the gun. As a class, role-play this situation. (The teacher or a volunteer from the class can role-play the soldier.)

– The soldier, if possible, can use a different language.
– The soldier is armed; how will the confrontation take place in the attempt to communicate with the students?

Role-play the following situations.

– Create a legal hearing in front of a judge in which the students are charged with treason for hiding the gun and for associating with an enemy soldier.
– The air-raid warden is called in front of his supervisors for letting the machine-gun slip through the barrier.
– Create a scene with the whole class where three or four pacifists go back in time in a "time warp" and try to persuade the students to abandon the machine-gun and to withdraw from supporting the war.
– Draw up a list of rules to be pinned up at the hiding place to be obeyed by everyone who knows about the gun.

Drama Journal

How does a novel give you ideas that can be used in drama? Could you create a play from a novel, using several incidents to build up a series of scenes?

How can the problem of narration in a novel be handled in drama?

Did you relate to the youth in this excerpt? Although the novel is set 40 years ago, do the problems of these young people still apply today?

What films do you know were made from novels? Can any novel be used for drama?

Examine a novel you have studied. Which incidents could easily be dramatized?

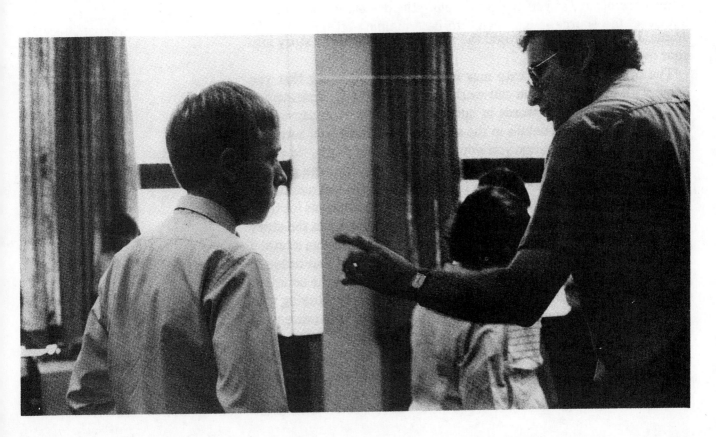

Beyond the Print

The use of story is exciting and satisfying when it permits the discovery of challenging possibilities, where the participants reshape a story to suit their own interests and purposes.

Tom Stabler
Drama in Primary Schools p. 134

The last chapter of Section C and the first chapter of Section D were about dramatizing stories. You were given some background information and excerpts from novels so that everyone would have the same frame of reference as you began to explore the drama. In this chapter, however, the source is only going to be a jumping-off point for the drama. Here, you will go beyond the words and ideas of the story into your own experiences.

The drama that you create may not resemble the story that you begin with in any way. You can work behind the words, beneath the words, and expand the words in building the drama. You can invent your own drama from details in the story that relate to your own life. You may know of a situation you would like to present that is similar to that of the story, or you may choose to present the opposite point of view to that expressed in the story. Characters who are just mentioned in the story may be developed fully as you explore the reasons for their behaviour. You can examine questions that have come up in the story and deal with them through the drama. Within a story, you can stop at a particular problem that needs to be solved, or a decision that needs to be made, and then take a look—through your drama—at the solutions and choices that might be given. You can create drama by working with what might have happened before the story begins, or dramatize what you think might happen after the story ends.

The beginning point for drama in this chapter is a legend based on a kingdom of long ago, where the king's decision was final.

Workshop

Tribute

Get in groups of five. Each group improvises a scene where a tribute is given to someone in authority. Consider the following:

– Who will the authority be?
– Who will the people be who are offering the gift?
– Why are they presenting the gift?
– What will be offered?
– How will it be presented?

In front of the other groups, each group presents its gift to the authority. In order to involve everyone in each tribute, each group can instruct the rest of the people where they should stand and how they should behave.

After all the groups have presented their tributes, the class can discuss who they thought the presenters were, what the gifts were composed of, and what they felt the situation was about.

As a class, discuss if people present tributes in contemporary society. Do wealthy people ever give tributes to others?

The King's Fountain

Read the following story.

A king once planned to build a magnificent fountain in his palace gardens, for the splendour of his kingdom and the glory of his name.

This fountain, however, would stop all water from flowing to the city below.

A poor man heard of it, and said to his wife:

"Soon our children will cry for water, our animals will sicken, and all of us will die of thirst."

His wife answered:

"A man of highest learning must go to the King, speak to him out of wisdom, and show him the folly of his plan."

So the poor man went throughout the city, to the most learned of scholars, and begged him to plead the cause.

But the scholar, deep in his own grand thoughts, barely listened. He pondered lofty matters and had no interest in humbler ones.

And the scholar lectured him with so many cloudy words that the poor man could make no sense of them at all, and went away downcast, saying to himself:

"Alas, the grandest thought quenches no thirst. Besides, what good is all the learning in the world if there is no one who can understand it?"

He realized that someone must present the cause clearly and winningly, with a golden tongue, so the King would listen and agree.

So he went to the marketplace, to the merchants whose words were smooth as pearls and who could string them together endlessly.

But when these merchants heard what he wanted, they choked with fear and their glib words failed them. While they gladly offered clever advice, not one dared face the King.

The poor man left them and went away dismayed, saying to himself:

"Alas, the finest words are empty air without the deeds to fill them. Besides, what good is a golden tongue without a brave heart?"

Then he realized that a man of strength and courage must go and force the King to change his plan.

Again he went throughout the city, to the strongest of all brave men: a fearless metalsmith who could knot an iron bar as easily as a shoestring.

The metalsmith, eager to stand against the King, swore that once inside the palace he would smash every window, crack every wall, and break the King's throne into firewood.

The poor man sadly shook his head, knowing the palace guards would strike down the rash metalsmith before he did even one of those deeds. And the King in his wrath would be all the more determined to build his fountain. So,

leaving the metalsmith still pounding his fists, he went away in despair, saying to himself:

"Alas, the strongest hand is useless without a wise head to guide it. Besides, what good is all the bravery in the world if it serves no purpose?"

He trudged home, hopeless and heavy-hearted, and told his neighbours and his family that he could find no one to stop the building of the fountain.

The poor man left his home. Alone, he slowly climbed the steep and seemingly endless hill.

Finally, he reached the King's high palace and for a long while stood outside, fearful and hesitant.

When the palace guards roughly seized him and threatened his life for intruding, the poor man trembled in such terror he could scarcely speak. Desperately he blurted out that he had an important message for the King alone.

The guards marched him to the throne room, where the King angrily demanded why he had come.

Knees knocking, teeth chattering, the poor man began to tell as well as he could of the suffering that the fountain would cause.

"Enough!" roared the King. "How dare you question what I do? I am the King!"

The poor man wished for the smallest crumb of the scholar's learning, but he could only stammer:

"Majesty—thirst is thirst, a poor man's no less than a king's."

Then his tongue dried in his mouth and he wished for even one of the merchants' golden words.

The King looked scornfully at him. "You come to trouble me for that? I need only snap my fingers and my swordsmen will cut you to pieces and be done with you."

The poor man wished for one drop of the metalsmith's bravery. With his own last ounce of courage, he answered:

"You have the power to kill me. But that changes nothing. Your people will still die of thirst. Remember them each time you see your splendid fountain."

The King started up, ready to call his guards. But he stopped and fell silent for a time, his frowns deep as his thoughts. Then he replied:

"You are too simple for clever debate with me; but you have a wiser head than a scholar. Your speech is halting; but there is more true eloquence in your words than in the golden tongue of a cunning counsellor. You are too weak to crack a flea; but you have a braver heart than anyone in my kingdom. I will do as you ask."

The poor man returned to the city and told the news to all. The scholar wrote a long account of the matter in one of his books, and misplaced it. The merchants never stopped ornamenting tales of the poor man's deed. The metalsmith was so excited he tossed his anvil into the air and broke one of his own windows.

The poor man, glad simply to be home with his rejoicing family, was hardly able to believe what he had done.

"A wise head? A golden tongue? A brave heart?" he said to himself. "Well, no matter. At least none of us will go thirsty."

1. After reading the legend silently, get into groups of five. Discuss the King's reasons for deciding to use the waters to create a fountain. What could the hidden reasons be for such an action? Create a tableau that demonstrates your ideas of the King's motive for building the fountain. (At this point you are beginning to leave the shelter of the story, to build a new story through drama.)

Each group can present its tableau, and the class can attempt to explain what each group is depicting.

2. In this exercise you will be creating your own plot, using the story as a beginning point, but going in your own direction.

Choose one group to act as the King's councillors. This group will explain the reasons for building the fountain. The other groups will work on presenting cases in anticipation of what they will be told by the councillors. All groups should consider these points:

– Will the councillors give "real" reasons or will they choose a political stance and mask the true motive?
– How will the people respond? Being tribal peasants, with few weapons and no military strength, what arguments and strategies will the tribe use to persuade the councillors to leave them the river water?
– After hearing the people, will the King's councillors remain loyal to the King?

Have someone from the class or your teacher role-play the King, and hold the meeting between the councillors and the tribespeople.

– How will the confrontation be staged?
– Where will each group stand?
– How will the tribespeople state their case?
– Will they use stories from the tribe's past to foretell the future?

3. You can continue to build your drama by using your own experiences of confronting authority. Here are some suggestions:

– Set the drama in today's world where a group of people are dealing with a person in authority and are sick with fear.
– Choose one situation from these ideas that the class agrees to work on. Then, in small groups, improvise scenes inspired by this idea. You may be surprised by the variety of reactions.
– Have a group from today's world travel to the original kingdom of *The King's Fountain*, and build a drama on their confronting the authorities with a different solution. Who will the group represent? How will they be treated by the people of the kingdom? How will the visiting group persuade the people of their plan?

4. Discuss as a class whether or not there are countries where there is no democratic sense of justice for the people. Are there still places where a ruler dictates without fair laws? What safeguards does your country have against such conduct?

5. If another country wanted your country's water, what could your people do today to prevent it?

Drama Journal

At what point in the dramatization did you feel unsure of the direction and focus of the drama?

What drama techniques help a group to keep moving forward in the drama?

Explain how the process you have gone through is the same as what happens to a playwright who is writing a script.

"Making a play through improvisation is full of difficulties, but can be a fulfilling process which requires the same skills as doing a play by Shakespeare. We still have to find our way through." Do you agree?

How can a group create a play that becomes a script?

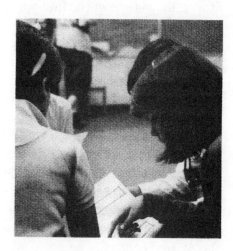

Storytelling

I don't hesitate to dramatize when I read or tell stories. I explore the full range of emotions open to the characters in the story, since mastering the story means personalizing it for the storyteller as well as the listener.

Bob Barton

Storytelling is one of the first ways we develop an awareness of others and of ourselves as spectators. As children we liked having stories read or told aloud to us. We also enjoyed taking on the role of storyteller, telling our favourite stories to others. In drama, the technique of storytelling is one way of communicating with an audience, and it is a technique that every audience can identify with.

With the storytelling technique, you will be role-playing, shifting your point of view, and exploring different language patterns as you tell the story. Your group may decide to tell a story beginning with one member at a time and then signalling for others to continue. You may decide to work in narration, improvising with the existing dialogue and creating new dialogue. Your storytelling may be an exercise in drama, or it may be the beginning point for the drama. It may reveal an idea in the drama, or it may be a review of what has already taken place. In role, you can tell a story as a summary of what has gone on. Sometimes you can tell a story in the role of a character within the drama. Storytelling allows your group to explain what has gone on before or to present another point of view.

As you begin to communicate with your audience, you will become more aware of your skills of communicating in all of your drama work.

The selections in this chapter give you the opportunity to tell stories as games, as group activities, and as part of the situation in the drama.

Workshop

The Snakebit Hoe-Handle

The tall tale or yarn is an exaggerated story intended to make people laugh. Such stories flourished when people had very few sources of entertainment other than the stories they told each other. Telling tales is a good way of practising your improvising skills and of beginning to think about the listener as an audience.

Do not read the following story until three people have volunteered to leave the room. Now the story can be read aloud to your class by your teacher.

THE SNAKEBIT HOE-HANDLE

A copperhead snake made for me
one day when I was hoein' my corn.
Happened I saw him in time,
and I lit into him with the hoe.
He thrashed around,
bit the hoe-handle a couple of times,
but I fin'lly killed him.
Hung him on the fence.
Went on back to work,
and directly my hoe-handle felt
    thicker'n common.
I looked it over good and it was
    swellin'.
The poison from that snakebite
was workin' all through it.
After I tried it a few more licks
it popped the shank and the hoe-head
    fell off.
So I threw that handle over by the
    fence;
went and fixed me another'n.
Got my corn hoed out about dark.
Week or two after that
I was lookin' over my cornfield,
and I noticed a log in the fencerow.
Examined it right close
and blame if it wasn't that
    hoe-handle!
Hit was swelled up big enough for
    lumber.
So I took it and had it sawed.
Had enough boards
to build me a new chicken house.
Then I painted it and, don't you
    know:-
the turpentine in the paint
took out all that swellin',
and the next mornin'
my chicken house had shrunk
to the size of a shoe box.
Good thing I hadn't put my
    chickens in it!

Ask one volunteer to come back into the room. Someone who heard the story now retells it to the volunteer, who in turn tells it to the second volunteer, now brought back into the room, who then tells it to the third volunteer. The third volunteer tells it to the class. The rest of you listen to the various versions, and notice:

– how different words are used to replace words in the story;
– whether the storyteller uses the first person I in the telling or switches to third person "he";
– if the dialect is used or is changed;
– if any details are altered;
– if the punchline remains; and
– if the storyteller understands his or her own telling of the tale.

Taller and Taller!

This activity is based on the "Liars Club," an organization that conducts annual tall tale competitions. Read through the following tales.

DALBEC'S WONDERFUL SHOT

There was once a very famous hunter named Dalbec, who lived in the village of Ste Anne. He had been hunting all day and was returning home when he came to a little round lake, on the opposite side of which he saw a fox. Just as he raised his gun to fire, six ducks came sailing from under the bushes nearer to him. He hesitated at which to shoot, and decided to try his chances at both. Placing the barrel of his long gun between two trees, he bent it into a quarter of a circle, fired at the ducks, killed them all, killed the fox also, and the bullet came back and broke the leg of his dog that was standing by him.

DALBEC AND THE GEESE

He had been ploughing one day, and at night, just as he was going to put his horse in the barn, he heard a flock of wild geese in the air over his head. He went into the house and got his gun, but it was so dark he could see nothing. Still hearing the noise, he fired in the direction from which it came. As no birds fell he concluded he had missed them, so he went into the house, ate his supper and went to bed. In the morning he was going for his horse again when just as he was stepping out of doors a goose fell at his feet. It was one of those he had shot at and it had been so high up it had been all night in falling.

DALBEC FLIES THROUGH THE AIR

It was the morning of the 'Toussaint' (All Saints' Day) that Dalbec had gone out early, shooting. He had expended all his ammunition and was returning home when he saw a flock of wild ducks swimming about among the timbers of raft that had gone ashore at the mouth of the river. The water was cold, but Dalbec went into it up to his neck and waded round until he could reach under the logs and get hold of the legs of a duck. When he caught one he pulled it quickly under the water and fastened it to his belt. In this way he secured about a dozen. All of a sudden he felt a commotion, and before he knew what was happening he found himself raised into the air and carried off. A strong northeasterly gale was blowing and away he went up the St. Lawrence. Just as he passed the church at Ste Anne he heard the first bell of the mass sound, and he wished he had stayed at home instead of going shooting. At the rate at which he was going he had not much time to think; but presently he realized that something had got to be done. He reached down and twisted the neck of one of the ducks. That let him down a little and he twisted another. So he kept on until, when he had done with them all, he found himself dropped on the ground in front of the church at Sorel, and heard the second bell of the mass. He had been carried seventy-five miles up the river in just half an hour.

THE GRASSHOPPERS WERE VERY THICK up here last summer. They destroyed everything.

A farmer was driving by our house one day and stopped in to get a drink of water. He was driving a mule and wagon. He left it sitting out in front of our house and walked around back to get his drink at the well.

When he came back he couldn't find his wagon or mule. He discovered that the grasshoppers had eaten up his mule and wagon, and were pitching horseshoes to see who would get to eat the harness.

Ruth Roat

WHEN I WAS IN THE NAVY, the captain ordered me down to Key West. As we were sailing along nicely into the open sea, we got under a big cloud, and what do you think this cloud was? Why, it was a flock of mosquitoes. They lit on our ship and cleaned us out of every bit of tarred rope and canvas we had aboard.

A month later, we saw this same cloud of mosquitoes down in Vera Cruz. How did I know it was the same bunch? Every one of those mosquitoes had on canvas overalls and tarred rope suspenders.

Harry Zatorski

THE BIGGEST TREE in Canada—an elm—took timbermen six days to cut down. And when it started to fall they ran back for two miles to get out of the way. They waited till dark but the top of the tree still hadn't hit the ground yet.

Edwin Carr

A MAN LIVING WEST OF TOWN here tried to raise a watermelon this summer. He had very bad luck. The soil was too rich. The watermelon vines grew so fast that they wore the watermelons out, dragging them along on the ground.

One of the boys from town went out one night to swipe a melon. He got the melon all right, but the vines were growing so fast that warm night that the boy had to be taken to the hospital. It seems before he could break that melon off the vine, it had dragged him half a mile and he was in bad shape.

Arthur R. Kirk

MY POP USED TO LIVE at the foot of a perpendicular bluff in the mountains. In the spring he'd sit out on the front porch, take out his slingshot and shoot potato seeds into the bluffs in rows, running from top to bottom. Then, in order to be sure they had enough moisture, he'd shoot an onion in above each potato. The onions made the potatoes' eyes water. And so my pop had a good crop every year.

Warren Hemenway

1. Choose one tale, and, on your own, practise telling the tale several times, first by reading it aloud privately, and then by attempting to tell it without the book.

2. Choose a partner, and tell your tales aloud to each other. Then help your partner make that tale "personal" by adding information that makes the story "owned" by the storyteller. For example:
– What details could be elaborated?
– What information could be changed?
– How could the storyteller make the story about his or her own region?

3. Get into groups of four or five, and try telling your own personalized versions.

4. As a class, arrange your own Liars Club, and have all of the stories told aloud. There should be no order to the telling; volunteers should begin when they can connect their story to the one previously told. For example, if the last story were about a cold winter, then the next storyteller could begin by saying, "Cold! I'll tell you what cold means," and then tell his or her story. In this way, the Liars Club will be a collective process, flowing from one story to the next.

How Big Was That Dog?

Little children sometimes tell wonderful "tall tales" quite unintentionally, because they perceive things like size, colour, weight, volume, and age from a different perspective than do grown-ups. Invent an incident or observation which might seem insignificant to an adult, and tell your group the story first from your own point of view. Tell it again, as if you are ten years old, then four years old, and finally as if you are a baby (if we could hear the baby's thoughts).

You Won't Believe This...

Think of something that has happened to you recently, or of something you saw happen. It can be something fairly ordinary. Now rearrange the characters and circumstances and exaggerate the details until you have invented a "tall tale" of your own. Tell the tale to your group, and choose one of the following reasons for doing so:
– Explain why you were so late.
– Persuade them how unusual you are.
– Stall for time!
– Make them laugh.
– Make them feel sorry for you.
– Save your own life.

(Remember: if you don't "believe" your story the others won't either!)

Whose Story Is It Now?

Investigate, if you can, some of the popular fantasy or adventure video games. Choose one that appeals to your imagination and make a list of the characters it involves, their qualities and abilities, and the obstacles and creatures they encounter. Make some brief notes about how the game's story begins.

Working in small groups, share your individual findings and select a game outline that appeals to the group. Divide up the roles, and use the basic story as a starting point for your improvised drama. In this situation, however, all of the obstacles and creatures get to be fully developed characters—each has as much ability to affect the story as the player has in the video game. You can include roles like avalanches, invading armies, swarms of frogs, and collapsing bridges, as well as black knights, warrior heroes, and damsels in distress.

You can use mime, sound effects, music, narration, and tableaux to heighten your fantasy drama as it develops.

Share your work with the other groups. If another group has chosen the same game as their point of departure, you may be surprised by the differing results!

Drama Journal

Were there times you told a story by yourself? in partners? in small groups? as a whole class? Which did you prefer?

Was it easier to tell a story in the first person (I), or in the third person (he, she)?

Is it necessary to memorize a story in order to tell it? Is this the same process as learning lines from a script?

Is a storyteller an actor?

Why is storytelling one of the oldest forms of theatre?

Heritage Drama

Drama connects us with the past and makes it available at the moment. True historical awareness requires a sensitivity to the fear and tensions of human events of the past.

Cecily O'Neill
Drama Structures p. 17

Drama is concerned with finding out why certain people behave as they do in a particular situation. You have already been investigating this a great deal in this book. However, in this chapter, you are going to look at a new way of establishing the *situation*. You are going to research a topic using such factual resources as interviews, letters, stories, and documents. You will gather all of your information with a view to gradually building a drama.

Once you have the material, you will have to interpret the information that you've found. You will want to examine it from different angles in order to determine the focus for your work. You will need to select, edit, and finally arrange your information. When you have structured your material, you can start exploring your topic through the use of different drama strategies. Your goal is to actually "live through" the situation you are investigating and to discover the motives of the people in the situation. As you work, you will find other sides to the issue and develop new perspectives about the meaning of the information you have found. Indeed, you may even find that you disagree with the decisions and conclusions reached by the people whom you are researching. Although you should always be faithful to your sources, it is quite possible to show "alternatives" provided that such alternatives are clearly signalled as your own views.

Work of this kind is often called "docudrama." The material in this chapter is based on actual stories that the students heard from their relatives. In other words, the drama was based on their own heritage. This chapter presents, as a model for your own work, heritage drama created by secondary school drama students.

Workshop

In Their Own Words

A secondary school dramatic arts class in the City of York worked with a Youth Theatre Director, Gary Schallenberg, to develop a theatre project based on stories from the heritage of the students involved. Each student was asked to provide five stories from personal experience or from the background of his or her family. The director helped the students interpret and expand the stories and deepened the students' understanding of the stories.

First, the students told their stories to the rest of the class. Then, after questions and comments from those listening, some of the stories were reworked and adapted, until they became the basis for dramatic exploration. In small groups, the students explored the dramatic ideas in each story, and, finally, these stories became the basis for a theatre presentation to an audience in the community.

The following four stories are some of the original material.

THE CREEPY PEEPERS

When my mother was a little girl, about three or four years before she came here from Italy, they didn't have funeral homes around, they simply brought the bodies into the house.

Whenever a person would die, she, and a little friend, used to hide behind the bushes and wait for the funeral cars to come so they could see the body. They knew the body would be upstairs, so they used to sit around and stare at the window of the room where the body was, to see if anything would happen.

One time somebody screamed and my mother, thinking it was the dead person come back to life, took off! The next day she came back and found out what really happened: It was a little girl who had died in the house, and her body had rolled off the bed. It was the mother who had screamed.

FAMILY REUNION

My grandparents were first married during the war and they were separated for two years. At this time the Ukrainians were sent to Poland to work and live while Russia took it over. My grandfather stayed in a camp where he worked the farm and did chores all day. At night he said that he used to have nightmares about his wife and children. He probably worried about their safety.

The camp was close to where they kept the women and children. Although they weren't prisoners at the time, the government wanted them close together. At night my grandfather actually dug a hole under a barbed wire fence. He and some of his friends would escape to go visit their families.

Grampa said that if he had only known better he wouldn't have done it. He said that he would leave the camp for about an hour and sneak back when the spot lights weren't shining on the yard. This went on for about a month. Then grampa got sick. He had tuberculosis. He was put in the hospital for about a month until he got better.

While he was in hospital he didn't know anything about his family. He was informed that his brother had been shot in the war and his nephew was reported missing. When my grandfather returned to the camp and was put back to work, he found out that the men who used to sneak out of the camp with him had been sent away to another camp. He never found out where. He suspects that they had been caught and killed or sent to a prisoner of war camp.

About six months ago, last Thanksgiving, my aunt was on the subway sitting beside two Polish ladies. Naturally, she joined in the conversation and gabbed about what Polish ladies usually gab about. She was shocked to find out that one of the ladies she was talking to had been her mother's maid of honour. This wasn't even the most exciting thing. The lady said that when my aunt's parents (my grandparents) left for Canada their nephew was found. Since he had only a mother, they were also sent to Canada.

Thirty years had gone by and no one knew that there was still more family in Canada. That day my aunt called her cousin and asked him over. He was identical to my father, but he had his brother's name. It was fun meeting my father's new relatives. Everyone was crying and laughing at the same time, and speaking Polish. It was the loudest and most emotional Thanksgiving I'd ever had.

A SKUNK FOR DINNER?

Many years ago, my Nanna and Poppy came over to Canada from Ireland. They moved to Barrie, a small town at that time.

Since my Poppy had always hunted over in Ireland, he decided he would also do so here. So off he went and shot a skunk (for dinner). The skunk didn't have time to spray, but as my Poppy began to walk home, whatever was in the skunk began to leak out. As my Poppy walked through the town he received many strange stares from people. He himself wasn't quite sure where this strange smell was coming from but he held on to his catch.

When he arrived home, he was greeted by my Nanna who threw him and the skunk out.

HOW MY MOTHER AND FATHER MET

With fate and a little luck, my dad married his dream girl. You see, my dad had first met my mom at a mutual friend's wedding. Upon meeting her, he fell head over heels in love. My mom at that time had a steady boyfriend and my dad was terribly disappointed. After the reception, he saw her leave with her boyfriend and my dad had thought that that would be the last time he'd ever set eyes on her. But luck was on his side because four days later he had put an ad in the paper for a full-time position in his shop. Guess who answered his ad? The girl of his dreams had answered his ad and he hired her on the spot. And it just so happened that my mom and her boyfriend had broken up the night before, leaving her available for my dad. A year later my dad married his dream girl and they've so far lived happily together for 30 years.

1.   In the first phase of this work, you are going to use these heritage stories as sources for drama. In small groups, select one of these stories for dramatization.

– Why do you think this story is important to the author?
– How will your group dramatize the story?
– How can you bring this incident to life and yet retain the story's original flavour?
– What drama techniques will you use? For example—will one of you be a storyteller while the others mime the action? Will all the members of your group role-play the story?

2.   Share the various dramatizations with the class. Then in a discussion, examine how the story became the basis for drama.

– Who spoke the narrative in each group?
– Was dialogue used?
– Where did movement fit into the telling of the story?
– How did each group involve all of its members?
– Did the group demonstrate an understanding of the significance of the story to its author?

What's Your Story?

In this phase of this work, your class goes through the same process as the group who originated the heritage presentation.

1. By yourself, decide on a family story. It may be about when you were younger, or it may have happened recently. It could also be a story about something that happened to your parents or grandparents. Often family get-togethers provide opportunities for hearing these kinds of stories.

2. Tell your story to a partner, and listen to your partner's story. Tell your story to a new partner, and listen to your new partner's story. Now tell the story that your partner told you, as if it had happened to you. You may have to make some minor adjustments. With your partner, clarify any details that were needed in the second telling of the story.

3. In small groups, tell your expanded stories, one member at a time. Then select one that the group would like to work on. Using this story as the basis for your work, begin to investigate all of its drama potential.

- What incidents could be dramatized?
- What roles will the members of the group play?
- How will the drama begin and end?
- Can you use mime, tableau, or movement along with your story? Could you use music?

4. The groups then share their stories. Some may have been exploring the same story. If so, you can combine the efforts of both groups.

As the stories are polished, they can become the basis for a class presentation. If this happens, consider the following:

- Who will the audience be (another class in the school, parents in the community, an old folks home)?
- What theatre crafts will be necessary in order to communicate with the audience?
- How will you open and close your presentation?

Rehearse, and then present your work at least twice, so that your class can discuss the effect of the audiences on what was happening in the drama.

These dramatized stories can be written down as a script that can be made into a class booklet. Perhaps your class could interview members of a particular community, such as an ethnic group, one specific family, or members of a club. These interviews could form the basis of a drama presentation to the original interviewees.

Drama Journal

Why do we enjoy hearing again and again our relatives tell familiar stories from our lives?

Will future generations have tape or video albums rather than just photographs?

How did your group decide on which stories to dramatize? Did the storytellers feel that their stories were depicted accurately and with the same depth of feeling?

Keep a journal of stories of your own heritage which you could use as the basis for drama or writing.

What can a narrator bring to a dramatic art form that is not available in dialogue?

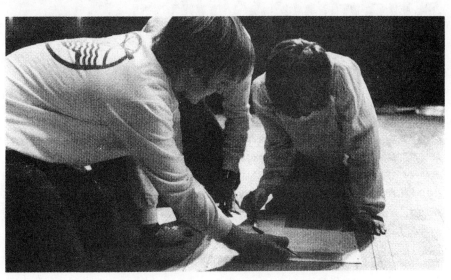

Sharing Within the Drama

Creating theatre is rarely accomplished without considerable difficulty and even conflict between members of the group. We are bound
to encounter differences of opinion; problems that are hard to solve.
All of these problems are potentially sources for inspiration and
opportunities for creativity as long as we communicate freely about
them. Through sharing, mutual problems can turn into mutual
opportunities.

Robert Benedetti
The Actor at Work p. 120

152

As you progress through drama and start to communicate your learning to others, you begin by sharing with an audience *within* the drama lesson. In this way you become both spectator and participant at the same time.

There are many ways of including an audience within the drama. Your class may decide on a theme that it wants to explore, and, in small groups, you each prepare a short scene that expresses your view. As you shape your ideas, you can ask the other groups to watch your work while it is still in progress. The others, through sensitive side-coaching, can make suggestions and help with problems. Try to explore all suggestions offered, even if they do not figure in your final work.

When all the groups have shaped their work, you can each present your ideas in turn. But first, you can decide on how the other groups fit into your work as role-playing spectators. For example, perhaps each group is presenting its interpretation of a crime. Those watching can role-play townspeople, and decide which interpretation they think works best. They can then—like a jury—decide on the guilt of an individual.

A third way of involving an audience is to ask people to write down the dialogue and action as you perform your work. Your improvisation can then be turned into a script which you and the observers can polish. The script can then be used by other groups.

This chapter allows you to build and share drama based on the Canada flu epidemic of 1918. Because this source contains so many beginning points for drama, you will be able to develop, explore, and present many interesting aspects of this difficult period in Canada's past.

Workshop

Dead One Arise

1. Variations of this game are found in Sicily, Czechoslovakia, and Germany. Choose one person to lie on the ground and be entirely covered with a blanket, sheet, or a pile of jackets. The rest of you walk round the body, calling solemnly, "Dead one, arise!...Dead one, arise!...Dead one, arise!" You do not touch the body, and you pretend not to look at it. Then, when least expected, the "dead" man or woman answers your call. He or she rushes at those who have done the "resurrecting," trying to touch one of you and make you the dead one in his or her place.

2. Add the following variations to the game.

– When a victim is caught, he or she joins the "dead" body. Continue until everyone is part of the dead body.
– Add music, and perform the game in slow motion.

3. Extend this game into drama by using some or all of the following ideas.

– Create a story about the dead person—who he or she is, how he or she died.
– Add a ritual to the dramatization in order to indicate that this ceremony is hundreds of years old.
– Extend the story: what happens after the dead person arises?

Epidemic

The next several activities are based on the book *The Silent Enemy,* which describes the flu epidemic that swept across Canada in 1918-19. First read the following newspaper article describing Eileen Pettigrew's book and the excerpts from the book itself.

Supply of coffins ran out

Book recalls flu epidemic of 1918-19

EDMONTON (CP)—The supply of coffins was quickly exhausted when the killer Spanish influenza swept across Canada in 1918-19, says author Eileen Pettigrew, whose book, The Silent Enemy, describes the horrors of the flu.

Residents of Alliance, Alta., southeast of Edmonton, erected barricades to ward off the disease, which eventually infected one in six Canadians and killed more than 20,000.

"They pulled a granary across the street and townspeople manned it to keep people out," Miss Pettigrew said in an interview.

Their efforts proved futile: Alliance's first flu death was the town's only doctor.

The book outlines the fear which swept across Canada after First World War soliders brought the deadly virus home with them.

Officials in Calgary ordered all residents to don masks in public while sidewalk spittoons were abolished in Edmonton, Miss Pettigrew said.

To write the book, she reviewed old newspapers and interviewed people who remember the devastating epidemic.

Schools were closed before the influenza hit Edmonton in October, 1918. Churches and theatres followed and stores were permitted to be open only between 10 a.m. and 3 p.m.

"You could be talking to a man on the street, turn around and walk down the street...you'd look back and he had fallen over," said one Edmonton resident quoted in Miss Pettigrew's book.

Native communities were hard hit by the flu during the winter. In some northern areas the dead lay on cabin roofs until the ground thawed in the spring, Miss Pettigrew said.

Before people developed an immunity to the new flu strain, the epidemic had killed about a third as many Canadians as the First World War.

The severity and high fevers caused by the strain of flu left people open to fatal complications.

"The thing that killed people was the pneumonia which followed," the author said.

Volunteers had to care for the sick because many of the country's trained medical personnel were in Europe with the Armed Forces.

Throughout Alberta, schools were turned into emergency hospitals and volunteers did the best they could with whatever medical supplies were at hand, Miss Pettigrew said.

Each tale of tragedy and sorrow is matched by another of courage in the face of a disease no one understood, she said.

"I found the bravery of the people quite remarkable."

The epidemic of 1918 struck hardest at young adults, and was followed by a high incidence of pneumonia. It affected almost every populated area in the world and it is thought to have killed between twenty and twenty-two million people in just a few months.

Spanish Influenza reached its height in Canada in the fall of 1918. It affected one in every six Canadians and killed between thirty thousand and fifty thousand; yet in the majority of history books it doesn't rate even a mention, and in others it is dismissed in a paragraph or two. Perhaps, as one writer suggested, compared with dying a glorious death defending your country, dying of 'flu was just not the way to go.

The scourge that was raging all over the world was well entrenched in eastern Canada, and it was carried rapidly across the country. Returning servicemen disembarking from crowded ships at Atlantic ports boarded trains that would take them home to cities, farms, and little towns from Newfoundland to British Columbia. Those who were not ill on landing were sometimes incubating the germ, and had to be taken off trains and hospitalized at cities across the country.

The western provinces, having seen what their neighbours to the east were enduring, put up what defenses they could by refusing to allow trains to stop or by placing inspectors on board to give passengers a clean bill of health before they were allowed to detrain, and some instituted total quarantines. Feelings ran high on the subject. "You can fence your town and put out your men to stop the traffic on the roads, but YOU CAN'T DEFEAT THE PLAGUE THAT WAY," wrote A.F.A. Coyne in the *Edmonton Bulletin* on November 12. "It is in the air—and you can't fence that."

Individual reactions ranged from fatalism to what one Saskatchewan woman described as "fear so thick than even a child could feel it." Coming after the losses so many had suffered in the war, for some there was only one way to deal with this new horror; they had to develop a shell over their emotions. "We were inured to sorrow"; "Every day there was someone we knew in the obituary columns"; "We got so we didn't even mourn." But if emotions were kept under control, compassion blossomed. In trouble as never before, the social barriers of the time were forgotten. Women who had never come closer to the mechanics of housekeeping than to instruct their cooks and chauffeurs, nursed people they didn't know, changed beds, cooked, and did laundry. The influenza epidemic cut across every stratum of Canadian life, affecting the rich as severely as it did the poor, and the just and the unjust suffered together.

Rumours were the order of the day. Stories circulated that Indians had been issued with unwashed blankets that had been used by infected troops. It was the cold; it was the unseasonable warmth; electricity was blamed; and, most of all, the enemy. A *Manitoba Free Press* editorial writer had this to say about the rumor that 'flu germs had been released by U-boat crews: "The Huns are sure handy people to blame anything on, but it is to be questioned whether one can blame them for everything that happens that does not seem just right."

Kingston theatre owners received notices from the medical officer of health that, after consultation with the Kingston Medical Society and under the provisions of the Ontario Health Act, it had been decided that the theatres must close on October 16. The president of the Canadian Theatre Managers' Association responded with an impassioned plea for reconsideration, pointing out the serious hardship such a closing would create for actors, who were not, in general, known to save their money. The medical officer of health remained unmoved, and ten days later notified poolroom proprietors that their establishments too must be closed to the public until further notice.

Travelling players were in difficulty everywhere. Members of the companies of "Furs and Frills," "It Pays to Advertise," and Ben Welch and his Burlesquers waited out the ban in Toronto. Chorus girls from the Stuart-Whyte Company, which had been presenting "Cinderella," didn't waste their time. Some became salesladies, some stenographers, and some got jobs with the hard-pressed telephone company.

The farmers of Lochalsh, near Ripley, were big, strong men of Scottish descent, stubbornly unwilling to accept the idea that they might become ill. A young doctor who had been serving overseas and returned to this, his home community, despaired of getting them to stop work and go home to bed when they had fevers. Dr. H.O. Howitt had the same problem at Guelph, chiefly with Italians and Austrians, who were splendidly strong and refused to stop work when they became ill. He told the annual meeting of the Canadian Public Health Association in Toronto: "We lost fathers of young families, fathers who felt they had to work on, and young mothers who would not take care of themselves because they thought they had to work or nurse 'for their children's sake'."

At Beaver Indian Reserve, near what is now the town of Fairview, Alberta in the Peace River area, some 85 percent of the people, who lived in tiny log cabins or wigwams, died between November 1918 and April 1919. Traditionally, each successful hunter shared a big feed with his fellows, so there was no stored food to draw on during the epidemic. Sick men went out in a desperate attempt to catch a rabbit—or anything at all—and often didn't make it back. The Indian agent, who lived fifteen or twenty miles from the reserve, was sick himself and couldn't help. There were not enough strong people left to put the dead bodies up on roofs to keep the dogs from consuming them.

Dr. O.D. Weeks of Calgary, who volunteered to help the Cree Indians in the Fort McMurray and Lac La Biche areas of northern Alberta, found them in dire straits, huddled together "in fear, and in sympathy," with the dead and the dying all together. At one cabin he found a delirious woman on the floor, clutching an eight-month-old baby who had been dead for forty-eight hours. "The woman protested strongly when the child was taken away," reported the *Edmonton Bulletin*. At another cabin a woman and three children were ill. Also in the cabin was a baby two-and-one-half weeks old, unwashed and untended since its birth. At the home of the chief at Beaver Lake Reserve seven people lay on the floor, all dead except the chief himself.

At Big Bay there were at least twenty bodies unburied, stored in a vacant cabin, with no one strong enough to dig their graves. Dr. Weeks, a strong supporter of inoculation, pointed out that at one Indian mission where there were

fifty children, five adult sisters, and one priest, all of whom had been inoculated, none had contracted the disease even though it was all around them. He credited his own ability to keep going night and day to taking weekly inoculations against the germ.

When she was seventy-nine years old, Emelia Merkuratsuk looked back on the winter of 1918. "There were many belongings and clothing lying around outdoors. Even now I don't like to see clothing lying around outdoors. Also I don't like to see people sleeping on the floor. Those things are reminders of the horrible sickness that once happened when I was still in my young life."

1.   In groups of four create a scene using tableaux which depict family life during the epidemic.

– What information will you use from the excerpts?
– How can you suggest that one family's problems symbolize the problems facing the population?
– How can your group create a sense of foreboding concerning their health?
– What conflict can be brought into the drama to heighten the impact of your work?

2.   With your whole group create a scene in which carts collect the bodies of the dead in the city. Some of you can role-play the "undertakers"; others can role-play the dead. Try using two people to role-play each body—one as the corpse and one voicing the story of that person's life.

3.   Get into groups of six. You are all actors who have been forced to find new jobs since the theatres have been closed. As you mime your work activity, discuss with each other, in role, what you miss about life in the theatre world.

4.   In small groups, enact the hearing where the priest is appealing the fine for defying the order to close the churches. What roles will each of you play? How will you react to the priest? Take turns playing the role of the priest.

5.   As a class enact a scene in which the need for vaccination is discussed. A panel made up of the mayor, the doctor, the magistrate, and the school principal can address a village meeting about vaccinating everyone against the flu. The rest of the class will be the people of the village.

– How will the people respond?
– Who will assist the sick?
– How will the children be protected?

6. Set the room up as a train. Most of you are passengers on the train, some of you can be the people who work on the train. Be prepared to tell other passengers something about yourself and about why you are travelling west from Ontario.

Using storytelling techniques, begin circulating rumours about the origin of the flu germs. Is there someone on board who might contaminate the others? Add to and elaborate on the information given in the excerpts until the whole train is talking, giving vent to their fears and suspicions.

At some point during the work a group of students, role-playing health inspectors, board the train and refuse some of you permission to leave the train, quarantining you on board.

– What will be your reaction?
– Will you plead with the inspector?
– How will the scene conclude?

7. Use your explorations of the flu epidemic as the basis for a polished presentation to an audience unfamiliar with this information.

As a class, list the various scenes that could be used. Divide into small groups, and each group explore one or two scenes until you are satisfied with the results. Then various scenes and interpretations can be shared with the class and final versions chosen.

Now create a framework for the various scenes so that the resulting play will be unified. One idea, for example, is to begin the play with a scene showing all of you lying on the ground role-playing flu victims. Then, one by one, you could sit up and begin a narration of the facts. You could intersperse the small group scenes with this individual work. During the work any of you could develop improvised monologues or scenes as you react to what others are saying.

When you present your work there are two things you will have to pay attention to—because of so many groups at work: one is continuity in certain details. For example, how will you set the time period in the drama? How will you co-ordinate factual information? attitude? language? The other is finding ways in role to help focus attention on each piece of work as it arises.

Because you are working in the improvisational style, each time your presentation is played it will be different. This allows you and your classmates to invent and explore new ideas. It is important that you find ways of bringing life to each exploration by exchanging roles, trying new physical actions, and by listening carefully to what the other actors are saying and responding appropriately and sensitively.

Remember that a game or exercise will often breathe new life into your class's work, giving extra energy and new ideas for a scene you thought was polished. One of the rhythmic games learned in another chapter might work well here. Such a game would also contrast with what is being presented through dialogue. Contrast (and impact) could also be achieved by adding sound and music.

When your improvised play is polished to your satisfaction, you can present it to one or two different audiences so that the dynamic of each presentation can be discussed.

Drama Journal

What is the difference between a person watching the drama and a person being an observing participant inside the drama? Which do you prefer?

What techniques used by other groups were most effective in drawing you into the dramatic situation? When did you feel that you were an audience member outside the drama?

How were you able to help someone overcome inappropriate behaviour in the drama?

At what time were you able to step outside yourself and watch yourself in role, inside and outside the drama at the same time?

Would you go to a play where you knew the audience would be involved inside the drama?

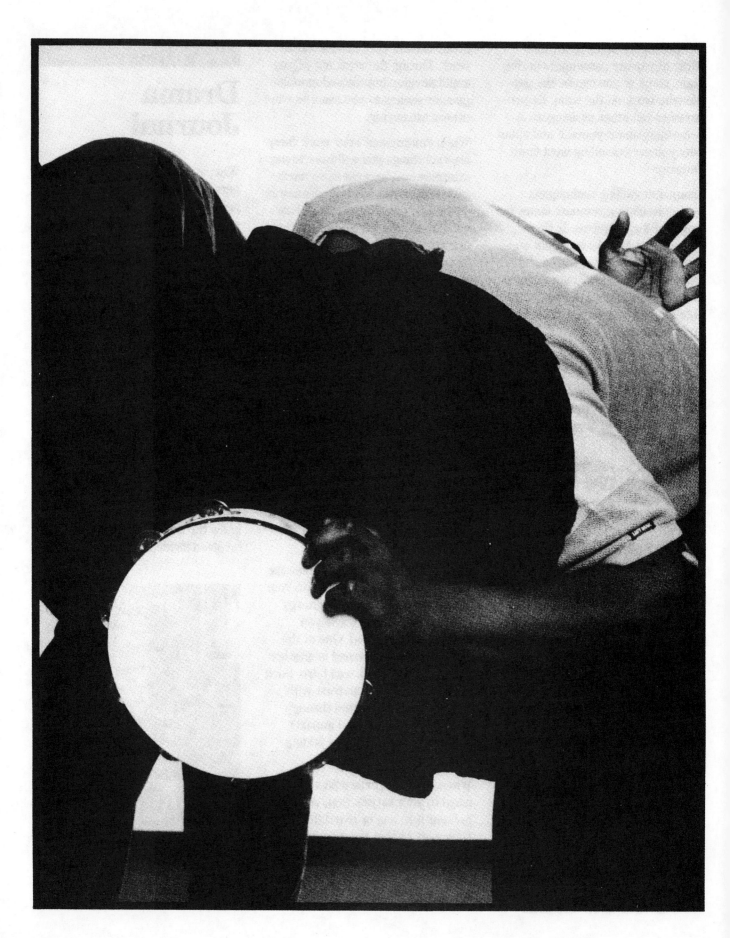

Drama Projects

An actor cries and laughs, and at the same time watches his crying and laughing.

Sonia Moore quotes
Stanislavski in *Training an Actor* p.96

At a very advanced stage, the class may become a kind of drama workshop in which the sub-group expect to improvise before the others, so that everything can be discussed—the dynamics, the content, the roles, the styles, the acting.

James Moffett
Drama NCTE p.27

Every drama group should do a performance project, because there are aspects of improvising that you can't learn any other way. But it is pointless to embark on such a project until that project feels like a logical *extension* of your work in improvising. When you can recognise improvisation as it is happening—in small and large groups—then you are probably ready to share your work. The following series of improvisation activities have been selected to give you a sense of two areas of improvisation that your group will need to explore in planning a performance:

1) theatre crafts
2) audiences

After that there is a choice of three performance projects. The first involves working with children; the second is for an audience of your peers; and the third is built around working with senior citizens.

Just as in the earlier sections of the book you started with games and activities that could be played for their own sake and progressed through these to the drama, here too you start with straightforward exercises and build on these to create the performance piece.

Theatre Crafts

Make-up was originally a mask to show the features. Painting the face now combines this purpose with compensation for powerful lighting; like costume, it is an extension of personality. Costume within a proper setting is an integral part of ceremony. Ceremony is the clothing of an idea. The clothing of an idea is theatre. And theatre is about people.

Esmé Crampton
A Handbook of the Theatre p. 183

Here are some of the instruments [of one theatre production]:

A Japanese dinner gong, a wooden Tibetan drum, eight pieces from a Balinese gamelon, tambourines, a hand-made replica of a medieval court harp, a dinky xylophone, slide whistles, Indian bagpipe flutes, Latin-American bongo drums, a saw, a bugle, rattles made from bean pods, a toy piano, one raunchy harmonica, recorders, two conches, Iranian flutes, kazoos, sandblocks, maracas, Jews' harps, claviors, Indian stomach tasangers, a Chinese circus drum, wood block cymbals and ratchets, crystal glasses, various pieces of scrap metal, and specially designed tuned cow-bells from Wonderful Copenhagen.

John Heilpern
Conference of the Birds p. 62

One of the pitfalls of getting involved in a performance project is that it brings into play factors that don't seem to have very much to do with the improvisation process. It's important, therefore, to explore the connection between improvising and theatre crafts—properties, staging, light, sound, costumes, and sets.

This book does not cover these topics in detail: there are other books for that. The point of the following activities is to demonstrate the way that a group committed to improvisational work can approach these topics, so that finding the drama remains the most important commitment in what you do.

You are not going to look at all theatre crafts: sound and properties have been chosen as case studies. But the principles are the same for the others.

Workshop

About Properties

Properties can help you create a belief in your drama, but only if the "prop" is more than just an object: it must be a symbol of something important in the drama, a focus that helps build the tension and the power of the moment. For example, in actuality, the prop may be a simple key ring, while symbolically, it may represent a wedding, or an inauguration. A bowl may mean home; a candle—shelter, darkness, faith; a cloak—authority or strangeness; a cup—sharing, healing or a ritual; a flower—life or growth; a fire—destruction or superstition; a key—security or privacy; and a sword—power, conquest, revenge or justice.

One item can have many different symbolic meanings, depending upon the situation that is being represented. You may use a simple necklace in ten different ways as you try to deepen the drama. Using properties in this way helps you to realize that it is the drama that creates the power; the prop is only a help.

Here is an exercise revolving around properties. Note that there is an audience role here. Make sure that everyone gets a chance to play both roles.

Look for items with interesting texture, colour, shape, and smell. There should be at least one for each person.

PERFORMER:

Pick a prop and use it to discover at least ten different possibilities. Try not to use it as it would really be used. A long, round piece of wood should not be used as a cane because this is what it most closely resembles. Work by yourself but if you get stuck, ask for help from the group. Interact with another person, each of you finding ways of using the props in an integrated fashion. Use sounds without mouthing words. Switch objects. What makes one object easier to work with than another? What does it take to relax and enjoy playing? Do you have to justify this activity in order to concentrate? Work in small groups to create a scenario with a beginning and end, doing as much as possible without talking. Work with your third or fourth choice and away from what you remember doing at other times.

AUDIENCE:

Watch to see the variety of ways that the performers are using object and to what degree they are limited by the object's shape, colour, or size. Are people dependent on TV for their ideas? Are they aware of where they got their ideas from? Are people able to work with give and take?

Exploring Sound

Work in pairs. One person suggest a sound-making machine, creature, or experience such as a locomotive, cricket, or gurgling brook. The partner then makes the sound. The sounds can be played with in a variety of ways—made faster, slower, louder, softer, or with a new rhythm. The person making the sound then suggests an emotional tone such as a locomotive carrying a funeral train, a cricket with an injured leg, or a brook being dammed up, and each partner makes this sound. Each partner takes turns suggesting sources for sound. Each in turn tries all the sounds. They can be imaginative, such as dew falling on a leaf or the sound of a thought passing from one person to another. Go outside the building and imitate street sounds or those heard in nature. Each person listen to your partner and note whether there is observable tension, general ease, or discomfort when the sounds are being made. The partner doesn't have to prescribe remedies; it is enough just to say where in the body the tension is. It is also helpful to have habits pointed out such as lifting the eyebrows as the pitch gets higher, pushing the head forward as the sound gets louder, or not using the lips to articulate sounds.

Sounds can also be built around outrageous situations such as someone getting a hand caught in a door. Each person can create for the partner the most outrageous sound-creating situation possible. Everyone should try all of the sounds. Don't strain or push when you get tired. Each person has a different time limit for careful work and this should be respected.

It Walked in the Woods

Read the following excerpt.

It walked in the woods.

It was never born. It existed. Under the pine needles the fires burn, deep and smokeless in the mould. In heat and in darkness and decay there is growth. There is life and there is growth. It grew, but it was not alive. It walked unbreathing through the woods, and thought and saw and was hideous and strong, and it was not born and it did not live. It grew and moved about without living.

It crawled out of the darkness and hot damp mould into the cool of a morning. It was huge. It was lumped and crusted with its own hateful substances, and pieces of it dropped off as it went its way, dropped off and lay writhing, and stilled, and sank putrescent into the forest loam.

It had no mercy, no laughter, no beauty. It had strength and great intelligence. And—perhaps it could not be destroyed. It crawled out of its mound in the wood and lay pulsing in the sunlight for a long moment. Patches of it shone wetly in the golden glow, parts of it were nubbled and flaked. And whose dead bones had given it the form of a man?

It scrabbled painfully with its half-formed hands, beating the ground and the bole of a tree. It rolled and lifted itself up on its crumbling elbows, and it tore up a great handful of herbs and shredded them against its chest, and it paused and gazed at the gray-green juices with intelligent calm. It wavered to its feet, and seized a young sapling and destroyed it, folding the slender trunk back on itself again and again, watching attentively the useless, fibred splinters. And it snatched up a fear-frozen field-creature, crushing it slowly, letting blood and pulpy flesh and fur ooze from between its fingers, run down and rot on the forearms.

It began searching.

1. Divide your class into two groups. Group A begins, and everyone in the group must be part of a single attack. For example, everyone may be part of a great tidal wave. Group A does not tell group B what the attack is. Group B begins by being the defence against the attack. Everyone agrees on the defence plan. Now, if Group B decides to be humans wearing gas masks, they would have been defeated by Group A's tidal wave attack.

Group A and B must plan in secret, and choose theatre crafts which will

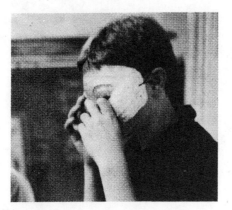

help dramatize their method of attack or defence. When each group is prepared, the drama begins.

At the conclusion of each attack, both groups attempt to discover what they felt the other group was portraying, and who should have won.

Before each new episode begins, groups reverse roles.

2. In groups of three to five, create the character of "it" using theatre crafts.

– Physically create the character using one or more students.
– Use make-up or mask to indicate its face.
– Incorporate costume to some extent by using an old sheet or cloak to give shape. You could paint it or attach things to it.
– Create a property for the character to use that will indicate the origin and nature of the character.
– Decide on the appropriate lighting for your character so that the entrance will convey its nature to those watching.
– Develop a sound collage that will help the audience interpret the reason for the character's existence as well as its mission.

Share the "character studies" with each other, then discuss the various ways the group used theatre crafts to build their characters. If you had an unlimited budget, what would your group invent?

Aliens

Read through the descriptions of the following four extraterrestrial creatures.

WANTED

BY THE ISB

MURDER

EARTH AIRBOT 408G

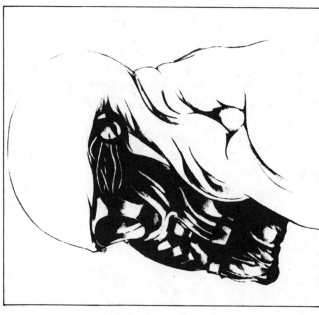

Two Dimensional Bureau
Schematic Side Face

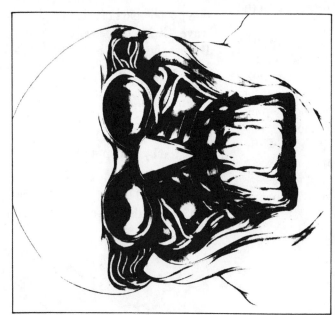

Two Dimensional Bureau
Schematic Front Face

DESCRIPTION:

ORIGIN: Planet Earth, Quadrant 4; Manufactured by General Dynamics Airbot Construction, New Jersey Plant.

HEIGHT: 5 ft. 8 in. (Earth gravity), 5 ft. 10 in. (Weightless state)

WEIGHT: 322 lbs.

COLOR OF EYES: Purple

COLOR OF HAIR: None

VISION: Infra-red, Shielded Auto Focal Tracking (c 2472 General Dynamics Airbot Construction).

MOST PROMINENT SURFACE COLOR(S): Purple, Blue and Black.

DISTINGUISHING CHARACTERISTICS: Visible identification markings located on lower back. Left side reads "408." Right side reads "G".

REMARKS: Airbot 408G is a tragic victim of circumstances. It is believed that during a routine servicing, this Airbot was the victim of a computer error. A malfunctioning logic circuit was mechanically replaced incorrectly, causing a series of thought command panels to re-organize within the Airbot's dome. This new equation process has created criminal thought commands similar to those harbored by common organic criminals. Following this incident, Airbot 408G displayed erratic behavior, was taken out of active Armed Forces duty (as an SPA-Space Pilot Attack-Ronin Class Fighter Pilot) and given a job as a "bouncer" at a Humanoid Status Armed Forces Officers' Club. One fateful evening, Airbot 408G simply refused to stop "bouncing" the clientele. The results: 15 dead, 40 injured.

CAUTION:

NO ONE IS SURE HOW FAR THE MENTAL DETERIORATION PROCESS HAS PROGRESSED. AIRBOT 408G IS ARMED AND EXTREMELY DANGEROUS. TERMINATION CIRCUITS ARE ACTIVE BUT EARTH COMMANDS HAVE FAILED TO PRODUCE ANY RESPONSE.

An Intergalactic League of Worlds Warrant was issued on December 31, 2480 at ISB HQ 4, Quad 4, charging Airbot 408G with 15 counts of murder, violation of Bureau Statute 120 (see: being extermination, first degree).

IF YOU HAVE ANY INFORMATION CONCERNING AIRBOT 408G, PLEASE NOTIFY YOUR LOCAL ISB OFFICE. VISOPHONE NUMBERS AND LOCATIONS OF ALL ISB OFFICES LISTED ON BACK.

ADAM HAWKINS

INTERGALACTIC SECURITY BUREAU
QUADRANT 4, TERRAN DISTRICTS
NEW WASHINGTON COLONY
VISOPHONE 23120019

WANTED

DESTRUCTION OF PRIVATE PROPERTY, DESTRUCTION OF PUBLIC PROPERTY, VANDALISM, CROSSING INTERDIMENSIONAL LINES ILLEGALLY, MANSLAUGHTER

DWEEZYL

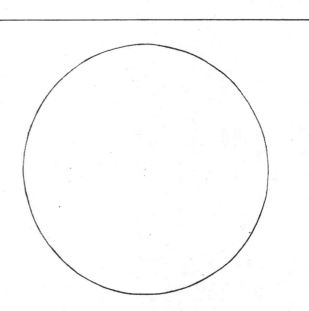

Two Dimensional Bureau
Schematic Side Face

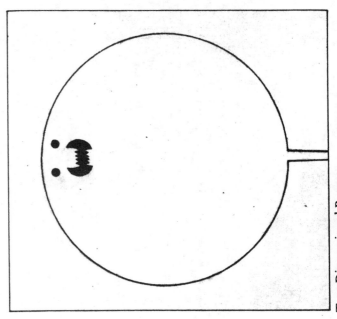

Two Dimensional Bureau
Schematic Front Face

166

DESCRIPTION:

ORIGIN: 4D

HEIGHT: Variable

WEIGHT: Variable

AGE: Unknown

COLOR OF EYES: Blue-yellow-black

COLOR OF HAIR: None

MOST PROMINENT SURFACE COLOR: Blue/violet

RACE: Unknown

DISTINGUISHING CHARACTERISTICS: A resident of one of the dimensions beyond The Portal, Dweezyl has been known to alter its shape, size and visibility factors at will.

REMARKS: Residing somewhere beyond The Portal, Dweezyl is a being apparently obsessed with the idea of destroying three-dimensional property. Slipping into League territory from point or points unknown, this creature has been known to appear unexpectedly in any and all quadrants and on any and all planets.

Known as the consummate graffiti artist, Dweezyl has been known to cover entire roadways, private homes and business structures with a thick ink obviously produced from somewhere within its bodily system. On the planet Fedra (Quad. 13), its high jinx inadvertently caused the death of a family of six Fedriopods when Dweezyl's sense of design totally inundated a small Tentacle-Ball court with ink. As of yet, law enforcement agents have not come up with a motive for Dweezyl's inky antics. However, several inter-dimensional psychologists have noted that, since the ink is apparently secreted from some point within the being, its graffiti scrawling may be political in nature.

CAUTION:

DWEEZYL HAS THE TEMPERAMENT OF AN ARTIST AND, HENCE, DEFIES ALL FORMS OF LOGIC.

An Intergalactic League of Worlds Warrant was issued on November 2, 2480 at ISB HQ 13, charging Dweezyl with Destruction of Private Property, Destruction of Public Property, Vandalism, Crossing Interdimensional Lines Illegally and Manslaughter, violations of Bureau Statutes 110 (see: vandalism), 111 (see: vandalism), 108 (see: vandalism, minor), 350 (see: tourism, passport requirements) and 115 (see: murder, near).

IF YOU HAVE ANY INFORMATION CONCERNING DWEEZYL, PLEASE NOTIFY YOUR LOCAL ISB OFFICE OR THE NEAREST PORTAL AUTHORITY OUTPOST. 4-D SCANNERS AND NETS WILL BE DISPATCHED TO YOUR AREA IMMEDIATELY. VISOPHONE NUMBERS AND LOCATIONS OF ALL ISB OFFICES LISTED ON BACK.

ADAM HAWKINS

INTERGALACTIC SECURITY BUREAU
QUADRANT 4, TERRAN DISTRICTS
NEW WASHINGTON COLONY
VISOPHONE 23120019

167

WANTED

MURDER

MAKAU THE WARRIOR

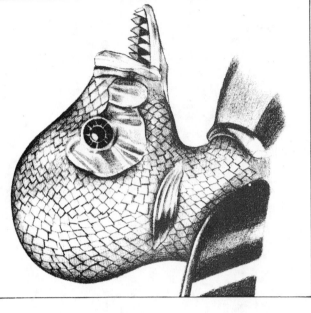

Two Dimensional Bureau
Schematic Side Face

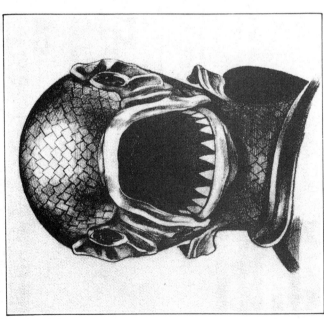

Two Dimensional Bureau
Schematic Front Face

DESCRIPTION:

ALSO KNOWN AS: Makau the Terrible, Makau the Magnificent, Mack, "Lips"

ORIGIN: Planet Moana, Quadrant 21

HEIGHT: 8 ft. 2 in.

168

WEIGHT:	320 lbs.
AGE:	early 30s
COLOR OF EYES:	Red
COLOR OF HAIR:	None
COLOR OF SCALES:	Green
MOST PROMINENT SURFACE COLOR:	Green
RACE:	Moanan
DISTINGUISHING CHARACTERISTICS:	Makau has a holographic tatoo of his first victim located on his chest.
REMARKS:	Makau the Warrior was born on the watery world of Moana. A planet inhabited by sea dwellers, Moana was known for its tranquil existence until war erupted on its surface two decades ago. At that time, it was briefly invaded by the humanoid citizens of Terraformed Zon. The humanoids, clad in diving gear and armed with laser weaponry, slaughtered many of the Moanans before a successful counterattack could be launched. The humanoids were defeated, but not before many casualties on both sides had amassed. Two of the Moanan victims were the parents of young Makau. Hiding his deeply-rooted resentment of humanoid life forms for nearly twenty years, Makau completed a normal Moanan education, served in that planet's armed forces and actually earned dozens of military citations before embarking on his bloody career in crime. Today, seeking revenge for his parents' deaths, he stalks all 25 quadrants, killing humanoid life forms wherever he finds them. To date, he has dispatched over 80 victims.

CAUTION:

MAKAU IS AN UNDERWATER KILLER. HE CANNOT EXIST ON LAND SURFACES WHERE THE ATMOSPHERE IS COMPARATIVELY THIN AND EARTH-LIKE FOR MORE THAN AN HOUR AT A TIME. SHOULD THE GLINT OF HIS EBONY ARMOR BE DETECTED IN ANY BODY OF WATER, NOTIFY YOUR NEAREST LAW ENFORCEMENT AGENT IMMEDIATELY. MAKAU IS CRAFTY. ON HUMANOID PLANETS HE IS KNOWN TO HAVE HIDDEN IN LAKES, PUBLIC POOLS AND SHOPPING MALL FOUNTAINS IN SEARCH OF PREY. HE IS A FRESH-WATER DWELLER.

An Intergalactic League of Worlds Warrant was issued on April 1, 2480 at ISB HQs, 17, 19, 15, 4, 8 and 10, Quads. 17, 19, 15, 4, 8 and 10, charging Makau with 85 counts of Murder, violation of Bureau Statute 120 (see: being extermination, first degree).

IF YOU HAVE ANY INFORMATION CONCERNING MAKAU, PLEASE NOTIFY YOUR LOCAL ISB OFFICE. VISOPHONE NUMBERS AND LOCATIONS OF ALL ISB OFFICES LISTED ON BACK.

ADAM HAWKINS

INTERGALACTIC SECURITY BUREAU
QUADRANT 4, TERRAN DISTRICTS
NEW WASHINGTON COLONY
VISOPHONE 23120019

WANTED
BY THE ISB

DESTRUCTION OF PRIVATE PROPERTY
MR. MUND

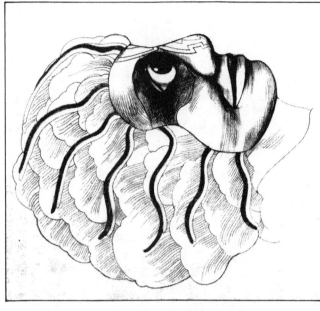

Two Dimensional Bureau
Schematic Side Face

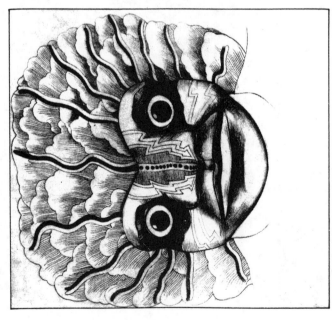

Two Dimensional Bureau
Schematic Front Face

DESCRIPTION:

ORIGIN: Crabtree Industrial Park; Wook, Iowa – Planet Earth, Quadrant 4

HEIGHT: 77 ft.

WEIGHT: 10 tons

AGE: 6 years

COLOR OF EYES: Brown

COLOR OF HAIR: Red, Yellow, Blue and Purple

HEIGHT OF MOUTH: 6 ft. at its widest point of opening

MOST PROMINENT SURFACE COLOR(S): Red, Yellow, Blue, Purple, Green and Pink

RACE: c 2474 Crabtree Industries

DISTINGUISHING CHARACTERISTICS: Mr. Mund eats cars.

REMARKS: Mr. Mund is a true case of science gone awry. Created and grown by Professor Harold Mund of Crabtree Industries, Mr. Mund was originally designed for use on the space habitat Earth IV; a scenic environment popular with vacationers and patterned after the original planet Earth during its 20th Century period. Earth IV, it seems, like its prototype, was having trouble in disposing of its waste metals in an environmentally safe manner.

A bionic-mammalian creation, Mr. Mund was designed to consume all scrap metal on the surface of the space habitat and then turn them into biodegradable waste via his natural digestive processes. After six months on the colony, Mr. Mund had succeeded in eliminating all signs of scrap metal but showed no signs of growing tired of his metal munching. For five years he has remained the scourge of the colony, appearing out of nowhere, pouncing on and devouring stray autos.

CAUTION:

VACATIONERS BEWARE; MR. MUND IS PARTICULARLY FOND OF SPORTY COUPES.

An Intergalactic League of Worlds Warrant was issued on January 6, 2480 at ISB HQ 4, Quad 4, charging Mr. Mund with 18 counts of Destruction of Private Property, violation of Bureau Statute 110 (see: vandalism).

IF YOU HAVE ANY INFORMATION CONCERNING MR. MUND, PLEASE NOTIFY YOUR LOCAL ISB OFFICE. VISOPHONE NUMBERS AND LOCATIONS OF ALL ISB OFFICES LISTED ON BACK.

ADAM HAWKINS

INTERGALACTIC SECURITY BUREAU
QUADRANT 4, TERRAN DISTRICTS
NEW WASHINGTON COLONY
VISOPHONE 23120019

1. Divide into groups of four and decide the following:

– which one of the four characters will your group choose to work on;
– will all of your group be part of the character chosen, or will one or two members be other characters mentioned in the description;
– how will you create the character? which theatre crafts will you employ?

You can start to create your characters using make-up, mask, costumes, properties, lighting, and sound. Because of time and money, you may have to limit your materials, but you can use simple symbolic items to present your character. (For example, a line of charcoal or lipstick can divide a face in half.)

2. Once you have developed your character, you can create a scene that presents the story behind the brief synopsis.

– Will you share with other groups the origins of the creature?
– Will you depict the scene where the creature got into trouble?
– Will you demonstrate the situation from the creature's point of view?
– How will you stage your scene using levels, lighting, and sound so that your character can be presented?
– How will you reveal the problems and experiences your character creates?

3. Each group can share its presentation of its character. As audience, note the following:

– how are the theatre crafts being used to develop the drama as well as the characters;
– if more than one group has selected the same character, how do the interpretations differ;
– has the group attempted to create the "meaning behind the make-up";
– what has been expressed about the lives and motivations of these beings?

4. Develop an improvisation based on the creatures meeting each other.

– What reasons can you think of for having the creatures meet?
– What will be the focus of the drama?
– How will you structure the beginning of the improvisation?
– Who will refocus and channel your work?
– How will theatre crafts be used to deepen the experience?

5. Because improvised drama develops through participation and exploration, redoing the drama with a different focus can bring about new understanding. With the improvisation just created, your class can begin to isolate sections that need developing, working in small groups on different aspects. The drama will be deepened when the groups bring back their ideas to use in the whole class improvisation. In drama, the significant learning happens most frequently when you are working in role, using spontaneous improvisation as the way of finding meaning.

6. When you have refined and clarified your ideas, you can present your polished improvisation to another audience, such as a class that has been studying a science fiction unit, or to a group of students who are studying drama. Use theatre crafts only as much as necessary to help the audience understand your drama and what it is really about so that they will be looking at more than cartoon characters and more than simplistic situations. Because you will be using improvisation, although polished, you will have opportunities to continue learning and exploring in role.

Drama Journal

Does drama happen without theatre crafts?

Explain how theatre crafts can *enhance* the drama, but not *be* the drama.

What effect did using the theatre crafts have on your role?

How can a simple "prop" acquire symbolic importance in the drama?

Explain how in using the crafts of the theatre that "less is more."

An Audience for Drama

Little by little, an audience might be brought to the point where a totally natural event takes place. The actor and spectator become partners. For both will have been transformed simultaneously.

John Heilpern
Conference of the Birds p. 133

Change and develop with each audience or you're lost.

Peter Brook
Conference of the Birds p. 128

When you are improvising in a performance situation, the audience is like another participant because it affects your feelings and experiences within the drama. Therefore, it is as important to understand the role of the audience as it is to understand the roles of each of your fellow performers. Start with the audience you know: your own group.

In the drama class, you explore and express ideas and images that allow the whole group to become part of the work. The risks you take in presenting are worthwhile when your group plays a positive part in the development of the drama, and you find yourself able to sustain the action in ways that alone, you could not have discovered. The audience can affect the drama when it is part of the experience on both a thinking and feeling level. This happens when the people presenting the drama are also living through and learning from the experience. If the audience understands the problem or issue being explored and can relate to the roles that are being represented, both the audience and the actors feel the tension of the situation, and drama occurs.

Sometimes the tension will be caused by the relationships between the people in the dramatic situation. But this tension may be the result of having to wait for the sound effects to start, or working against the clock to complete a task! If you feel the tension of the moment, you will communicate this to others watching. And each of them in turn, audience and actors alike, passes the feeling on.

It is important in your drama work that performers and audience talk after the sharing, so that the work will be judged not only on what looked right, but also on the inner experience that everyone can then clarify. The following activities are improvisations as much as they are performance pieces.

Workshop

The Island

In this activity the teacher will act as narrator. You will work alone at times, and in groups at other times. Keep in mind that the narration is only to give you points of departure for your improvisations.

Narrator: You are lying down, eyes closed. Your whole body is loose, floating on warm, green sea. Think of fish swimming around the rocks under the water. Coloured, patterned. All going away, getting smaller, going into the distance in the dark water. The tide is washing you up onto the beach, lifting up first one side of your body, then the other. Feel the sand under you, touch it with your hands, run your fingers through it. Open eyes. Stretch. Get up slowly. Walk about. Feel the sand under your feet. The surface of the beach changes (pebbles, rocks, sharp shells, soft wet sand). Look about the beach. What can you find? Look inland. What can be seen? What are the others doing? Come together on the sand.

Let's explore the beach. Don't go too far off alone. What do we need? What can we eat or drink? What does that fruit taste and smell like? Is there danger? Where can we sleep? Is there wood for a fire? Can we light it? Are there signs of animals or humans?

Look for materials to build a shelter. Will there be room for everyone? Can some sleep out in the open? Who will take turns as guards? What dangers should they watch for—animals? High tides? Hurricanes? Look for things to use as pots, bowls, drinking cups: shells, gourds, old tins. How can we build a fire and keep it lit? Can someone rig up a spit?

Look for fruits, roots, berries. What about fish—how can they be caught? Any animals that can be caught? What weapons do we have? How can we prepare animals and fish for the pot? Look for water. Is it salty or fresh?

Let's explore the island. To be safe, stay with a group. Split off, survey different areas and report back here on your findings. Look out for marsh, quicksand, potholes. Are there mountains? Chasms? Ruins? Is there gold? Precious stones? Hidden treasure?

Come back to the beach. It's getting dark.

Come together and sit on the sand. How can we plan an escape or hope to be rescued? Can we make signals? Build a raft or a boat? We might salvage things from the boat wrecked on the reef. How far is the next island?

How will we pass the time? Does anyone know any songs? Word games? Can someone tell stories? How could we make musical instruments?

How will we deal with accidents or illness? What if someone gets a mysterious fever, food poisoning, or breaks a limb? What will we do about snake bite? Are there any medicinal plants here familiar to anyone?

There are people on the island! Why have they come? Are they hostile or friendly? Will they help us? Will we understand each other? Does anyone know any sign language?

Suppose we are rescued. Imagine: a ship, a plane, a helicopter. Imagine arriving back in port or at the airport. Will there be interviews with reporters? What stories will you have to tell?

The Expedition

The author of the picture book *The Expedition* uses a series of pictures in a cartoon fashion to tell a story about what happens to an island tribe when other people arrive. In only a few pictures the reader enters a new world and constructs a society that is only hinted at, never seen in actuality. The islanders' life, work, celebrations, problems, and the conflict that results when strangers representing another culture arrive in their land, are left to you to imagine.

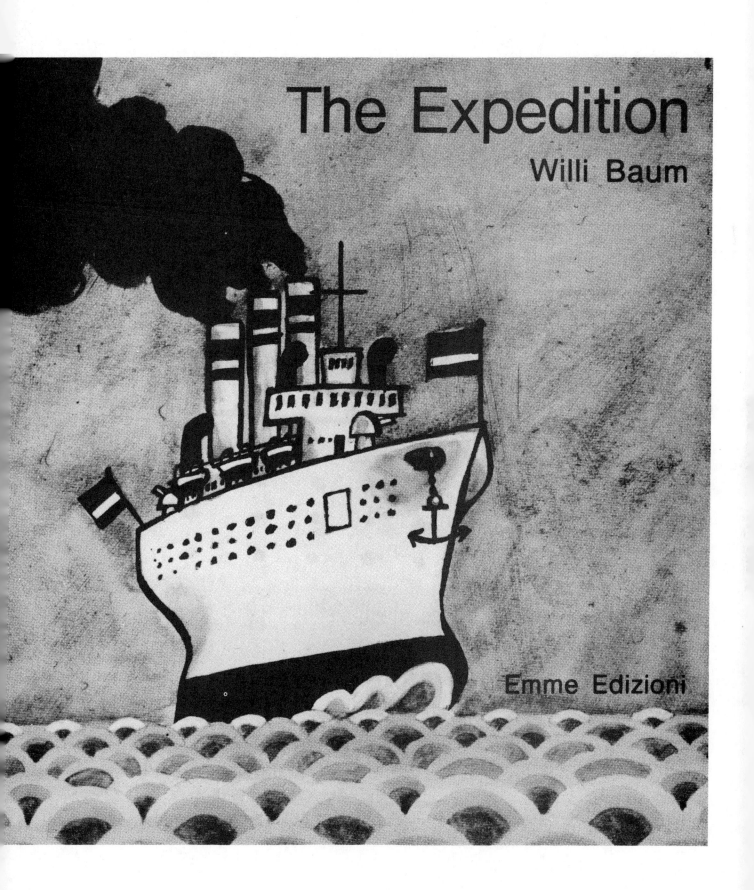

The Expedition

Willi Baum

Emme Edizioni

181

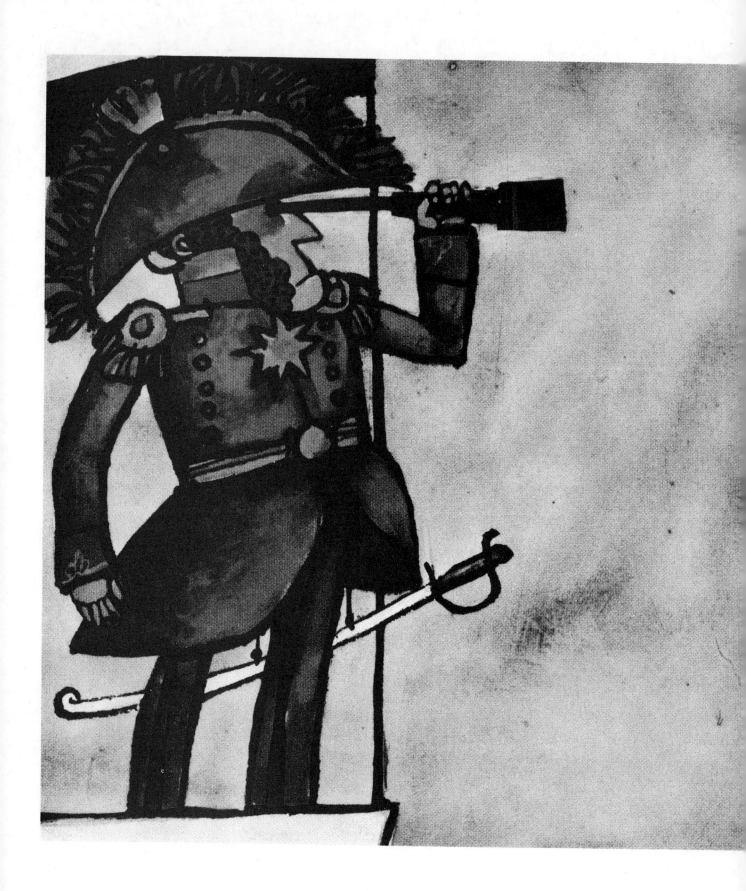

188

190

196

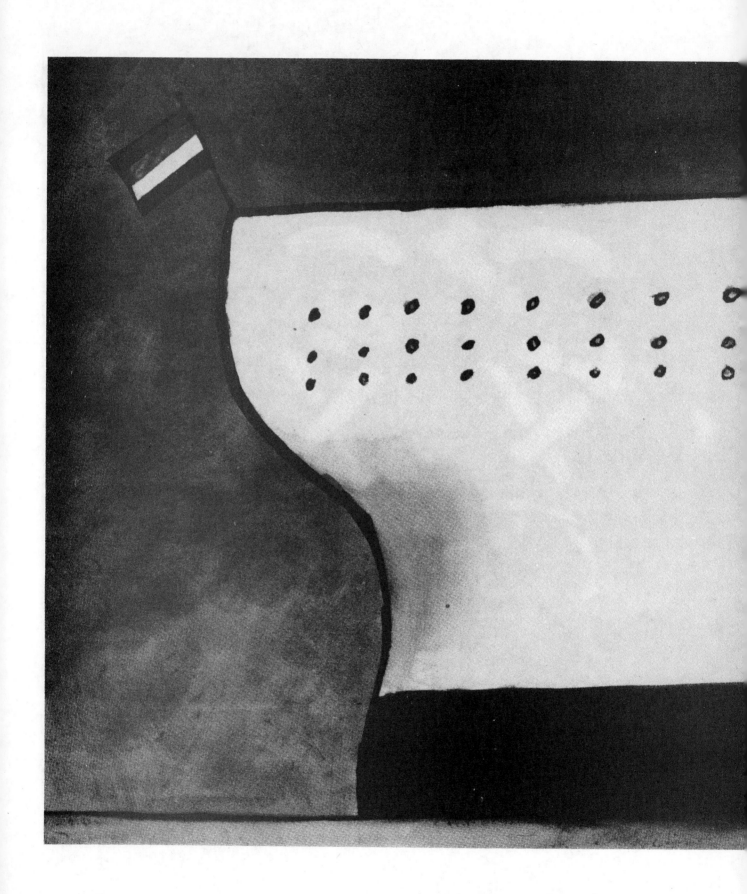

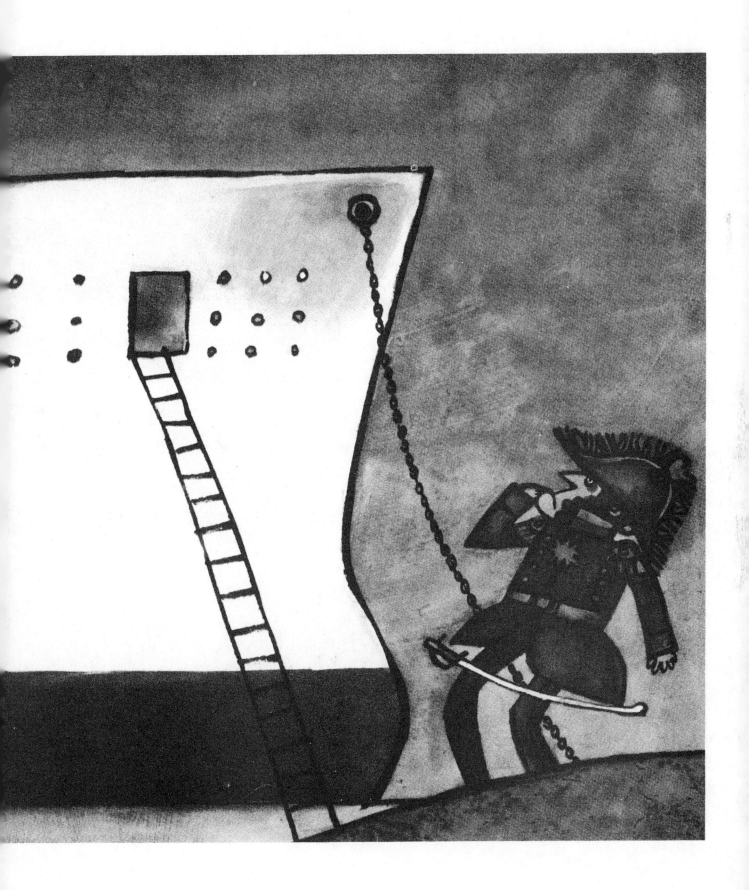

206

Because the people of the island were not pictured, you can develop their lives and their civilization any way that you wish. Divide your class into two groups, and find the space for each group to work independently. Each group will "build a people," using the next three activities.

1. Gathering Information: You can explore many aspects of the life of your chosen people, such as: business, communication, clothing, education, family, food, health, law, leisure, shelter, travel, war, work, and worship. Each of these items can be broadened or made specific. For example, if food is the topic that your tribe chooses to explore, you can demonstrate:
- how food is found—fishing, hunting, trapping, gathering;
- who finds the food;
- who distributes the food.

However, since drama is more than simply portraying any one aspect of life, you must work your way through the many problems and situations that arise when you are living in the real world. For example, what would happen to your tribe if there were a famine?

Choose one of these topics (or come up with your own), and establish your tribe's traditions, rules, etc. When you are satisfied with your work, present it to the other group.

In this presentation, the others will be a "spectator audience," and not an "audience-in-role." When you are finished your presentation, discuss with your audience what they understood about your work. Were you able to communicate clearly to them?

When you are finished your discussion, the second group presents its work.

2. Using Rituals: All peoples have certain rituals to help them mark the stages in life. For example, in examining the rites of marriage in your tribe, you might create the text of a wedding ceremony and use various properties (ring, rice, confetti, veil, white dress). You might stage a tableau which shows how the ritual is:
- the celebration of the couple's commitment;
- the formalization of the commitment to each other;
- the public acknowledgement and acceptance of the couple's commitment;
- the legalization of the contract;
- a religious rite for some couples;
- the satisfaction of fulfillment of cultural expectations;
- the fulfilling of role expectations.

Similarly, using various improvisational techniques, you can examine the rituals surrounding birth, coming to maturity, setting out on a journey, or homecoming. You needn't look at all of these and there may be others more important, but in order to develop the nature of your tribe, you will have to decide on *some* of the important rituals in the people's lives.

In your group, choose and develop your ritual. Decide how the temple (the one that was taken apart in the story), is used in your particular ritual. As you work, keep in mind that you will be presenting your ritual to the other group—not as a performance for the others to watch, but as a ritual which you want them to be part of. How can you develop ways of drawing them into your work without having lengthy out-of-role directions and instructions? For example, most cultures have some rituals where the "initiate" does not know what will be expected of him or her during the ceremony: the rites have been kept secret to protect the power of the ritual. So now it is your group's turn to initiate the others into the ritual. In this way, your audience is in role as members of your tribe.

When both groups are satisfied with their work, decide which tribe will perform its ritual first.

3. Using Movement: With your same group, discuss the fact that your tribe was visited by something long ago. If not human, what could the visitors have been? What effect did the visitors have on your tribe? Did they leave a legacy of some sort? Did they influence the way in which your tribe lived?

Using only movement, tell the story of what happened long ago. When you are satisfied with the story being told, plan how three or four tableaux which represent the story could be "painted" on the temple walls.

When you are ready with your tableaux, you can present the frozen scene to the other group. If you are a member of the second group, then, as audience, you have to observe the actors closely to attempt to learn as much as possible about the tribe. This means that the actors will have to be aware of the audience and take into account what the audience is seeing and making sense of. After the second group has had a chance to study the scene, have a discussion so that both groups are very clear about what is being depicted. Now, using movement, present your story a second time. This time the other group, as an *involved* audience, portrays the visitors that discover your world.

When you are finished, the second group begins with its frozen tableaux.

Drama Journal

What are the difficulties in communicating to an audience?

Analyse the times when what you intended to communicate was not what your audience understood.

As a member of an audience, what elements draw you into the performance, and which block your participation?

When you are working with an audience, how aware are you of their presence, and what effect do they have on your work?

How do you know when your work is ready to share with an audience?

23

Moving the Drama Out

It was the first public performance the group ever gave. And it was for children. It's not just that children don't set up defences and barriers. The child asks the question 'Why?' The child forces the sophisticated actor to relearn the steps. Faced with the natural openness and spontaneity and perhaps the cruelty of children, actors have much to learn. The actor, like any adult, can't fake it for a child. But when Brook's group gave their first children's show, they thought it wouldn't take much effort. They thought it a low-level form of work. Hadn't they joined the centre to find the key of life?

Unfortunately for the actors, the children ran riot. They were so dissatisfied with their show that they set on the group, chasing and beating them with the bamboo sticks. No matter what the actors tried, it wasn't good enough. The kids had been patronised and taken for granted, dished up second best. The kids charged at the terrified actors again and again, lashing them with the sticks.

John Heilpern
Conference of the Birds p. 280

An important aspect of learning through drama involves working with people who have not been part of your drama workshops. By moving into the community with your drama explorations, you can examine the role of participation in the drama as well as work with the spectators and help them become involved in what is happening.

The three models of drama that are presented in this chapter are based on a novel for children (*The Iron Man*), a script (*The Crucible*), and oral stories told by senior citizens. These workshops form the basis for your work in the community. Discuss the different projects as a class, and then focus on one project that you can carry through to completion. Taking drama outside the classroom will allow you to explore the potential of working with others in this art form. By engaging others in the drama project—communicating and working with them in this medium—you will come to appreciate and understand your own development as a drama student.

Workshop

The Return of the Iron Man

In this project, the children will work inside the drama along with you, the actors. By bringing theatre into education, you can use specially created material to encourage the children's participation, and still be using and practising your ability as an actor.

This excerpt is from an excellent children's novel by Ted Hughes, called *The Iron Man*. It contains enough information for you to create the improvisation you wish to introduce to the children.

THE RETURN OF THE IRON MAN

One evening a farmer's son, a boy called Hogarth, was fishing in a stream that ran down to the sea. It was growing too dark to fish, his hook kept getting caught in weeds and bushes. So he stopped fishing and came up from the stream and stood listening to the owls in the wood further up the valley, and to the sea behind him. Hush, said the sea. And again, Hush. Hush. Hush.

Suddenly he felt a strange feeling. He felt he was being watched. He felt afraid. He turned and looked up the steep field to the top of the high cliff. Behind that skyline was the sheer rocky cliff and the sea. And on that skyline, just above the edge of it, in the dusk, were two green lights. What were two green lights doing at the top of the cliff?

Then, as Hogarth watched, a huge dark figure climbed up over the cliff-top. The two lights rose into the sky. They were the giant figure's eyes. A giant black figure, taller than a house, black and towering in the twilight, with green headlamp eyes. The Iron Man! There he stood on the cliff-top, looking inland. Hogarth began to run. He ran and ran. Home. Home. The Iron Man had come back.

So he got home at last and gasping for breath he told his dad. An Iron Man! An Iron Man! A giant!

His father frowned. His mother grew pale. His little sister began to cry.

His father took down his double-barrelled gun. He believed his son. He went out. He locked the door. He got in his car. He drove to the next farm.

But that farmer laughed. He was a fat, red man, with a fat, red-mouthed laugh. When he stopped laughing, his eyes were red too. An Iron Man? Nonsense, he said.

So Hogarth's father got back in his car. Now it was dark and it had begun to rain. He drove to the next farm.

That farmer frowned. He believed. Tomorrow, he said, we must see what he is, this iron man.

His feet will have left tracks in the earth.

So Hogarth's father again got back into his car. But as he turned the car in the yard, he saw a strange thing in the headlamps. Half a tractor lay there, just half, chopped clean off, the other half missing. He got out of his car and the other farmer came to look too. The tractor had been bitten off— there were big teeth-marks in the steel.

No explanation! The two men looked at each other. They were puzzled and afraid. What could have bitten the tractor in two? There, in the yard, in the rain, in the night, while they had been talking inside the house.

The farmer ran in and bolted his door.

Hogarth's father jumped into his car and drove off into the night and the rain as fast as he could, homeward.

The rain poured down. Hogarth's father drove hard. The headlights lit up the road and bushes.

Suddenly—two headlamps in a tall treetop at the roadside ahead. Headlamps in a treetop? How?

Hogarth's father slowed, peering up to see what the lights might be, up there in the treetop.

As he slowed, a giant iron foot came down in the middle of the road, a foot as big as a single bed. And the headlamps came down closer. And a giant hand reached down towards the windshield.

The Iron Man!

Hogarth's father put on speed, he aimed his car at the foot.

Crash! He knocked the foot out of the way.

He drove on, faster and faster. And behind him, on the road, a clanging clattering boom went up, as if an iron skyscraper had collapsed. The iron giant, with his foot knocked from under him, had toppled over.

And so Hogarth's father got home safely.

BUT

Next morning all the farmers were shouting with anger. Where were their tractors? Their earth-diggers? Their ploughs? Their harrows? From every farm in the region, all the steel and iron farm machinery had gone. Where to? Who had stolen it all?

There was a clue. Here and there lay half a wheel, or half an axle, or half a mudguard, carved with giant tooth-marks where it had been bitten off. How had it been bitten off? Steel bitten off?

What had happened?

There was another clue.

From farm to farm, over the soft soil of the fields, went giant footprints, each one the size of a single bed.

The farmers, in a frightened, silent, amazed crowd, followed the footprints. And at every farm the footprints visited, all the metal machinery had disappeared.

Finally, the footprints led back up to the top of the cliff, where the little boy had seen the Iron Man appear the night before, when he was fishing. The footprints led right to the cliff-top.

And all the way down the cliff were torn marks on the rocks, where a huge iron body had slid down. Below, the tide was in. The gray, empty, moving tide. The Iron Man had gone back into the sea.

SO

The furious farmers began to shout. The Iron Man had stolen all their machinery. Had he eaten it? Anyway, he had taken it. It had gone. So what if he came again? What would he take next time? Cows? Houses? People?

They would have to do something.

They couldn't call in the police or the Army, because nobody would believe them about this Iron Monster. They would have to do something for themselves.

So, what did they do?

At the bottom of the hill, below where the Iron Man had come over the high cliff, they dug a deep, enormous hole. A hole wider than a house, and as deep as three trees one on top of the other. It was a colossal hole. A stupendous hole! And the sides of it were sheer as walls.

They pushed all the earth off to one side.

They covered the hole with branches and the branches they covered with straw and the straw with soil, so when they finished the hole looked like a freshly-ploughed field.

Now, on the side of the hole opposite the slope up to the top of the cliff, they put an old rusty lorry. That was the bait. Now they reckoned the Iron Man would come over the top of the cliff out of the sea, and he'd see the old lorry which was painted red, and he'd come down to get it to chew it up and eat it. But on his way to the lorry he'd be crossing the hole, and the moment he stepped with his great weight on to that soil held up only with straw and branches, he would crash through into the hole and would never get out. They'd find him there in the hole. Then they'd bring the few bulldozers and earth-movers that he hadn't already eaten, and they'd push the pile of earth in on top of him, and bury him for ever in the hole. They were certain now that they'd get him.

Next morning, in great excitement, all the farmers gathered together to go along to examine their trap. They came carefully closer, expecting to see his hands tearing at the edge of the pit. They came carefully closer.

The red lorry stood just as they had left it. The soil lay just as they had left it, undisturbed. Everything was just as they had left it. The Iron Man had not come.

Nor did he come that day.

Next morning, all the farmers came again. Still, everything lay just as they had left it.

And so it went on, day after day. Still the Iron Man never came.

Now the farmers began to wonder if he would ever come again. They began to make up explanations of what had happened to their machinery. Nobody likes to believe in an Iron Monster that eats tractors and cars.

Soon, the farmer who owned the red lorry they were using as bait decided that he needed it, and he took it away. So there lay the beautiful deep trap, without any bait. Grass began to grow on the loose soil.

The farmers talked of filling the hole in. After all, you can't leave a giant pit like that, somebody might fall in. Some stranger coming along might just walk over it and fall in.

But they didn't want to fill it in. It had been such hard work digging it. Besides they all had a sneaking fear that the Iron Man might come again, and that the hole was their only weapon against him.

At last they put up a little notice: "DANGER: KEEP OFF," to warn people away, and they left it at that.

Now the little boy Hogarth had an idea. He thought he could use that hole, to trap a fox. He found a dead hen one day, and threw it out on to the loose soil over the trap. Then towards evening, he climbed a tree nearby, and waited. A long

212

time he waited. A star came out. He could hear the sea.

Then—there, standing at the edge of the hole, was a fox. A big, red fox, looking towards the dead hen. Hogarth stopped breathing. And the fox stood without moving—sniff, sniff, sniff, out towards the hen. But he did not step out on to the trap. Slowly, he walked around the wide patch of raw soil till he got back to where he'd started, sniffing all the time out towards the bird. But he did not step out on to the trap. Was he too smart to walk out there where it was not safe?

But at that moment he stopped sniffing. He turned his head and looked towards the top of the cliff. Hogarth, wondering what the fox had seen, looked towards the top of the cliff.

There, enormous in the blue evening sky, stood the Iron Man, on the brink of the cliff, gazing inland.

In a moment, the fox had vanished.

Now what?

Hogarth carefully quietly hardly breathing climbed slowly down the tree. He must get home and tell his father. But at the bottom of the tree he stopped. He could no longer see the Iron Man against the twilight sky. Had he gone back over the cliff into the sea? Or was he coming down the hill, in the darkness under that high skyline, towards Hogarth and the farms?

Then Hogarth understood what was happening. He could hear a strange tearing and creaking sound. The Iron Man was pulling up the barbed-wire fence that led down the hill. And soon Hogarth could see him, as he came nearer, tearing the wire from the fence posts, rolling it up like spaghetti and eating it. The Iron Man was eating the barbed fencing wire.

But if he went along the fence,

eating as he moved, he wouldn't come anywhere near the trap, which was out in the middle of the field. He could spend the whole night wandering about the countryside along the fences, rolling up the wire and eating it, and never would any fence bring him near the trap.

But Hogarth had an idea. In his pocket, among other things, he had a long nail and a knife. He took these out. Did he dare? His idea frightened him. In the silent dusk, he tapped the nail and the knife blade together.

Clink, Clink, Clink!

At the sound of the metal, the Iron Man's hands became still. After a few seconds, he slowly turned his head and the headlamp eyes shone towards Hogarth.

Again, Clink, Clink, Clink! went the nail on the knife.

Slowly, the Iron Man took three strides towards Hogarth, and again stopped. It was now quite dark. The headlamps shone red. Hogarth pressed close to the tree-trunk. Between him and the Iron Man lay the wide lid of the trap.

Clink, Clink, Clink! again he tapped the nail on the knife.

And now the Iron Man was coming. Hogarth could feel the earth shaking under the weight of his footsteps. Was it too late to run? Hogarth stared at the Iron Man, looming, searching towards him for the taste of the metal that had made that inviting sound.

Clink, Clink, Clink! went the nail on the knife. And

CRASSSHHH!

The Iron Man vanished.

He was in the pit. The Iron Man had fallen into the pit. Hogarth went close. The earth was shaking as the Iron Man struggled underground. Hogarth peered over the torn edge of the great pit. Far below, two deep red headlamps

glared up at him from the pitch blackness. He could hear the Iron Man's insides grinding down there and it sounded like a big lorry grinding its gears on a steep hill. Hogarth set off. He ran, he ran, home—home with the great news. And as he passed the cottages on the way, and as he turned down the lane towards his father's farm, he was shouting "The Iron Man's in the trap!" and "We've caught the Iron Giant."

When the farmers saw the Iron Man wallowing in their deep pit, they sent up a great cheer. He glared up towards them, his eyes burned from red to purple, from purple to white, from white to fiery whirling black and red, and the cogs inside him ground and screeched, but he could not climb out of the steep-sided pit.

Then under the lights of car headlamps, the farmers brought bulldozers and earth-pushers, and they began to push in on top of the struggling Iron Man all the earth they had dug when they first made the pit and that had been piled off to one side.

The Iron Man roared again as the earth began to fall on him. But soon he roared no more. Soon the pit was full of earth. Soon the Iron Man was buried silent, packed down under all the soil, while the farmers piled the earth over him in a mound and in a hill. They went to and fro over the mound on their new tractors, which they'd bought since the Iron Man ate their old ones, and they packed the earth down hard. Then they all went home talking cheerfully. They were sure they had seen the last of the Iron Man.

Only Hogarth felt suddenly sorry. He felt guilty. It was he after all, who had lured the Iron Man into the pit.

1. Your group are to role-play the farmers whose crops, fields, and equipment have been damaged by the Iron Man. One member of your group will role-play the Iron Man. This character can be as elaborately costumed, masked, and made-up as you like. This person should, however, be introduced to the children when they first arrive, and they should know that he or she will be playing a character later on in the drama and needs to go away to get ready. In this way you run no risks that any child will be genuinely frightened.

The children are to role-play "expert scientists." These scientists are brought in because they are experienced at dealing with monsters.

2. This drama is designed to allow the children to decide on, explore, and try out a variety of plans for coping with the Iron Man. It is *not* a test of them to see if they can arrive at the same solution as your group. The purpose of the drama is to challenge the children and to get them thinking, but not to force them into defeat. If you go for the first solution that the children offer, the drama will be over too quickly. You need to be sensitive and to know when to apply pressure and when to relax.

In order that you feel secure when you work with the children, it is useful to have tried out in action some of the solutions that the children may offer. Therefore, split your own group into two and experiment. As you explore, use a flow chart to record your ideas. Your flow chart might end up looking something like this:

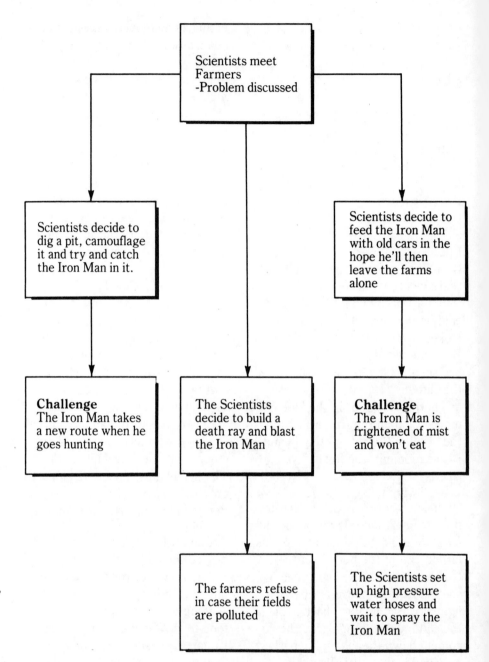

Notice that as well as possible courses of action for the children, the chart also includes ideas for ways in which the Iron Man or the farmers can challenge the children's ideas.

214

3. Development of your project involves giving some thought to the following:

– how will you begin the drama;
– how much of the actual *Iron Man* excerpt—words, characters, situations—will you use;
– how will you bring the children into role;
– how will you encourage the children to think of different solutions;
– how will you finally bring the drama to a finish?

While you are at work on the framework of your drama, you must also give some thought to the presenting of the work. Is there a suitable grade in your own school? in a school nearby? Will your teacher make the arrangements, or is everything your responsibility?

Outsiders in History

For your own learning and growth, this project is best suited for presentation with a non-drama class. Based on Arthur Miller's play "The Crucible," the project has genuine cross-curricular potential. Choose a class, and make sure that the necessary arrangements for working with this class are taken care of.

1. Read through all of the following material, keeping in mind that you are going to build with the non-drama class a role-playing situation based on this topic. You will probably want to do some preparatory work with the class, and therefore you should pull some suitable games and activities out of this text. In order to help the new group commit to the drama, you will want to do some work in advance with the framework of the drama, and with the development of your own roles.

2. When you join up with the other class, first draw a large-scale map of an imaginary coast-line. Explain to the group that you need their help to create a new settlement in the year 1750 somewhere in North America.

Organize the major buildings of the township—church, inn, mill—and add them to the map. Name the township and any important features of the landscape.

3. Everyone will be villagers in this settlement. From within your own group organise the following roles:

– Village Elder
– Minister
– "Suspicious Person"

The "Suspicious Person" will eventually be suspected of being a witch. The person playing this role is uncommunicative with the other villagers and carries a box at all times which was previously filled with an assortment of objects: a medallion, small doll, sea-shell, key, small glass bottle, large needle, etc. Neither the box nor the objects inside it should work against the period you are trying to create. (No plastic, for instance.)

All other members of both groups are villagers and are free to decide their own family groups and occupations. (Ask the non-drama group to avoid role-playing children, and, where possible, include one of your own group in each of the family groups formed.)

Once the family groups are organized have them mark their homesteads on the map.

4. Each group should now go and improvise the start of their normal day in the village. After the groups have had time for some discussion and experiment, all groups should be asked to start their day together on a given signal. From this point on the drama has started.

The non-drama group may find this work in role difficult; only through your commitment to your role and your concentration can you help them believe in their roles. Therefore, as the village comes to life and the day progresses you should interact with members of the non-drama group. By talking to them as if the village is "real," and as if the simple everyday problems of life in the village have really to be faced, you can help them develop belief in their roles.

5. When the drama appears to be running smoothly, two previously chosen members of your group should subtly introduce the following rumours:
a) the hens seem to have stopped laying;
b) the cows seem to have stopped giving milk.

For the *best* effect these rumours should spread naturally through the whole group. It should not be necessary for your own group to undertake total responsibility.

As the rumours spread they will tend to grow and to become exaggerated. This will be helpful to your drama. Once the rumours are established the Village Elder should call a meeting to discuss the problem. At this point the question of witchcraft has to be raised. If it seems unlikely that the non-drama group will do this, a member of your own group has the responsibility for introducing the idea.

6. From this time on the drama could take a number of directions, and you should, in your rehearsal period, explore the most probable possibilities. However, the most likely direction for the drama is that the group will look for a scapegoat and that they will find "Suspicious Person" a suitable choice.

If this is the direction of the drama then the question of what is inside the box will become important. The group will want the box opened.

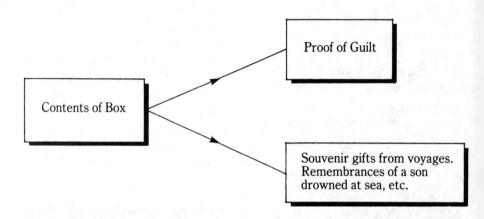

It is important that the scapegoat has both of these options regarding the box's contents available. The performer can choose the argument he or she will use according to how the drama has developed so far.

Your group should have a loose framework ready for the rest of the drama. Some members may choose to narrate a story about a past incident, or to present tableaux of past cave drawings concerning a similar problem. The class may be divided into two groups to demonstrate two different solutions.

At the conclusion of the drama, it is important that your group sit with the children and let them express their feelings and ideas about what has happened in the drama.

Reminiscences

Many of our old people live in institutions which, while providing proper care, are also highly organized. This tight organization tends to create routines which, in their turn, create boredom and a lack of a need for people to communicate. "Reminiscences" uses the memories of senior citizens to create drama which stimulates discussion, problem-solving, decision-making, and laughter.

There are four major steps in this project. Stopping at any point in the progression will still pay dividends and be of value, but the logical end-point of this work is reached when the group you are working with are involved in the role-play as participants rather than simply as audience.

Step 1:

Initial contact should be made with a senior citizens' home by your teacher. You will need to know:

a) the average age of the people you will be working with;
b) the kinds of disabilities you can expect in your group;
c) the time available for your session, and if this time is free from interruptions.

When you have this information, you can set about collecting photographs, books, and objects to be used as discussion points on your first visit to the senior citizens. Pick material which interests you and which is from the years when the people you will be working with were young.

Step 2:

On your first visit explain that you are interested in collecting:

a) any information that the group might have to offer on the background of the materials you have brought with you;
b) any stories which the senior citizens might like to tell as a result of their talking about these materials with you. (If you think that you might need a note book or cassette player to help you remember the information, make sure that you are prepared.)

Explain beforehand that, provided the contributors agree, you intend to take the stories away with you and turn one or two into a performance which you will then bring back to show.

Remember to always respect confidentiality regarding these stories if you are asked to do so. If you are told a story which is clearly upsetting the person telling it, try as tactfully as possible to change the topic through asking a question about the material you have brought.

Step 3:

Provided that you have the agreement of the senior citizens' group, share the stories back at school, and find those which have sufficient detail and dramatic potential to be turned into short theatre pieces.

Look for ways which will allow some members of your class to remain out of role and in contact with the senior citizens.

During rehearsal, practise taking side-coaching from your drama group. (You will be accepting side-coaching from the seniors.)

When the scenes are ready, return to the senior citizens' home and explain to the seniors that although you have tried to bring their stories to life, you really need their expert knowledge. Make it clear that if they have any suggestions to make they can call them out during the performance. The members of your group not performing should encourage this audience participation.

Step 4:

The final step in this project involves the move from side-coaching to full participation. Your group should be on the look-out for those members of the audience who seem ready to join in at this level. When someone is ready to take this step there are two possibilities:

1) that one of your members drops out of the improvisation and is replaced; and
2) that a new character is invented and introduced to the action.

If the senior citizen who wishes to join the improvisation cannot move easily, then it should be possible for you to move the action to that person.

One student, who had been part of "Reminiscences," stated:

The sight of an 80-year-old man who, during the drama, role-played an auctioneer in charge of a box-social, holding up a book (because we had no real boxes) to his nose and sniffing, "chicken and lemon meringue pie" will live in my heart and mind for a long time to come.

Drama Journal

How much should performers care about the audience?

How did the audience you chose affect the preparation work you did?

Now that you have performed for an audience, how have you changed as an audience member?

Why do you think professional actor-training programs do not allow beginning actors to perform in front of an audience?

"You have completed the course, but just begun the journey." Why does each exploration in drama require the participants to experience again the techniques of improvisation, both in drama and in life?

Epilogue

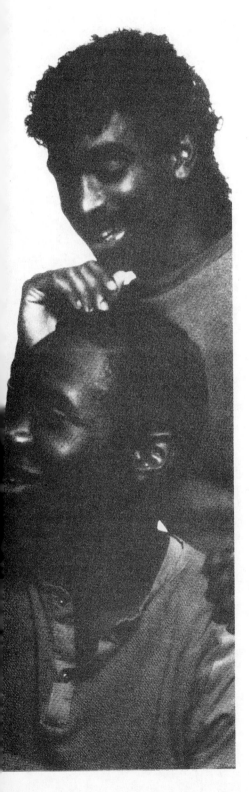

It is time to look back on your year's involvement in improvisation and to reflect on what you have accomplished. Each person brings to a drama class a particular set of experiences, a personal background that is the basis on which to build the drama work. No two people will develop in the same way from taking part in improvisational drama classes, but there will be common areas of growth for everyone.

Drama has presented you with opportunities for understanding your own strengths, and for using this knowledge in making decisions about changing and growing in the future. The work in improvisation is just a beginning for the rest of your life. The strategies you have explored are there for you to use again and again. It is not a matter of finishing one technique; it is necessary to use what you have gone through as the learning points for your next experience, so that you can continue to develop throughout life. By understanding "another" in role, you get to know "yourself" better and better.

Discovery through drama can lead you into the wider community, where you will be able to interact with younger children, peers, and members of the community at large, such as senior citizens. As you communicate with others through drama—by participating in workshops, by attending theatre presentations, and by performing for trusted audiences—you will continue to develop and change your perceptions of the world, to become truly educated about the rest of society, to think and feel "as if" you were seeing life from a whole new perspective.

Drama is an art form, and like the other arts, it helps us as humans to take another look at ourselves and at the world around us, so that we can better appreciate the complexities of life, and begin to understand our place in the world. If you are to earn your living from working in the arts, then you will have begun your career on a healthy basis. If you are to use the arts in your private life, then you will have understood the process from the inside. In either case, you will have been part of the world of drama, and you will have knowledge of this powerful medium.

There is no limit to the art of drama. You need the understanding of all human nature, the sense of beauty of the artist and poet, the sense of rhythm of the dancer and musician, the mentality of a philosopher and scientist.

It is the universal art.

Director of the *American Academy of Dramatic Arts*
Charles Jehlinjer

Acknowledgments

Our thanks to Alan, April, and Chris who appear on the cover and throughout the book. Thanks as well to the students and teachers at Albert Campbell Secondary School, and to Peter Gallagher and Young People's Theatre for allowing us to take photographs of the drama classes.

For the use of the selections below, listed in the order in which they appear in *Improvisation*, grateful acknowledgment is made to the copyright holders as follows:

Excerpts by John Heilpern are taken from *Conference of the Birds* by John Heilpern, Copyright 1978, published by A.D. Peters & Co. Ltd.

"Tangles" by Nancy King is adapted from A MOVEMENT APPROACH TO ACTING by Nancy King, Copyright © 1981, page 160. Reprinted with the permission of Prentice-Hall, Inc., Englewood Cliffs, New Jersey.

"Following a Leader" and "Listen Through the Dark" are adapted from *Development Through Drama* by Brian Way, published by and available from Longman Group Limited, Longman House, Burnt Mill, Harlow, Essex CM20 2JE, England. Reprinted with the permission of the publisher.

Excerpts by Kay Hamblin (appearing in adapted form as "Transformations," "Stuck!", "Flying," "Tightrope Wobbling," "Butterfly," "Snake Charmer," "Alter Egos," "Buried Alive!", "The Gift," "Masquerade," "Erase a Face," "Garbage Picker," "Stationary Journey," "Magic Box," "Movers," "Mime-in-the-Box," and "The Flight of Icarus") reprinted from *Mime: A Playbook of Silent Fantasy* by Kay Hamblin courtesy of The Headland Press, Inc., P.O. Box 862, Tiburon, California 94920. Copyright © 1978. All rights reserved.

"Horses" is taken from Peter Shaffer's play EQUUS, Copyright © 1977, 1984 by Peter Shaffer.

Excerpts by Nancy King (appearing in adapted form as "Statues," "Silent Movie," "Frozen Together," and "Statues Come to Life!") from *Giving Form to Feeling* by Nancy King, Copyright 1975 and published by Drama Book Specialists (Publishers), New York, are reprinted with the permission of the publisher.

Pantomimes 101 (pages 295-296, appearing as "Combination/Transformation" and "The Polluted") reprinted with special permission from The Dramatic Publishing Co., Inc., all rights reserved. This play may not be performed without clearance for royalties. For information contact The Dramatic Publishing Co., P.O. Box 109, Woodstock, IL 60098.

Peanuts cartoon by Charles M. Schulz, © 1982 United Feature Syndicate, Inc., is reproduced with the permission of United Media, 200 Park Avenue, New York, NY 10166.

Passage "You are a traveller in a far-off land..." in "Starting With Words" is taken from 100+ IDEAS FOR DRAMA by Anna Scher and Charles Verrall, Copyright 1975, and is reprinted with the permission of the author and Heineman Educational Books (publisher).

Excerpts, appearing in adapted form as "Starting with Feelings: Action and Reaction," "Nightmares," and "Fantasies," are from A MOVEMENT APPROACH TO ACTING by Nancy King, Copyright © 1981, pages 160-161, 162, and 163. Reprinted with the permission of Prentice-Hall, Inc. (publisher), Englewood Cliffs, New Jersey.

"The Ash Tree" and "The Creation of the World" are taken from *Exploration Drama: Legend* by W. Martin and F.H. Vallins, Copyright 1968. Reprinted with permission of the publisher, Bell & Hyman (Publishers).

"in Just–" is reprinted from TULIPS & CHIMNEYS by E.E. Cummings by permission of Liveright Publishing Corporation. Copyright 1923, 1925 and renewed 1951, 1953 by E.E. Cummings. Copyright © 1973, 1976 by the Trustees for the E.E. Cummings Trust. Copyright © 1973, 1976 by George James Firmage.

Excerpts by Gene Stanford from *Developing Effective Classroom Groups* by Gene Stanford are reprinted with the permission of Hart Associates (publisher), 255 West 98th Street, New York, NY 10025.

Excerpts (appearing in adapted form as "Persuasion," "A Day in the Life of...", "In Others' Shoes," "What Should I Do?", "Mood Swings" and

"Viewpoints") from *Games and Simuations in Action* by A. Davison and Peter Gordon, Copyright 1978, are reprinted with the permission of The Woburn Press (publisher).

"First Line/Last Line" is adapted from *Gamesters' Handbook* by Donna Brandes and Howard Phillips, Copyright 1979, published by the Hutchinson Publishing Group Ltd.

"Trans-Siberian Express" is reprinted from page 48 of *Drama Guidelines* by Cecily O'Neill, Alan Lambert, Rosemary Linnell, and Janet Warr-Wood with the permission of Heinemann Educational Books.

Myra Cohn Livingston, "Old People" from *The Way Things Are and Other Poems*. Copyright © 1974 Myra Cohn Livingston. (A Margaret K. McElderry Book.) Reprinted with the permission of Atheneum Publishers, Inc.

"The Chinese Checker Players" excerpted from the book THE PILL VERSUS THE SPRINGHILL MINE DISASTER by Richard Brautigan. Copyright © 1968 by Richard Brautigan. Reprinted by permission of DELACORTE PRESS/SEYMOUR LAWRENCE.

"Volunteers" is reprinted from pages 41-43 of *Drama Guidelines* by Cecily O'Neill, Alan Lambert, Rosemary Linnell, and Janet Warr-Wood with the permission of Heinemann Educational Books.

"It Only Comes Out at Night" is excerpted from *Drama Without Script* by Susan Stanley, published by Hodder & Stoughton Educational. Reprinted with the permission of the publisher.

"Underwater World" is adapted from *Drama Resource Cards* by Jay Norris and Mike Evans, published by and available from Longman Group Limited, Longman House, Burnt Mill, Harlow, Essex CM20 2JE, England. Reprinted with the permission of the publisher.

"The Wild Man" (appearing in the workshop "The Wild One") by Kevin Crosley-Holland is reprinted with the permission of Andre Deutsch Ltd., 105 Great Russell Street, London WC1B 3LJ, England.

"Down Below" from THE SKIN SPINNERS by Joan Aiken. Copyright © 1960, 1973, 1974, 1975, 1976 by Joan Aiken. Reprinted by permission of Viking Penguin Inc.

Quotation (page 87), "Investigating...the Police" (adapted), and "Women on Patrol" (adapted) are excerpted from TAKING ACTION: WRITING, READING, SPEAKING & LISTENING, THROUGH SIMULATION GAMES by Lynn Quitman Troyka and Jerrold Nudelman, Copyright 1975, pages *vi* and 52-65. Reprinted with the permission of Prentice-Hall, Inc., Englewood Cliffs, New Jersey.

"As the Stars Disappear" is adapted from *Drama Resource Cards* by Jay Norris and Mike Evans, published by and available from Longman Group Limited, Longman House, Burnt Mill, Harlow, Essex CM20 2JE, England. Reprinted with the permission of the publisher.

Byrd Baylor, "The Way to Start a Day" from *Anthology for Young People*. Copyright © 1976, 1977 Byrd Baylor. Reprinted with the permission of Charles Scribner's Sons.

"The Sun Dance" by Julian Salomon is reprinted from *Totem, Tipi and Tumpline: Stories of Canadian Indians* edited by Olive M. Fisher and Clara L. Tyner, Copyright 1955, with the permission of J.M. Dent & Sons (Canada) Limited.

Extracts from *Stanislavsky on the Art of the Stage* by David Magarshack are reprinted with the permission of Faber and Faber publishers.

"More Socks," "Bread Crumbs," "Cottage Cheese," "I Talk Too Much," "Joey Wants to Scream," and "Worst Moment" are reprinted from HOLD ME! by Jules Feiffer, Copyright © 1977 by Jules Feiffer, and published by the DRAMATIST PLAY SERVICE, INC., 440 Park Avenue South, New York, NY 10016.

"Standing Alone" and "A Little Too Verbal" are reprinted from FEIFFER'S PEOPLE by Jules Feiffer, Copyright © 1969 by Jules Feiffer, and published by the DRAMATIST PLAY SERVICE, INC., 440 Park Avenue South, New York, NY 10016.

From "Artichoke" by Joanna M. Glass, © Copyright 1979. Used by special permission of the Lucy Kroll Agency, NYC, NY.

Excerpt from "Ground Zero" by Brian Shein is reprinted with permission from THEATRICAL EXHIBITIONS, 1975, published by Pulp Press Book Publishers.